Praise for *TRASH*

"With deep sensitivity and nuance, Cedar Monroe invites us to go beyond what we usually hear—or what we think we know—about America's small towns and rural counties. Through the stories and lives of poor and dispossessed people encamped along the Chehalis River, *Trash* is an intimate portrayal of what it really means to be poor and white in this country. Monroe carries the unbearable loss of this community, beautifully and carefully. Yet *Trash* is not an appeal to pity or charity. Rather, it is a call to build organization and leadership in these forgotten places, among poor white communities. Given the threats of an emboldened white Christian nationalist movement to our democracy and fundamental rights, Monroe's call is a political necessity for our times."

—**Shailly Gupta Barnes**, policy director for the Kairos Center for Religions, Rights, and Social Justice and the Poor People's Campaign: A National Call for Moral Revival

"Here is a voice not often heard in our difficult but necessary conversations about justice and inclusion. Cedar Monroe reveals another layer of complexity in the quest for Beloved Community with this provocative study of poor white people in America and the forces that seek to prevent them from claiming solidarity across racial lines with others who are poor."

—**The Most Rev. Michael B. Curry,** Presiding Bishop of The Episcopal Church and author of *Love Is the Way* and *Songs My Grandma Sang*

"This deeply moving book blends memoir, history, and a razor-sharp analysis of the havoc that capitalism and white supremacy have wreaked on the natural world and Indigenous, Black, brown, and poor white communities. Through remarkable storytelling, Cedar Monroe recounts what resistance, organizing, and solidarity look like in the margins of empire and beckons us to learn from past movements, our elders, and the leadership of the disinherited. This book is a must-read that calls us all toward collective liberation."

—**Lindsey Krinks**, author of *Praying with Our Feet*

"*Trash* combines true and painful stories with thoughtful analysis of what happens to poor white people who fail to live up to the unwritten rules of white dominant culture. This is a must-read for those who care about the future of poor young adults in the United States."

—**Elizabeth Mae Magill**, author of *Five Loaves, Two Fish, Twelve Volunteers: Growing a Relational Food Ministry*

"With raw energy and honesty, Cedar Monroe offers an insider's view of the culture and struggles of America's poor working class and bears witness to their search for hope, home, and dignity amid violence, drugs, eviction, and death. This is a must-read to understand the human sacrifice of the American empire."

—**Dr. Kwok Pui Lan**, Dean's Professor of Systematic Theology, Candler School of Theology, Emory University

"At a time when our rich and varied identities are so often used to divide us, Cedar Monroe's book does just the opposite. Calling strongly, faithfully, clearly, and with tremendous heart for all poor and oppressed people to come together to demand change, Monroe insists that it is only when we reach across barriers of race and culture that we will come to realize the fullness of our power. This is an important, maybe even an essential book. Everyone should read it."

—**Rev. Cristina Rathbone**, author *of A World Apart: Women, Prison, and Life Behind Bars*

"*Trash: A Poor White Journey* is a highly personalized account of millions of poor people who have been victimized by the system that is supposed to protect them. I recommend this book as an organizing tool for all of those who want to learn the truth about the plight of our poor white brothers and sisters. I will use this book in all my organizing classes. Cedar Monroe gets a ten rating from me."

—**Hy Thurman**, author of *Revolutionary Hillbilly*; cofounder of Young Patriots Organization and First and Second Rainbow Coalition; and chair of North Alabama School for Organizers

"Reading *Trash*, from title to epilogue, made me more awake and more uncomfortable than I would choose to be. And it's so beautifully written, researched, and experienced that I could not stop. Monroe dives, at great personal risk, into the depths of their ancestry and culture, and emerges with a riveting narrative and compelling vision for action."

—**Rev. Dr. Deborah Little Wyman**, founder and missioner, Ecclesia Ministries and common cathedral

Trash

A POOR WHITE JOURNEY

CEDAR MONROE

Broadleaf Books

Minneapolis

TRASH
A Poor White Journey

Library of Congress Cataloging-in-Publication Data

Names: Monroe, Cedar, author.
Title: Trash : a poor white journey / Cedar Monroe.
Description: Minneapolis : Broadleaf Books, [2024] | Includes bibliographical
    references.
Identifiers: LCCN 2023016296 | ISBN 9781506486277 (hardback) |
    ISBN 9781506486284 (ebook)
Subjects: LCSH: Poor white people—Washington (State)—Grays Harbor County. |
    Whites—Washington (State)—Grays Harbor County—Economic conditions. |
    Whites—Race identity—Washington (State)—Grays Harbor County. |
    Social stratification—Washington (State)—Grays Harbor County.
Classification: LCC HC107.W2 M66 2024 | DDC 305.5/6908909—
    dc23/eng/20230523
LC record available at https://lccn.loc.gov/2023016296

Cover Design: faceout

Print ISBN: 978-1-5064-8627-7
eBook ISBN: 978-1-5064-8628-4

Some details and identities have been changed for people's privacy or safety.

Printed in China

To Jim Campbell (1952–2021)
and
To the residents of the River.

Before I begin this story about a place now called Grays Harbor County, named after the white explorer who docked his boat here over two hundred years ago, I want to offer my respect and acknowledgment to the sovereign nations who have lived here always: the Quinault Indian Nation, the Shoalwater Bay Tribe, the Confederated Tribes of the Chehalis Reservation, the Quileute Nation, the Hoh Tribe, the Squaxin Island Tribe, and many others in the region. They continue to fight for their sovereignty over land they have cared for since time immemorial.

CONTENTS

Part Five
Building

FOREWORD

You do not need to look far to see the connection between poverty and death in the United States. Before the pandemic hit, two hundred and fifty thousand people were dying each year from poverty and inequality, according to the Columbia University Mailman School of Public Health. That's seven hundred people a day. In 2023, researchers at the University of California, Riverside, identified poverty as the fourth-greatest cause of death in the nation, writing, "Poverty kills as much as dementia, accidents, stroke, Alzheimer's, and diabetes."

Simply put, the United States has gotten used to death, especially when it comes to poor people. There are sixty-six million poor and low-income white people, twenty-six million poor and low-income Black people, thirty-eight million poor and low-income Latinx people, and two million poor and low-income Indigenous people in these yet-to-be-United States. The United States has an average of five abandoned houses for every person who is unhoused—and still allows for upward of ten million people to have nowhere to lay their heads.

This is an absolute indictment of our society. And these are the contradictions raised and stories told in *Trash: A Poor White Journey*, Cedar Monroe's indelible book about the pain and power of the poor. Although our country may have accustomed itself to death, we don't have to. Monroe's bracing prose forces us not to look away from either the suffering or the promise of those living in poverty.

As an antipoverty organizer for three decades and cochair of the Poor People's Campaign: A National Call for Moral Revival, I have visited Grays Harbor County, Washington, the community in which *Trash* is set, a number of times. My second visit occurred in 2017, with a delegation of Black Lives Matter activists from Ferguson and Miami, veterans from the Iraq and Afghanistan wars, Union of Homeless organizers, faith leaders, and a Student Nonviolent Coordinating Committee activist still organizing poor white and Black people in the rural South today. On our first day, we attended a memorial service for a young homeless man who had died from poverty and inequality. Although it was only January, he was not the first resident of the area to die that year. Here in the richest country in the world, deaths like his have become unremarkable.

Before the service, community members prepared food and readied the church. Monroe, as chaplain to those of the area who were unhoused, led us in a meaningful service of remembering. After the memorial, we ate together, told stories, and made music. One member of our delegation commented that the way the community came together in the face of poverty and death must be what heaven looked like. I still use this as a touchpoint many years later.

This book tells an untold story in America. It's a story of people who have been abandoned amid abundance, who hold in their hands the power to transform society from the bottom up. It is a story not dissimilar to the stories from sacred texts and traditions from more ancient times, including the letters of the apostle Paul, who writes, "Isn't it obvious that God deliberately chose men and women that the culture overlooks and exploits and abuses, chose these 'nobodies' to expose the hollow pretensions of the 'somebodies'?" (1 Corinthians 1:27 MSG).

Trash exposes the hollow pretensions of those who have benefited from the status quo. It finds hope in the very humans society has left out, looked over, and locked up. This is not an easy story to read; it has no pretty bows or decorations. But the truth and grit of the "nobodies" may just be the hope for the nation. May we have eyes to see and ears to hear it.

—Rev. Dr. Liz Theoharis, director of the Kairos Center for Religions,
Rights, and Social Justice and cochair of the Poor People's Campaign:
A National Call for Moral Revival

INTRODUCTION

THEY SAY WE are trash people. White trash.

My story is part of the story of the sixty-six million poor white people in the United States. We live scattered around the country, from rural towns and farms to inner cities, from trailer parks on the edge of towns to tent cities in our largest urban areas. I come from these people, variously called, in popular culture, white trash, rednecks, poor whites, or crackers. My wife calls us broke-ass white people.

Like many poor white people, I cannot easily trace my ancestry back to Europe, but I know I come from people leaving land in Europe, displaced by greed and believing the promise of free land and work in a "new world." My ancestors scattered across this continent as mechanics, factory workers, farm laborers, grocers, housekeepers, and the occasional outlaw. Will Campbell, a pastor and activist during the civil rights era, wrote that "rednecks"* like me had spent generations "searching but never finding a secure life in a land of plenty."

Poor whites have often been the surplus people of the United States. We are uniquely privileged by our skin color—because if we can garner some level of respectability, either through college or through respectable trades, we can at times gain entry into the American Dream. We are also barred from that dream more often than not, left to struggle for survival.

I was born to poor white people in a suburb of San Jose, California. My people had moved from the Great Lakes region, from the South, from Appalachia, and from the US-Mexico border, all during the Great Depression. We

---

*The term *redneck* is used as a slur toward poor white Southerners, and by extension poor white people in any part of the country. There are many theories as to its origin, but it almost certainly refers to the red necks of white people who worked outdoors, thus separating Southern white workers from a white landed elite who never needed to redden their necks with manual labor. Will Campbell and others have sought to reclaim this term as a self-identifier. I use it in quotation marks, as a term that I consider both a slur directed at poor white people like me and an uneasy self-identifier.

moved when I was twelve to the Pacific Northwest, to Grays Harbor County, on the coast of Washington State. As I grew up, as jobs dried up and prisons filled up, vast tent cities also began to line the coastlines of the United States. Poor whites, always pushed westward as the vanguard of land acquisition by large corporate interests, finally went as far west as possible. There, many of us were thrown away, just like the trash heaps that surrounded the tent cities spreading up and down the coastline. Trash people living among trash: that is the dominant narrative about our lives.

At the same time, I was raised to see myself as a citizen of a republic designed to bring freedom to the world, with ancestors who took a God-ordained mission to spread civilization from sea to shining sea. No matter my economic situation, no matter my struggle to survive, I could still take comfort in the fact that I belonged to the people of a great nation. These stories we are told serve to both control us and to motivate us to continue to support a system that is destroying all of us.

My people have much to repent from. We have often been recruited to do the empire's dirty work. We have fought in genocidal wars against Indigenous peoples and in imperial wars around the globe. We have too often stood below the lynching tree, choosing whiteness over solidarity, choosing unprovoked violence over liberation. We did it for the promise of a better life that we rarely received, and, in the process, we helped to decimate Black and brown and Indigenous communities, along with our own best chance of liberation. Instead of the secure life in a land of plenty so many poor whites sought, Will Campbell explains further, we found the "freedom to flounder, to drift, to wander westward in a frustrating search of what had been promised but never delivered."

Poor whites are the largest group of poor people in the United States. Some 33 percent of white people are poor. That is roughly 20 percent of the US population. We have also been intentionally pitted against poor Black, brown, and Indigenous people, in a competition for land and work, something that has short-circuited any struggle for an end to poverty. The system of capitalism unique to the United States has been wildly effective, both at creating wealth for those in power and at keeping poor people fighting among themselves in the process.

I was raised during the heyday of the Religious Right and in its most extreme fringes. When I left home and came out as queer, I spent decades trying to unlearn the lessons of my childhood and find my place in a world not meant for me. I was lucky to learn from communities outside the United States, in Oaxaca and on the US-Mexico border, immigrant communities in the United States, liberation movements south of the border, Palestinian resistance movements, and some truly stellar professors of color in seminary. I learned how my community had been pitted against communities of color, at home and abroad, as a highly successful way to maintain profit. I realized that I, as a poor white person in the United States, could recognize the terrible results of capitalism on poor communities and begin to imagine common cause across race and nationality.

As I started to develop my ideas, I almost immediately ran up against opposition, not just from the conservative white religious groups I had grown up in, but also in liberal higher education. I realized that I was expected, once educated, to leave behind my past and the poor white communities that had raised me. I resisted this expectation and returned home to the community in which I had been brought up.

I was ordained in the Episcopal Church and have worked as a chaplain to an incredibly poor community in Grays Harbor County, Washington, for the past decade. Majority white and bounded by multiple Indigenous nations, this community in the middle of nowhere sits on the very edge of the western coast. We are as far west as you can go.

As I visited people on the streets and in jails, I realized how many young people in my generation had been thrown away. We have discovered through bitter experience that the promises given to poor white people in the United States are empty, that the promise of a "secure life in a land of plenty" was an illusion all along. Young poor white people are caught between white supremacy, which demands we succeed under capitalism, and the lack of a future that is becoming more and more evident as poverty rates climb and tent cities and prisons warehouse so many of us. My generation of poor white people, and the generations after us, get to choose: between the empty promises of white supremacy, on the one hand, and solidarity with poor people across race on the other.

This book is about that choice.

I began writing this book two years into a worldwide pandemic, two years after uprisings for Black lives forced a racial reckoning five hundred years in the making, and more than a year after armed protesters swarmed the US Capitol in an attempt to topple the Biden presidency before it began. Those of us in the United States are still trying to make sense of the events of the past few years. It is hard, because we do not have the education and perspective of many other parts of the world. We are stuck in our own bubble, with American exceptionalism functioning as the primary narrative of both major political parties and most academic and popular discourse.

What is the role of poor white people in the social order of the United States? Liberals have been convinced that poor white people, the so-called rural working class, elected Donald Trump to the presidency and formed his base. Conservatives have been convinced that poor white people are fundamentally flawed, failed white people who made their own bed and now must sleep in it.

A century ago, W. E. B. Du Bois noted that poor white people, who he calls the "white worker," have few revolutionary leaders. If poor white people get some power, they cease to be poor, and their best interests seem to align with the planters, the business owners, and the current political and social order. Du Bois is right. The leading commentator on poor white people in the last decade has been J. D. Vance, author of *Hillbilly Elegy*. A poor Appalachian kid with an addicted mom who got out of poverty through military service and entered law school, Vance wrote a book that has provided Americans on both the left and the right with a convenient explanation for white poverty. While Vance writes from his personal experience, he also promotes a perspective, used heavily on both sides of the aisle, that blames poor people for their own poverty. He maintains that poor white people have developed a pessimistic, fatalistic culture that makes them poor workers, unproductive, and prone to addiction. He argues, from his introduction onward, that the culture in which poor white people are raised is to blame for their lack of initiative and failure to thrive under capitalism. They need to follow Vance's advice: work hard, get out of their slump, and become productive citizens of these United States. Like most narratives fed to poor people in the United States, Vance's suggests that if he got out of poverty, anyone can.

This is the story told by most media outlets and on most college campuses. This is the story poor white people tell ourselves, every single day, as suicide and overdose rates cripple our communities. This is the story carefully crafted by the American empire, in its single-minded quest for the almighty dollar. The power of this story in upholding the status quo is illustrated by J. D. Vance's rise to political power, as a Trump-supporting Republican senator now back in Ohio.

In this book, I will paint a different picture. I grew up as the social programs that regulated the market were stripped away. I saw the results every day: in my dad's sense of failure, in the steep decline in jobs, in my own despair and homelessness, in the crumbling communities around me. Driven by a conviction that there was some reason for all of this—beyond the right-wing conviction that queers like me were ending the world as we knew it—I read everything I could and I listened to the communities around me. Eventually, when I returned to Grays Harbor as a chaplain, I began to use our stories to ask questions of the J. D. Vances of the world. These questions form the basis of this book.

So who am I, as a poor white person? What is my history? Why are poor white people pitted against people of color? Why are 33 percent of white people poor, and why are 43.5 percent of Americans poor? And why don't we join forces across various divisions—and across the globe—to end our poverty?

The air we breathe is saturated with the narrative of the American empire and Manifest Destiny. Today, this empire seems to be buckling under the weight of its many indiscretions, failing both as a world leader and at taking care of its own people. We only need to look at the insipid leadership of both parties and the homeless camps lining our coasts to see its failure. Some 140 million people in this country, about 43.5 percent of Americans, are poor and low income.

Meanwhile, capitalism is alive and well, functioning exactly as it was meant to. Two of the wealthiest men in the world, Bill Gates and Jeff Bezos, live in my state, guzzling up resources and labor with unrelenting greed as the average person struggles to keep a roof over their head and as tent cities ring Seattle and every other city and town in the state. The housing market is sending the cost of shelter soaring, but we are already hearing of "robust economic recovery."

Poor white people have a complicated story, and telling it is a complicated task. As poor people, we suffer under all the institutions at work in our society to keep us in our place. We are workers, either employed in low-wage jobs or forming that vast army of the unemployed that capitalism needs as a surplus labor force. We are brutalized by policy and often also by vigilantes, police, prisons, and even the church. We die often and young, denied medical care, flooded by drugs, denied housing and basic human dignity.

Yet we were promised land—the land of Indigenous people—by virtue of our whiteness. Even though most of the land sits in corporate hands for profit, and always has, there has always been *just* enough incentive to keep poor white people at war with others: Indigenous people first, and then all other people of color who sought to meet their needs. The justification for the seizure of land in North America, after all, was that its conquerors were white and Christian. From the Homestead Act to the present day, poor white people have been taught to see their struggle for a place to live and belong as fundamentally at odds with the rights of Indigenous, Black, and brown people.

It is a serious tension. We as poor white people are told that stolen land is ours, as potential homesteaders or homeowners, yet so many of us are denied even basic housing rights and are run out of the shacks we build on riverbanks to survive. We often join the ranks of the police and military, forming the backbone of those institutions, even as militarized police and prisons brutalize poor communities and bodies across race, including our own.

White supremacy teaches white people that they are superior to people of other races and have a special duty to rule and subjugate the world. It provides the motivation for poor white people to uphold capitalism and carries in it a continued promise of jobs and land if they comply. Poor white communities are at high risk for recruitment into all the extremes of white nationalism and white extremism, as illustrated not just by the confederate flags flying from trailer parks and the rise of far-right militias in small towns but also by both Christian and pagan versions of white nationalism gaining traction everywhere.

The other side of the coin is also part of white supremacy: if white people fail to either uphold capitalism or succeed in it, we are failed white people.

We must deserve whatever violence, death, or suffering comes our way. We must deserve our own poverty and degradation because of our own mistakes. In other words, we are trash and deserve to be treated like trash. Divided by race, in wider society, in the prison system, by every system around us, we have sunk into a sense of despair as we watch our communities fall apart.

I am most grateful to Ms. Ruby Sales, civil rights leader and Black elder, who challenged the white theological community when she said this: "What is it that public theology can say to the white person in Massachusetts who's heroin-addicted? I don't hear anyone speaking to the forty-five-year-old person in Appalachia who feels like they've been eradicated, because whiteness is so much smaller today than it was yesterday. Because there's nothing wrong with being European American; that's not the problem. It's almost like white people don't believe that other white people are worthy of being redeemed."

This book describes my experience of being a chaplain in a poor community. In many ways, it is my attempt to respond to Ruby Sales's questions. In my work, I often confronted the question of whether the white heroin addict or the aging white guy in a poor town was worthy of a good life. The entire system, from business interests to local politicians, said no. But my faith, and my belief in the fundamental dignity of every human being, said otherwise.

This book is a story of confronting the history of this country and the marks of its devastation on one corner of the world. It is the story of learning from the Indigenous people of this place, whose land this is, as they suffer the continued effects of genocide. It is the story of confronting white supremacy, in my own heart and in my community, as we seek a way forward in a country that has betrayed us. It is the story of poor white people, my own people, who are marked as failed white people and treated accordingly. It is the story of the punishment meted out to those who fail white supremacy.

Those of us who escape the worst of poverty in white communities rarely tell our stories. Perhaps we are hampered by shame and a Vance-like need to frame our own story as triumphant, distancing ourselves from the distasteful stereotypes of white poverty and degradation. I want, instead, to tell the story of my community, to offer a counter-story to the prevailing narratives of poor whiteness that press in on all sides.

At the same time, I approach this work with a great deal of trepidation. There is so much more that needs to be said that this book does not cover. There are so many blind spots I bring, some of which I've corrected and others that will be glaring to many readers. I run many risks: the risk of centering white people at a time when it is so important to listen to Black, Indigenous, and brown voices. The risk of oversimplifying the racism that has been part of the warp and weft of this nation from the beginning.

I know I will make many mistakes in this work. Any time white people, poor or not, talk about racial realities, we speak from our own social location, a location that hampers our ability to see the systems that benefit us. I am aware of the way that whiteness, even poor whiteness, hampers one's vision, and every time I think I understand how these systems work, I find that I have so much more to learn.

So in these pages I attempt to tell the story of poor white people not to detract from the real and terrible struggles of communities of color but to add another dimension to the devastation of white supremacy. White supremacy is not good for anyone, even those it seeks to redeem. In the end, it destroys us all. It is a system rotten to its core, to its root, used to shore up a system of greed that is killing us all and threatening the earth itself.

This book is an attempt to start a conversation, not define it—to openly talk about the intersections of race and class when it comes to poor white people, something white people are rarely keen to do. I hope this book sparks a much longer conversation. It's a small attempt to tell my story, and the story of a community dear to my heart, as honestly as I can. And I hope, in telling that story, that we can have a wider conversation about poverty and racism, capitalism and colonialism, imperialism and militarism, and how to end the systems that oppress us.

$$\text{♁ ⸙ ♄}$$

In this book you will meet a community of struggling people, the people who taught me, people who endlessly and courageously fight for life. My first place of learning was "the River," a strip of land along the Chehalis River in the center of Aberdeen, Grays Harbor's largest city. Here, the largest homeless encampment in the county faced sweeps and evictions, and here, they fought back with all the resources they had. In this book, you will meet a few of those people and hear about their fight for some place to exist and live.

You will meet a community living in the abandoned zones of late capitalism. You will see young people suffer in prison, and you will walk with us as we bury our loved ones who die of untreated illness, overdose, suicide, police brutality, and street violence. You will see what happens when whole communities are abandoned and left to die, denied their basic human right to life.

You will also witness our courage and resolve to live and struggle for life in the most desperate circumstances. You will meet people in this book who are choosing solidarity with other poor people, joining with others who are resisting the political and social institutions that oppress us. You will watch as we take the fight for survival to the courts and to the US Capitol. You will meet people who are standing up in protest against policies that ensure that poor people die often and early. Who are reclaiming their children and learning to care for them in a world where they never were shown how. Who are standing up to vigilantes at a risk to their own lives. Who are clawing their way to sobriety in a world full of drugs and poison. Who are finding healing as they grow vegetables and tend the land.

If poor white people are to choose solidarity with other poor people, we must dream of a better future and an end to this centuries-long experiment in death and destruction. We must realize our history and what brought us to this point, learning from Black and brown organizers to understand our history from the underside. We must learn to see ourselves in a radically different way: not as the trash of a global empire nor as foot soldiers in the American experiment. We must realize that we are not, in fact, trash. No human being is, and no human being deserves to be treated as such.

Part One

ORIGINS

❦ 1 ❦

CANARIES IN A COAL MINE

ZACH, A SKINNY white kid, was lounging back in an old office chair on wheels. His dark hair was cropped short, and he looked restless, even bored. If you looked close enough, you'd see the chair's cracking surface had his nickname carved into it: "Squawk." His name was all over the jail—chairs, walls, tables.

They say if you write your name on jail walls, it is a bad omen: it means you'll be coming back. Zach always came back.

He held his wrists out to me with a silly grin. "See?" In a rough prison tattoo, his wrists said, "Fuck cops." If you drew his hands across his back in handcuffs, you would definitely notice that one. "They always tighten up the cuffs when they see that." His grin broadened.

"How do they treat you here?" I asked.

"Aw, they are all right," he shrugged. "The guard is always telling me to read the Bible and believe in Jesus. I told him I already have a pastor—one who don't tell me what to believe."

I grinned back. We had bantered that way for almost a year, as I visited him every few weeks at the county jail. Zach had his share of felonies. He was twenty-two and had caught his first felony at around eighteen, when he was sent to Walla Walla, the oldest and worst prison in the state, one of many that provides a labor force for corporations and state contracts.

Incarceration started much earlier for Zach. Washington State had the toughest truancy laws in the country, and Grays Harbor County implemented them with uncompromising zeal. Zach's brushes with juvie began when he was thirteen, and, in his own words, he spent more of his life locked up than out. He spent most of his teens in and out of jail and the youth shelter, using harder and harder drugs. I saw Zach last in the summer of 2016, in jail again on a probation violation, dope sick and miserable, bemoaning his varied love life.

On November 8, 2016, as a deeply divided country prepared to vote, I was spending the night at our church shelter in Westport, a tiny coastal town, where a dozen or so homeless people were sleeping in our first ad hoc shelter. The unease surrounding the election touched our small community, but most people in the shelter that night had not voted and were preoccupied with the more pressing needs of food and shelter.

Every once in a while, an argument would break out over who might be the best candidate for the presidency. Hillary Clinton was not well loved in our part of the world, since it was under Bill Clinton's presidency that the national forests were closed for logging and the North American Free Trade Agreement (NAFTA) offshored much of our industry. Also, under the Clinton presidency juvenile incarceration had exploded, and, in our community, that left deep scars.

Donald Trump was also deeply suspect, with his open criticism of welfare and the Affordable Care Act (ACA). Everyone remembered how impossible it was to get medical care without insurance before the ACA, and numerous people were coming up to me to strategize how to get medical procedures or dental work done quickly—because, as they told me, "We might lose health care soon."

Around midnight, as everyone slept and the shelter was actually quiet for once, I glanced at my phone. A text flashed across my phone. "Zach died yesterday."

At first I didn't believe it. Street rumors of death are common and just as often false. But when I was able to get in touch with his girlfriend and best friend, they told me what had happened. Zach had been to two hospitals, complaining of a sprained ankle and difficulty breathing. At least one of those hospitals assumed he was drug seeking and sent him away. After the last hospital visit, he went home to an abandoned, damp trailer, wheezing, his chest bruising, barely able to stand. When his friend came to check on him, he was unconscious. "The doctor said there was nothing he could do," they told me. "He tried, but he said he should have been treated earlier." Later, the coroner would rule that he died of pneumonia with severe abscesses in his lungs, likely due in part to his drug use, although friends suspect his living conditions may have played a part as well. Zach had just turned twenty-four.

I found myself on my knees in the sanctuary, tears streaming down my face. My memory of November 8, 2016, the day Donald Trump was elected the forty-fifth president of the United States, is now dominated by the death of a young man I had visited often in jail. He was dead because he fell through the cracks of every system, dead because he was thrown away by the community at thirteen when he entered the juvenile justice system, dead because he didn't have adequate housing, dead because of the opioid epidemic, dead because it is nearly impossible to get adequate medical care when you are poor in the United States.

⸱ ⸱ ⸱

I left Grays Harbor in my early twenties and, for some time, never looked back. When I did return, it was to the realization that so many of my generation who did not get out ended up on the street. While many people's stereotype of homeless people is of older men panhandling on corners, the reality of homelessness is much more complex. The majority of people I met on the streets were between sixteen and thirty-five and had lost jobs, never gotten one, or aged out of foster care. Young women always point out that there are more women than men on the street; they just hide better.

The numbers of people who experience homelessness are hard to track, largely because the Department of Housing and Urban Development uses point-in-time counts to calculate data, relying on a one-night volunteer count organized by each county. By that count, 553,000 people were counted nationally in 2018, half of whom lived in California and Washington. But the National Law Center on Homelessness and Poverty concludes that this is a vast undercount. Anyone with eyes in any city in the country can see that it is. In Aberdeen, with just over 16,000 residents, the most accurate data that I have been able to find is a report in 2018 through the public health department. This report revealed that 512 people seeking social services were unhoused and another 535 were couch surfing. That means one in sixteen people are experiencing homelessness in this small town.

Poverty in Aberdeen is stark. It is starkly visible in the mansions on the hill overlooking the town and the run-down tract homes and apartments on the flats, built over the fill of the logging industry. It is starkly visible in the churches, where Sunday morning is as segregated by class as it is by race. It is most starkly visible on social media, where small-town commentators take to voicing their deepest fear of and hate toward their failing children.

In Aberdeen, the old brick buildings and tenement houses look like they were thrown together in a hurry, their foundation posts sunk into the mud and fill of the harbor. Now half are rotting and abandoned, and parts of the downtown corridor look like a ghost town. A few charming stores and breweries have opened in recent years, but the small business owners who fill the usable buildings are frustrated, trying to eke out a living in a place where the population is decreasing and few people can afford to buy things.

When Walmart moved in, the stores selling food and supplies dwindled to corner marts. Business owners want a thriving business district, understandably; they want packed pubs and artsy stores and a stream of tourists staying in renovated hotels. Because Aberdeen was built on sawdust fill alongside a harbor, it is a natural wetland. Capitalism might want to believe it can change the path of the ocean, but the earth will always defend its limits. Even greed eventually bumps up against natural limits. In 2015, Aberdeen was home to a devastating flash flood that covered the downtown district in three to six feet of water, and it became apparent that no one would invest in the tattered remnants of the old logging town whose downtown was destined to be reclaimed by the ocean. A levy project to hold back the constant flooding in downtown was started. It continues, now the last hope of a town teetering on the edge of destruction, people fighting for what is left of a place that holds their memories and history.

Most of the people who live in Aberdeen live in colorful places like "felony flats." A few Section 8 apartment buildings are full, always full, and everyone else fights for a place—an apartment, an old fixer-upper. So many of those fixer-upper houses are flop houses—homes owned by older people on Social Security or drug dealers. In a mix of generosity and black market ingenuity, they allow as many people who can pay for a couch or a piece of floor space or a closet to stay, as long as they do not cause trouble.

Perhaps the business that thrives most in Aberdeen is the street trade— in drugs and sex, for sure, but also in stolen items, food, skills in repair work or cooking, and sleeping space. A blow job might buy you a couch but so could buying the whole household food for a week with your food stamp card. All tradable items are worth half their legal market value, including stolen goods. To stay in a bedroom closet in a flop house for a month might cost you the value of $300. It would not be unusual for a young person desperate for shelter in the winter to rob the local Walmart of $600 worth of goods to sleep in a flop house closet not large enough to lie down in.

Now the business community and the homeless community are increasingly at odds. While it is more common to rob large supermarkets, small businesses and especially owners of vacant buildings are feeling the effect of increased property crimes. Most of the old abandoned buildings in Aberdeen are completely stripped of copper wire, for example, their already old plumbing and electrical systems destroyed. If a building is empty, people camp in it. Many of those buildings burn down as candles topple or propane tanks blow—or even occasionally from fires set on purpose, sometimes with their squatting residents still inside.

"The haves and the have nots," my dad always used to intone every time we drove through town on a farm errand. It was the way it had been for well over a century, since the timber barons moved in, built their homes and churches on the hill, and threw up cheap housing on the flats for the workers they needed for the forests and the mills. They hired people who migrated from Appalachia, from Finland, from Sweden and Norway, and then later from the American Southwest. Back then, at least, work was as plentiful as the poverty, even if it was incredibly dangerous and so many people lost life or limb. Now there is no incentive to ensure that the thousands of people who live on the flats have their needs even partially met.

My generation of poor millennials who were raised in this logging community expected that there would be work for us. But we came of age to find that there was very little industry left and very few good-paying jobs to be had. We were raised to work hard, but what was left were low-paying cannery jobs, service work, and temp jobs. Logging trucks no longer clogged the highway, and unless you owned your own fishing boat or business, you had few options beyond working for Walmart or the prison.

The other option is to join the ranks of the unemployed and end up on the other side of the bars. People who end up in the most extreme conditions—young men like Zach who are spit out of prison onto the street, who live in back alleys and on borrowed couches, in shacks and tents and abandoned trailers—are the canaries in the coal mine. They show, in living, breathing color, the effects of five hundred years of oppression, made visible in their bruised and broken and scarred bodies.

🐦 🐦 🐦

To understand the systems that made Zach's story possible, you have to understand the history of this place.

In Grays Harbor, the amount of profit generated by the felling of old growth forests was staggering. Men broke their bodies and often lost their lives doing incredibly dangerous labor, while the timber barons amassed incredible wealth. Workers lived in houses slapped together on a swamp, while the cities of the West Coast were built on their labor. This reality forms the backdrop to any understanding of the stories this book tells.

Capitalism relies on labor being as cheap as possible, to increase profits. In order for capitalism to regulate the labor market and maximize profit, a vast army of unemployed workers must be available when work does arise. Once the resource—in this case, trees—becomes more scarce, the communities built around that industry are cast off and become a sort of abandoned zone.

This forces a vast number of people to survive or die outside the formal economy. In its past, Aberdeen was a hotbed for union organizing among timber workers. But as less labor was needed, prisons expanded their population. In the last forty years, as extraction jobs like timber or fishing have either become less important or more mechanized, prisons have become a kind of warehouse for the unemployed, a place to funnel people from cast-off zones. Since 1968, the number of sentenced inmates in US state and federal prison of all races has grown exponentially: from 187,914 in 1968 to 1,458,000 in 2016. In practice, this means that young people in poor communities are forced into an illegal, underground market economy to survive because there are no jobs. Then they are fed into a prison system where they provide a nearly free labor force to corporate and government contracts.

For young people in Grays Harbor, the drug economy is king. Drugs are big business and becoming bigger business by the day. When I was young, Aberdeen was one of the meth capitals of the country, with hundreds of entrepreneurs mixing up batches of toxic chemicals to keep loggers and truckers awake and to make thousands dependent on a pipe or a needle. Now drugs stream into the region from all over the world.

If you are young and poor, or if you just aged out of foster care, or if you just got out of prison, the fastest way to find a bed or a couch to sleep on is to run drugs. This explains one reason that, even after a forty-year war on drugs, Aberdeen still has high addiction rates. It is easier to get drugs than food, and plenty of people trade their food, their bikes, their jewelry, and eventually their stolen property for their next fix.

Drugs, and particularly the opioid epidemic, are one of the great health crises of our time. Most people I have met got addicted to opiates through prescription OxyContin, medicating after surgery for injuries in logging accidents or for chronic pain. The link to the timber industry is important: logging results in frequent injuries, and many people older than me began using Oxy-Contin after serious injury on the job. Drug companies like Purdue Pharma, owned by the Sackler family, aggressively marketed their product and convinced many doctors to prescribe it with abandon. My childhood doctor lost her practice when it was discovered that physicians were distributing opiates under the table to clients, sometimes out of compassion for lack of availability of any pain management, sometimes for the extra money it afforded providers in poor towns. It was a short jump to heroin once OxyContin scrips became hard to get. More and more, they are replaced by mass-produced fentanyl, wildly increasing overdose rates.

Drugs are not just a health crisis, although they are that. Drugs now form a harsh and brutal economic system that has filled in the gaps of the crash of industry in Poor Town USA. While drugs numb the brutality and pain of poverty, they also provide brutal employment for hordes of young people with no other option and no job waiting for them out of high school.

The drug economy provides little stability or upward mobility. Everything you make can and will be lost, and any property you purchase will be seized by the US government once you get busted. It is a life of highs and lows: driving cool cars and flashing bling one minute, locked in jail the next. If you are an entrepreneur in this economy, you will likely end up shooting up heroin yourself in a muddy tent, breathing toxic fumes from the spills of long-gone industry. Or dying with a body riddled with infection, so alienated from society that the hospitals assume you are beyond care.

Zach was one of many of these canaries in a coal mine. Funny, creative, brilliant, and one who fell victim to the brutality of US capitalism, under which human life has no value beyond being useful or surplus labor. Young people especially are adrift, desperate for a future and aware that the promises given to their parents no longer apply to them.

Poor white people have drifted as far west as possible and found that there is no "secure life in a land of plenty" available for them, as Will Campbell says, after all. The promises of the United States to poor white people for so long are actually, for many of us, empty. There is no free land, no secure home for us in Manifest Destiny. There is only cheap labor and a prison cell or death if you do not survive it.

Zach's funeral was small. His friends drifted in and out of the church for hours after, lighting candles in his memory. The church probably hadn't seen so many Jordans or baggy jeans in its history. Zach was a decade younger than I am. He was born well into the economic crash in Aberdeen, right about the time Clinton gutted welfare and made child incarceration a priority. A decade earlier I had been born to working-class white parents. My parents and their peers, who helped to vote in Reagan's policies, still thought it was possible to pull themselves up by their own bootstraps. They were respectable enough to believe in the promises of land and work offered to white people.

My generation and those who came after me did not see the fruits of that belief. We knew we were being left to die.

2

POOR WHITE TRASH

"DO YOU WANT some homemade vegetables?"

I was a deeply shy eight-year-old, pulling my little red wagon through the maze of duplexes and apartments on our block. I meant to ask if people wanted home-*grown* vegetables, but the words didn't come out quite right. Our tiny backyard was full of vegetables—tomato plants, pole beans, squash, sunflowers, and cucumbers—and I would get up early every morning and water them, watching the sun rise and feeling the powdery dust beneath my feet. If I close my eyes, I can still smell the lemons ripening and the orange blossoms in the northern California breeze.

The grandma at the door, who was likely raising several grandkids, was usually kind and probably bought some zucchini or tomatoes for a few dollars. I was a scrawny white kid, and this was my first hustle. I'd drag that little red wagon up cracked concrete sidewalks to the grandmas raising their grandkids, the Korean family who was always nice to me, down past the apartments where down-and-out white men on motorcycles seemed to provide a steady stream of loud music, mechanic's work, and irritating grins. I hated cold-calling at people's doors as much as working-class people hate when people show up on their doorstep. I don't think that hustle lasted much more than a year.

Years later, my family kept up a steady stream of side hustles and then some decent business in rural Washington State. I kept my family in vegetables, and we sold everything from goat kids for the local Oaxacan families' quinceañeras to goat milk soap at local boutiques. I groomed dogs on the side to help my parents buy groceries.

Luckily I always ended up with legal side hustles or at least almost legal ones (small farmers are always trying to find loopholes within the heavily regulated food industry). I was surrounded by drugs—the family across the street seemed to always have a steady supply of meth and warrants—and many of the people I grew up with became addicted. But I never did dabble in that underground economy, which at the time provided the backbone for poor people's livelihoods.

In my own soul, however, in the private life behind the hustle and the hard work, I dreamed of throwing myself down a well or off a cliff. Poverty, abuse, and self-hatred were a daily part of my life as I helped raise my younger siblings and felt stuck in a world of little opportunity.

My parents often lived in fear of authorities getting wind that we were not in school, since homeschooling was not legal in California at the time, and I grew up deeply isolated, in part due to that fear. Once there was a sharp knock at our door, reverberating through the tiny duplex. I stood back in the hallway, waiting, with my two little sisters, the baby, only a year and a half, in diapers. "Get in the closet," my mom ordered from around the corner. I could see an officer's uniform through the old curtains that smelled like cooking grease. I ushered my sisters back to our room and slid back the closet doors. "Hey, let's hide!" I whispered to my little sister. "It will be fun!" I didn't catch the baby soon enough, and she went toddling out of the room. I held my younger sister, and we sat behind the clothes in the corner of the closet, waiting. My grandpa had been a cop, but I knew my parents were still terrified of them. I heard a deep voice wafting back into the room as we waited. Ten minutes later, my mom opened the closet. "You can come out now."

My dreams at night were full of silent screaming, of wandering lost down roads that led nowhere, and of the violence I encountered in daylight. I would wander off alone into the forest and hide under trees, digging my nails into my flesh.

At some point I was dissociating so often, staring off into space with my heart pounding, that my mom took me to the doctor, wondering if there was something physically wrong with me. Once, when I nearly severed my finger while grooming a dog, I calmly wrapped it, put the dog away, and went about my day. What drugs gave many of my neighbors—a sense of relief and escape from the trauma of poverty and violence—my own brain gave me freely. Even today there are large chunks of my memory missing, and I cannot construct a linear timeline of my childhood.

The worst memories I have are of the violence I witnessed. I had known this boy from church. His parents homeschooled their nine children;

the eldest girl had died years before, although no one really knew why. It was early summer, and the jasmine smelled heavenly as I opened the door for the mail carrier. A friend of our family, she burst into tears as she handed me the mail. "I should have known. I should have guessed it," she said, weeping. The boy, who lived just up the road, had nearly died after months of torture by his parents. They had taken his recent illness as a sign of rebellion, had beaten him regularly and force-fed him his own vomit. The boy was two years older than I was, twelve, and he weighed only fifty pounds when police arrested his parents. I remembered seeing him at church and now realized I hadn't seen him in a while. As the mail carrier told us the story, I felt nauseous.

Within days, my mom got phone calls as the church tried to raise bail money for his parents. All I wondered, over and over, was, What had happened to their other child, that older sister who had died? Why didn't the church parents ever notice or intervene? Why in hell did the Baptist church I grew up in support those parents?

It is easy for me to talk about the inhumanity and injustice I witness around me, not so easy for me to talk about my own experiences. The thing about all forms of captivity is this: There are always shocking moments of inhumanity and cruelty. But most days, and years, of my childhood simply run together in a haze of boredom and isolation and longing.

For my entire childhood and teen years, my world was small, relegated to the home I grew up in and the farm we moved to, the small circle of people I was allowed to see from church, and then, later, from a small cult group and the few neighbors who bothered to talk to us.

That time, still, is a blur. It is a long stretch of wondering if what you experience is normal or what normal might be. It is a lot of retreating into your own head and imagination, escaping the reality around you, tumbling question after question over in your own mind until you think you might go mad. It is finding refuge in self-harm. It is finding small things you can control: hiding forbidden books, imagining forbidden adventure. It is also conforming: learning to talk and walk and breathe and think the way you are supposed to. You police your own thoughts and your own dreams. You are dependent completely on the people who have power over you, and you seek their love and approval.

I lived and moved in a different captivity than the many children who grew up in Grays Harbor and experienced incarceration early. Mine was a world where everything I did and said was strictly controlled. With no community events, schooling, television, or even friends by which to measure social norms, our small homeschool group was completely cut off from the world around us, surrounded by an endless list of requirements and expectations and often swift repercussions should we fail to meet them.

I remember sitting with my jaw clenched as a young father in our group beat his eighteen-month-old child for somehow crossing him during a service. I knew multiple girls who were raped repeatedly by their fathers: isolated homeschool movements are amazingly safe places for rapists to hide. I knew children who died at the hands of their parents. Children like Hana Williams, adopted from Ethiopia by white Christian homeschool parents in Mount Vernon, Washington. Starved and beaten by her parents, she died of hypothermia and abuse in their front yard.

My childhood was intensely isolating and lonely. For such a long time, I thought of my experiences as unique and embarrassing, something few others experienced. Turns out I was part of a much wider history and much longer experiment than I had thought.

🐦 🐦 🐦

Once, long ago, poor whites lived on the land of Northern Europe. Before private property, before the rise of capitalism, most of us lived on what scholars call "common land." From the Roman invasions of Northern Europe to the rise of nation states in the sixteenth and seventeenth centuries, Europe was a place of intense war and conflict, a place of empire building, and a place in which it was incredibly difficult for Europe's poor and oppressed to live. However, most people remained connected to the land their ancestors had been on for hundreds or thousands of years.

Then European empires like Spain and England turned land-hungry eyes on the Western Hemisphere. Enriched with their own empire and nation building, with armed fleets ready for war—after Spanish forced deportation of thousands of Jews and Muslims, after English seizure of church assets, after land seizure that left English peasant populations wandering growing cities—they saw the potential to make a profit off the land and human labor of other continents.

For the first time in history, financial profit (capital) became the end goal of European economies. While money had always been one of many means of exchange, capital now became the sole economic goal, resulting in a five-hundred-year-old race to increase the bottom line. To satisfy that endless search for capital, vast amounts of land were needed for raw materials. And vast numbers of cheap laborers were needed to do the work of transforming raw materials into profit.

Northern Europe, and particularly the English empire, privatized their land, forcing peasants off the land they had lived on and farmed for generations, before looking for land across the sea. Thus began the American experiment. The population of the Western Hemisphere was subjugated, enslaved, or murdered, as European nation states swept aside cultures with thousands of years of accumulated knowledge, wealth, and history. For labor, European conquerors turned to the African continent, kidnapping and enslaving millions to work vast plantations of sugar, rice, cotton, tobacco, and whatever other product could make fast and easy money.

Europeans who would become poor white people had been tied to the land for millennia, sometimes as independent peasant farmers, sometimes as serfs who owed allegiance and labor to petty kings or lords, but usually able to eke out a living on the land. On English-controlled land, serfs became peasant farmers and were able to continue to care for the land they had been tied to, in the words of Karl Marx, "from time immemorial."

As capitalism took the stage, the land itself became a commodity. Historians refer to this as the "fencing of the commons," or the policy of enclosure: that is, the transfer of ownership title of lands to a wealthy aristocratic elite. They soon realized they could make money off large crops, livestock operations, extraction of trees or ore, or, later, factories, and so they drove the people off the land to which they were once indigenous. This was the origin of the capitalist concept of private property. European peasants were removed from the land, forced into cities where they often were labeled vagrants, and stripped of their regional languages, cultures, and ways of life. As the "new world" opened up, these landless peasants were often deported for petty crimes or rebellion or offered the opportunity to go to the "waste land" of America. As historian Nancy Isenberg writes, quoting the work of English aristocrat Richard Hakluyt:

> *It was not just land that could be waste. People could be waste too. And*
> *this brings us to our most important point of embarkation: Hakluyt's*
> *America required what he classified as "waste people," to corps of*
> *laborers needed to cut down the trees, beat the hemp (for making rope),*
> *gather honey, salt and dry fish, dress raw animal hides, dig the earth*
> *for minerals, raise olives and silk, and sort and pack bird feathers. He*
> *pictured paupers, vagabonds, convicts, debtors, and lusty young men*
> *without employment doing all such work . . . The bulk of the labor*
> *would come from the swelling numbers of poor and homeless.*

This was a classic colonial move: take the surplus population of one place—the "white trash," so to speak—move it into a newly conquered territory, and subjugate the people who live there. The English, Irish, German, and Scottish settlers proved useful as foot soldiers in this imperial project. They had the incentive to fight with Indigenous people for the land, clearing the way for corporations and the US government to seize it.

Marx gives several examples of this process. In the Scottish Highlands, the Duchess of Sutherland decided to clear her lands of fifteen thousand people to make way for sheep farms. From 1814 to 1820, she destroyed and burned villages and turned the land into a vast pasture, destroying both culture indigenous to the region and the land itself, and she appropriated 794,000 acres to use to produce wool for the English textile industry. Eventually, when the demand for wool was less, the land was turned into hunting preserves for the English aristocracy.

In Ireland, the English crown had subjugated most of the region well before the nineteenth century. In the 1840s, Ireland experienced what they call *An Gorta Mór*, or the Great Hunger. A million people died of starvation, and a million more fled to the United States, Canada, and Australia. While the country produced enough food to feed everyone (only the potato crop failed in that decade), English and Irish landlords preferred to sell their products on the market and watch their tenants starve, or even pay for them to leave the country on high mortality famine ships. *An Gorta Mór* opened up Ireland's land for plunder.

These displaced people were then free to become settlers, or indentured servants, in the Americas. Irish people in the United States faced their own discrimination, but they also were able to join the numbers of poor white people hungry for land settlement and willing to do whatever dirty work the American empire needed. For example, Philip Sheridan was born to first-generation Irish refugees and gained popularity during the Civil War. Known for his role in the Indian Wars and for spearheading the slaughter of the plains buffalo, Sheridan is infamous for saying, "The only good Indian is a dead Indian."

Poor white people were used to "open" the frontier: pushed to first settle on land still under the control of Indigenous people and then spark open warfare. The reality for families like mine, of course, was that very little of that land ever really benefited us. "Those untethered from the land, who formed the ever-expanding population of landless squatters heading into the trans-Appalachian West, unleashed mixed feelings," Isenberg writes. "To many minds, the migrant poor represented the United States' re-creation of Britain's most disposed and impoverished class: vagrants."

Thomas Jefferson wrote longingly of an Anglo-Saxon peasant republic, where European refugees and immigrants would settle on small plots of land across the country and recreate an old European ideal. This vision certainly inspired the people I come from. Yet Jefferson dreamed of such a republic while sitting as a Southern aristocrat and enslaver on a plantation that held captive more than six hundred Black people over the course of his lifetime. He and the rest of the founding fathers supported the business interests of large planters and large corporations who needed land to expand their profits.

So while my immediate ancestors were always trying to settle down on a small plot of land to make a living, they never really succeeded. They were pushed further and further west, until I was born, in a little rented duplex on the coast of California to parents who desperately wanted to go back to the land. They ended up buying a little plot of twenty acres in Grays Harbor where it was impossible to make a living—the trees had been cut and the topsoil had been pushed over the side of the mountain by Weyerhaeuser, the largest timber company in the world. True to form, the majority of land in the United States was, and still is, controlled by corporate interests and a handful of wealthy owners.

In Aberdeen, on the far West Coast of the United States, I realized that the stories I had been told about where I came from were lies. Instead of some Jeffersonian ideal, we had a history of sorrow and loss and one that left us squatters on stolen land.

We are the descendants of peasants and serfs, indentured servants and rebels, squatters and vagrants: the surplus people of Europe, forced economically or politically to seek survival on a new continent. In the South, we were unwanted and unneeded in a slave economy, pushed to the less productive mountain land. We were soldiers in the Indian Wars and members of the Ku Klux Klan. In the North, we were used for factory labor, until our numbers grew so large we were pushed west to live on land that was not ours to take.

Only today, there is no west left. I was born on the edge of the Pacific Ocean, and there is nowhere left for people to go. The worst off of us line the shores of the Pacific in vast tent camps, filling up the space under bridges and overpasses, along rivers and on beaches.

When I look back on my own childhood, moving along the West Coast, I remember my longing to belong to a place and knowing that I did not truly belong anywhere. I remember being taught my role as a white person in the United States. Our ancestors were justified in their seizure of Indigenous land for the benefit of their families, or so the story went. "We were just stronger," my dad would tell us, talking about white people. "It's how God wanted it to be." But in the end, we were left constantly struggling to make ends meet, in a death struggle for survival.

And I remember in my bones the dirt and the scent of ripening tomatoes, the rising sun, and the smell of the forest on the morning breeze.

3

THE FAMILY CURSE

"DO YOU WANT to come to the library with me?" my dad asked. I was sitting on the floor in front of the coffee table, bent over a book and my notebook and writing in carefully made, precise letters.

I loved going to the library with my dad. The libraries at San Jose State were amazing. While my dad was pursuing his own research projects, I would wander, chasing my own knowledge in the quiet, musty shelves on floor after floor of books. Yesterday I had spent several hours hiding in the closet at home as my dad's anger bounced off the walls, his teeth grinding in frustration. But today was a good day, and maybe tomorrow would be better.

Perhaps the single driving force in my father's life was his constant sense of failure. He was brilliant, every bit as brilliant as any professor I've ever met, but aside from a stint in Bible college, he had little opportunity to pursue his dreams. He had a wife, a wife he nearly lost bearing her third child, and three babies who needed food and a place to live. He hated his jobs, every one of them: every drudge job in a warehouse, every attempt to climb the corporate ladder. Even when he successfully made it into management for a few years in a computer company, having worked his way up from a warehouse clerk, he loathed the work.

My father loved living things. As a young man, he filled his dreary little duplex with potted plants, and, while he saved for his farm, he filled every backyard with growing things. My fondest childhood memories are of picking oranges and ripe tomatoes, and of the rows of sunflowers along the fence. Next to his love of plants was his love of books. His walls were always floor-to-ceiling bookshelves, from our shabby duplex to his double-wide.

Despite my father's passion for the things he loved, most of his life was spent doing tasks he hated, working for men with more wealth and power than he would ever see. He took out his frustration at home, controlling the only part of the world that was his to control. Often, his anger at the world and perhaps at himself would be unleashed in a tirade that would leave his daughters hiding and in tears.

His frustration at being stuck making money in jobs he hated filled him with a crushing sense of failure. In the world of the white working class, if you fail, it can only be your own fault. There is no sense that a system might be broken or needs mending—no sense that the world in which you are a cog might be the failure, not you.

He talked about himself as being cursed—cursed to constant failure—and his whole life was consumed by the anxiety and depression that engendered. My sisters and I, growing up in the shadow of that burden, were the usual recipients of his frustration, as he took out his fury at his own perceived failure on us. We learned to hide, in closets and in books, in the woods and in our own souls. We learned to expect failure ourselves. Having been created in our father's image, my sisters and I saw ourselves as his failed, cursed children.

My story begins with this sense of failure, this sense of unworthiness.

↓ ↑ ↓

I also inherited the struggle of my people: to prove themselves worthy of the American Dream, to work hard enough to live a secure life in a land of plenty. Some of us succeeded, if only barely, and others of us did not. For the sixty-six million poor white people in the country, a deep sense of shame that we have failed whiteness, that we have failed our destiny, remains.

Growing up, we always talked about ourselves as if we were different from the upper-class whites who ran most of the business and political world. We had some feeling that we were being left out, that we were despised by the elite. But we never quite could name it.

Most of what we felt was shame. If we did not make enough money: shame. If we could not keep a job or a house or a decent car: shame. If we could not pursue our dreams: shame. Surely it was our fault for not working hard enough.

My dad spent long hours at jobs he hated and saved for twenty years to buy himself a hardscrabble farm with soil so poor from clearcutting that it would barely grow anything. It took a few years to scratch some pasture and vegetables out of the ground. I learned how things were made, and I learned how to make them when the money ran out: food, clothing, shelter.

I learned that, when you are poor, land and the ability to make the things that humans need for survival is power. But life was a constant struggle, and my father split his time between maintaining a farm that could not make a living and a warehouse job he could not quit.

I have always believed that my dad's crushing sense of failure drove his constant quest to prove himself worthy and respectable. My dad was raised by a deeply Catholic mother and grandmother; my mother, by nonreligious parents. They were both converted to fundamentalist Protestant Christianity during the late 1970s, the so-called Jesus Freak years. They had an immediate fascination with the conservative theology of the rising Christian Right. They were seeking order in a chaotic world, redemption from their failures to whiteness, and refuge from terrible childhood trauma.

The presumed answer to the chaos of an uncertain and war-torn world, the answer to decades of drudgery, the answer to the suffering my family and others around us tried to keep at bay, was the return to "biblical family roles." If we could prove ourselves worthy, we would find safety and a better world. What my sisters and I found instead was a system designed to break our wills and crush our spirits. The scars of that remain forever.

I grew up in the middle of the conservative backlash against the civil rights movement. Central to this backlash, dubbed the "Religious Right," was a belief in the importance of the nuclear family. While liberals often suggest Christian conservatism is rooted in lack of education, the reality is that most of the leaders of the movement were, and still are, highly educated and very well-funded. My family took the Religious Right one step further and became part of the wing of the Christian homeschool movement dubbed the "Quiverfull" movement: a movement fostered by well-funded theologians who believed that it was white Christians' duty to have large families and become a national influence on the political direction of the nation. They believed that Western civilization, originating in the Ancient Near East of biblical times, continuing through the Roman Empire and then the Christian empires of Europe, found its culmination in the American experiment. More importantly, they believed that teaching children this history, enforcing traditional gender roles (specifically to encourage the production of more children), and mandating civic involvement could sway the direction of US politics toward a theocratic ideal.

At its core, white Christian nationalism was a path for working-class and poor white families to prove themselves worthy and respectable recipients of the land and work promised to them. It also, inadvertently but predictably, gave abusive parents and molesters a place to hide. My parents jumped with both feet into this movement and often played with its extreme fringes, surrounding us with often dangerous and abusive people. These spaces were havens for abusive, charming men filled with the conviction they were destined to take over the country for Jesus.

This appeal—for white American families to return to a fictional American Christian past—was just another iteration of the white supremacy that upheld settler colonialism and capitalism. It has been a powerful intoxicant for white people. We white people, both rich and poor, are taught explicitly or implicitly that we are of a superior race. Underneath all of that is the expectation that we will be given land and work. The United States, however, does not keep its promises. Instead, land is primarily in the hands of large corporations, living-wage jobs exist as an elusive incentive to keep people working, and poor white people are left to struggle for survival.

For poor whites, white supremacy remains an elusive, ephemeral thing. Whiteness is supposed to confer intelligence, status, success. So what about the white people on welfare, on drugs, those who are generationally poor or in prison? What about the white people who have not made it?

Poor white people live with this crushing shame. White people are taught to treat failed white people with contempt. But nothing is more crushing than the contempt we heap on ourselves.

My father's constant quest for redemption failed him and his children, and it blighted our childhood. It was in the best interest of white elites and business interests to support a white Christian nationalism that would maintain unbridled capitalism and white supremacy, but it paid harsh dividends to the struggling white families who joined in.

Occasionally, those of us who survived our childhoods talk about the memories of violence: of parents who were taught to beat their children into submission, of isolation, of loss, of children we knew died of abuse, of horrifying failure. Most of us are part of a wave of backlash against fundamentalism, as young people came out of conservative Christian strongholds into a world for which they were not prepared. Those of us who grew up white and poor have emerged with serious scars and even deeper shame.

As I began work as a chaplain, I realized that a central part of my work was to confront the devastation that white supremacy has wrought on my own heart and on my own people. Psychotherapist Resmaa Menakem writes, "Well before the United States began, powerful white bodies colonized, oppressed, brutalized, and murdered other, less powerful white ones." In some ways, this pattern continued in the United States, as we used white supremacy to brutalize not only poor Black, brown, and Indigenous communities but each other.

🕊 🕊 🕊

Even while we internalized the white supremacy of our upbringing, I still had contact with people across race as a child, particularly in San Jose. With my family sprawling across much of California, I was aware that my family was mixed race. It had become more so over time: my Filipina step-grandma, my African American uncle, Latina and Black cousins and second cousins. Some of them I know well; others I only met at my grandfather's funeral. It is increasingly common for white poor families to intermarry and form mixed-race families; in fact, I know few families where that is not the case.

Living in contact with people across race, of course, does not mean that white people are taught to be less racist. Raised in fundamentalist circles, I was taught not only the whitewashed version of history typical in American schools; I was taught to believe that the European conquest, and even the African slave trade, were works of God and brought true religion to uncivilized people. I was taught an unadulterated version of American exceptionalism. In an interesting twist, however, my mother bought books from a Mennonite publisher for years, and so I was also exposed to strong critiques of the genocide of Indigenous people, slavery, and nationalism.

My cousins introduced me to hip-hop and groups like NWA. My love of the natural world left me wondering how much knowledge had been lost through conquest and the loss of Indigenous traditions. While most of the textbooks I read sought to downplay the horrors of genocide against Native people, I tracked down the sources, from Columbus and Cortez to US Army officers, and was horrified by their bloodthirsty narratives.

At the same time, the dominant narrative in the Quiverfull movement was of the triumph of white civilization. For example, some leaders in the movement have openly praised Southern slavery, and their ideas have since gained a great deal of traction in the alt-right. Doug Wilson of Moscow, Idaho, runs a church and a school and has built a following of Quiverfull and homeschooling families for some time. I remember being exposed to his books and articles as a teenager. He openly praises slavery and advocates for strict gender roles, spouting neo-Confederate ideas like multiple other homeschool advocates.

My sisters and I were not wrong: we were followed by a curse. But it was not a family curse that destined us for failure; it was the curse of white supremacy, one that both held us responsible for our own failure and demanded that we prove ourselves worthy of whiteness.

❧ 4 ❧

NAMING MY STORY

I HAD ONLY left home, with all its isolation, a year before. Now I was volunteering at the local library, feeling restless in my new marriage, uncertain about how to connect with the world. Sitting on an old sofa in the sparse living room, a stack of books occupying my end table, I was reading Maya Angelou for the first time. *I Know Why a Caged Bird Sings.*

She was telling the story of her childhood rape. "Just my breath, carrying my words out, might poison people and they'd curl up and die like the Black fat slugs that only pretended," Angelou wrote. "I had to stop talking."

I stopped reading for a moment. A million images, a million memories, flooded over me.

I remembered the dreams that plagued me as a child: of my mother, as a child herself, afraid as she opened the door to her house. Hiding on stairs. Running away. Even when I had no knowledge of the events of her life, I saw her fear in my dreams. It stalked me for a long time. It wasn't until much later that my mother told me her story, a harrowing story of intense abuse and frequent flight from one home to another.

I remembered my own thirteen-year-old self. My own experience of sexual assault. The feeling of being dirty and ugly. My grandfather's defense of his friend. My mother's anger.

I had also stopped talking to all but a few family members. I remembered being in the grocery store in the time that followed and the cashier asking me a question. I opened my mouth, but no words came out. Long habit and fear stopped my tongue, time and time again.

I had lived with the memory and trauma of my childhood every day. Reading Maya Angelou was the first time I had learned a way to name it, to talk about it, and to see it in a larger context.

I was a poor white person who had been taught by white supremacy to internalize the shame of sexual assault and live into "pure womanhood," which means producing legitimate children and maintaining a subservient role. What particularly affected my sisters and me was the view of women in the Quiverfull movement, which is really just white supremacy's view of white "family values" taken to its logical conclusion.

Maya Angelou named that experience for me, a poor white girl who was never given a lens to understand my own experience. She explained my pain to me.

🕊 🕊 🕊

I am at least the third generation of women who did not graduate from high school. I never went to school as a child, my mother ran away from home and dropped out of school at fifteen, and my grandma started working to support herself at fifteen.

My maternal grandmas, like many poor white women, broke many of the rules for respectable white women. My great grandma, who I called "Purple Grandma" because she always wore as many bright colors as she could fit into an outfit, had migrated from Appalachia to Southern California during the 1930s. She lived her life as fully as she could as a housekeeper in a Beverly Hills hotel, eventually dying in her late seventies on a beach vacation with a new boyfriend. Grandma Jo, who worked my whole life at a casino in Reno, was also a woman who grabbed life by both hands. Born to a single mother who traveled across the country and apparently took many lovers, she swore off men after her second husband died, moved in with her best friend and shared a mortgage, and visited us kids at least twice a year with her carefully saved $100 bills to spend on us. She never questioned my parents in front of me about the choices they made, but she always made sure my sisters and I knew that we could choose independence over the closed family system in which we were raised. I miss her. Nearly every day, I wish I could call her again and ask her advice. Every conversation always ended with, "Well, darling, I just want you to be happy. Do what makes you happy." Even when I told Grandma Jo I was queer, she told me she just wanted me to be happy.

My queerness had come as a shock even to me. Raised with rigid gender roles and in deep isolation, I had found refuge in Louisa May Alcott's Jo Marsh and Polly Milton, and Lucy Maud Montgomery's Anne with an e, but it never occurred to me until adulthood that I did not fit into the gender and sexual roles in which I was raised. My upbringing, with rigid gender roles, was meant to keep me producing white children. Coming out as a queer and genderqueer person was part of what gave me the perspective to think critically about the systems white poor people often take for granted.

White women are expected to play a particular role in settler colonialism. They are the objects that white men are taught to protect—particularly from Black and brown men. From the genocidal violence of the Indian Wars to the lynchings of Black men in the post-Reconstruction era, the protection of white women has been used to justify racial and colonial violence. Even second-wave feminism centered the needs of wealthy white women who fought for the right to vote and to work, often openly demanding that they be given these rights before Black or Indigenous men.

Poor white women have rarely voted and have always worked. They maintain their protection by their proximity to respectability. A poor white woman is worthy of protection as long as she is a good wife or mother. Of course, this protection is usually from the *outside* world; many poor women experience a great deal of violence within family systems like the one in which I was raised.

All of the women in my family were children of trauma; addiction, loss, and abuse had marked each of their lives, sometimes profoundly. My grandmothers taught me that it was possible to throw off those expectations and live my own life. My mother, however, worked hard to raise her children to be respectable women who would be worthy of the very protection she was never afforded. My mother and I have always had a fraught relationship, especially after I came out as queer and took a very different path from her own. Even so, I have always admired her strength, her ability to survive intense trauma, her ferocious love for her family.

When I grew up and encountered white feminism, I found very little that was familiar to me and very little that spoke to my own experience. It wasn't until I read Black womanist and Chicana authors that I found language that spoke to me. These authors talked about the strange experience of loving men who both experienced injustice outside the home and brought their anger and rage into it, of internalized oppression, of the experience of violence against your body by people you thought you could trust. I knew that I did not understand or share the experience of racism. But insofar that class was also a factor in this reality, it made sense.

Maya Angelou spoke about the sexual abuse of children and how it left its mark, something white feminists seemed to avoid unless talking about statistics. Gloria Anzaldúa spoke about living between worlds and on borders. As a white person, I had no experience of actual border crossing. But I was living in a world that I, as a queer and working-class person and someone raised in the profound isolation of an abusive movement, had difficulty understanding.

bell hooks explained class to me, my first introduction to the subject. My Black womanist professor in seminary, Rev. Dr. Joan Martin, taught me how to see beyond white theological constructs of ethics. If it wasn't for the witness of these Black and brown women, I would have never learned to look at the world as I do. I would have never had the tools to assess my own life story and the story of my own people. Nor would I have been able to search for healing.

My own experience of queerness shapes how I frame both my own life experience and the stories of the people in my community. Rigidly constructed, gendered identity forms the basis of respectability and white supremacy. This is heavily and often brutally enforced within white families, white society, and the state. As a child in the Quiverfull movement, I would have imagined that being gay and trans, being queer, being married to a woman, would have been literally the worst thing that could befall me. Within that system, according to some authors like Gary North, it would make me worthy of death.

The brutality visited on queer, on female, on poor, on Black, on Indigenous bodies is not the way it has always been. It is a path to profit, carved into our own flesh, enforced by movements like the one in which I was raised, funded by wealthy and powerful men. Leaving Christian fundamentalism and coming out as queer was my first act of resistance to the systems that are killing us. I was beginning to reclaim my body, my flesh, as my own.

⚜ 5 ⚜

CLASS WAR IN GRADUATE SCHOOL

"I DON'T GET it. Fuck these small-town rednecks. They are everything wrong with America."

The woman's voice rose an octave as she continued her monologue, her hand flying and her voice reverberating around the seminary cafeteria. I focused on the feather necklace around her neck and gritted my teeth. I felt a sudden surge of self-consciousness as I pushed my Walmart shoes under my chair and toyed with the flannel shirt I always seemed to be wearing.

There were five of us at the table. I was in my first year of seminary, and everyone else was in their second. The guy next to me appeared to be zoning out. I could see the sun shining on the ancient brick buildings outside. Everything people were saying suddenly sounded muffled, far away. "Fox News . . . guns . . . behind the times . . . racist . . . They don't even understand what is good for them."

The room came sharply back into focus and I felt a surge of rage. The cafeteria lights were glaring on the metal table next to the salad bar, and a steady stream of conversations buzzed around us.

I pushed myself out of the plastic bucket seat and brought my hand down, full force, on the flimsy table. The blow echoed through the loud space. Suddenly, all eyes were on me. "That is *enough*!" I said, my usually quiet voice cutting through the space. I knew my face must be beet red with anger. Why did my face have to turn red when I was angry? The guy next to me moved his chair back a few inches, his eyes wide.

"My parents are not some stupid people for you to make fun of."

All of my suspicions that I did not belong here—here, in the halls of learning, here, on the richest street in the entire country, where the Episcopal Church located one of its seminaries—flooded back. Who did I think I was? A scholarship student, a theology student who hung out with homeless people more than anyone else, someone with no wealth and no social capital, with not a single family member who had ever gone to university or graduate school: Who did I think I was?

Then again, who did this girl—this New England white girl—think *she* was, to dismiss a whole people, people she never met and knew absolutely nothing about? I asked her: What did she know of the realities of people like my mother, who had run away from home at fifteen and had never graduated from high school? Or of my sister, back home, a single mom raising three kids? Or of my great-grandpa, who had been born a sharecropper and died on the streets of Los Angeles? What did she know of the drugs that had flooded my community, rotting our teeth and stealing our souls? Had she ever grown a family's food in the dirt left after a timber company had stripped the land of everything of value?

My voice shook with rage and pain. Finally, I took a deep breath and walked out. A friend from the table followed me outside, a little wary. They gave a short laugh as we reached the hall. "Man, don't get you angry, huh?"

"I told you that you never wanted to see me mad," I retorted. Yet it had felt good. The lack of emotion in university conversations puzzled and annoyed me. My dad and I, now that I was grown and no longer afraid of him, would have blazing arguments that always ended with my mom forcing us to stop for dinner.

It had also felt good to say what had been churning in my gut all year: I was in a place that openly despised the people from which I came. Decades ago, Will Campbell had reflected that "redneck" was the last acceptable slur in polite company. In 2018, NPR ran an article saying, "You can get away with calling something 'white trash' in polite company, on cable television and in the headline of a magazine article." Poor white people have long served as a mirror image for white liberal respectability politics. "White trash"—those who are supposedly uneducated, backward, usually rural, uncouth, white, and unwashed—are the stereotype white liberals can say they are *not*. Poor white people, deftly associated with anything liberals disagree with, become a way to keep their own hands clean, to claim to be the "good" white people.

But they were my people. I was white trash and I knew it. I saw it in the way people looked at me, and I felt it in my lack of polish in the posh circles of Harvard Square. More than anything, I heard it in the invective hurled by educated white liberals who knew absolutely nothing about my life or the people I came from.

☘ ☘ ☘

Books have always been my salvation, my escape from everything. They were my solace through the hardest years of my life, and they kept me alive as a teenager. I learned to request interlibrary loans at our tiny rural library, and I read voraciously, like a starving child, losing myself in other worlds when the world I lived in was too much. But it never occurred to me that college was a viable option.

Then I was twenty-five, married, and had saved enough money working at two daycares to pay for classes at a community college. I excelled and transferred to the Evergreen State College, survived a divorce, several moves, and grunt jobs, and graduated with the conviction that I was called to be a chaplain.

I received enough scholarships to attend Episcopal Divinity School in Cambridge, Massachusetts. I was thrust into a world foreign to me. Living on Brattle Street, known as the most expensive stretch of real estate in the country, I was surrounded by universities—from the sprawling Harvard compounds to smaller colleges like Lesley University—and surrounded by New England wealth.

In these halls—not just in my seminary, but in the classes I took across the theological consortium and the lectures and churches I attended throughout Boston and Cambridge—one thing was crystal clear: I was expected to leave my past and my people behind. I was expected to be grateful that the coffers of the Episcopal Church had ensured my path toward respectability. I would never again have to live with poor people, and I could enter the American Dream and never look back.

It was another proffer of salvation, not unlike the one my parents had grasped with both hands. I could leave behind my failed people and enter the world of the liberal reformers and the white saviors, far enough removed from the poor white trash of my birth. I could learn to enunciate words correctly— "no accents!" my liturgy professor urged us—and I could bargain for a good salary and live a good life. Poor white people were failures: beyond hope of redemption, racist beyond saving, best left to die out in their hollers and trailer parks. But maybe a few, like me, could be saved.

I quickly saw that the vision of salvation on offer from the academy was no less white supremacist than the version of success that captivated my parents. This was another reason why, like W. E. B Du Bois said, poor white people struggled to develop many revolutionary leaders. The Black community did more easily, with powerful leaders, including Du Bois himself, creating systems of thought and intellectuals who explained the Black experience. When poor white people enter the academy, we are expected to join its capitalist agenda. Our best interests, at least on the surface, align with that path. Our whiteness buys us opportunities for advancement—but only if we leave behind the experiences of our past or use them to prove that anyone who works hard can do the same. A few leaders did emerge over the years, however, and in seminary I continued to learn about poor white leaders—from John Brown to Will Campbell and Hy Thurman to leaders coming into their own today—people who have managed to organize resistance among poor white people against the systems that oppress us all.

I did not understand how the upper-crust academics of Boston got off thinking they had moved beyond racism. Brattle Street was the whitest street I had ever lived on. I watched rich white kids walk down the streets of Harvard Square while mostly Black and brown young people—some of them students too—begged at their feet every day. In the classroom, we often talked about poverty and social class as if poor people just had a different lifestyle, not that they were people locked in a class war with an owning class that made money off their labor and needed a vast army of unemployed people to keep the price of labor down. And we rarely talked about how many students—how many of us—were poor as well.

I went to Harvard lectures and fancy book launches to listen. But I went also because I was hungry and they had food. No one ever, not once, asked me if I had enough to eat.

In their nostalgia about the civil rights days, white professors and academics would often talk about the enemy as poor Southern white people. Rednecks were the enemy. They implied it so often I started openly calling myself a redneck just to provoke a conversation about poor white people. While some of the white professors openly criticized my lack of polish, I longed to find a way that embraced learning while refusing to turn my back on my people. Thank God for my Black and brown professors. Thank God for the wisdom they shared and the time they took to talk to me as I tried to navigate this foreign world. Professors of color gently gave me space to start talking about my past, to explore what liberation might mean for poor white people. Dr. Duraisingh's door was always open, as I would pour out my heart about my dreams of ministry; Dr. Cheng opened up class discussions around class and race, giving me space to voice my new understanding of who I was. He and others encouraged me to talk about the places I came from, the poverty I saw everywhere.

Luckily, I came to seminary with a clearer understanding of class, having been nurtured in those understandings in college and in communities that had taught me about how poverty worked in the Americas. Once, when a professor was explaining the difference between the owning class and the working class, I interrupted him. "So if my parents own their own house, does that make them owning class?"

He smiled. "Do they have to work for a living?"

Well, of course.

"The owning class *owns the means of production*," he explained. "They're the owners of corporations: the people who own the land and the factories and the industries of capitalism."

Even though many of the white professors, intellectuals, and church leaders of New England might have thought they were a world away from poor whites—and in some ways, culturally, they were—many of them were still workers, and some of them probably came from the ranks of poor white people. Just because they ideologically aligned with a certain sector of the economic and political elite who dominated Boston's institutions and thought of themselves as part of an "in" club, the reality was, they were as working class as the rest of us, even if more of their needs were met. In the United States, we think of class in terms of how much money we make and how much education we have, creating artificial divides between perceived working, middle, and upper middle classes. These artificial divides give a sense of false security and an opening to look down in judgment on people who have less money or education. I was taught, however, that if you can become homeless, if you have to work for a paycheck to survive, you are as working class as the rest of us. I was deeply frustrated by the pressure to see myself as something "more" than the people I came from. The classism I encountered in graduate school was often rooted in this false divide—this assumption that if you received a higher education, you "moved up" in the world and needed to both act like it and leave those in poverty behind.

The most important part of my education was to the see class struggle outside of the narrative of the United States. As I became involved in the Episcopal Church, my first internship was with a bilingual church. The church was vibrant, full of recent immigrants who rarely had documentation and constantly feared arrest. It was full of young families and young activists deeply connecting to their Indigenous heritage. They taught me, even before I read Octavio Paz and Eduardo Galeano, about the danger of US imperialism and the heavy cost that people in Latin America were paying for the greed of US corporations. They taught me how to live in a fractured world, to live as though liberation were possible. Every day, the men and women of that parish faced the danger of deportation across dangerous borders and separation from their children. And yet they insisted on living into a future where, in the words of Galeano, "your legs are your passport, valid forever."

I will never forget the twelve-year-old girl I met on a seminary-sponsored trip to Nogales and the US-Mexico border. Standing next to her quiet and exhausted mother, who was holding her two-year-old brother, she spoke a mix of fluent English and Spanish. "My grandpa died, and we wanted to go to his funeral," she told me. "Our family lives in California, and the only way back was to cross the desert."

We were standing in an outdoor tent next to a migrant shelter, where volunteers in Mexico were dishing out meals for the hundreds of exhausted people who lined the streets of the Mexican side of Nogales. Most of them had just been dropped by US Border Patrol agents, after being held in detention for twenty-four to seventy-two hours, brought before a judge, and then deported.

"We got caught by *la migra*," she told me. "There was a woman with us. She got kicked by a horse when they found us in the desert. She lost her baby, and *la migra* just threw it away in the desert. And she never saw a doctor."

An advocate I was traveling with asked where the woman was now. The girl shrugged. "She hasn't talked. She just wanders around the street, and we don't know where she is."

The United States, from the beginning, has seen itself as an empire. It has reached its imperial arm across the Americas, dominating the political and economic future of the countries south of its border. American corporate interests have written the future for most countries south of the US-Mexico border, from large banana and sugar plantations to maquiladoras.

Immigration in the United States, particularly across the US-Mexico border, is driven by the need for cheap labor. The North American Free Trade Agreement, brokered by President Bill Clinton, was held up as a triumph of global economic cooperation. Whatever else it was, it was a coup for neoliberal economics (another name for unbridled capitalism, or an unlimited market). It was a death knell for Indigenous agricultural methods and lifeways that had been practiced for generations. NAFTA, among many other things, opened up corporate agricultural exchange across the border. US agribusiness, having already consolidated and destroyed small farms in the United States, now flooded the Mexican market with cheap commodities. This essentially put Mexican farmers out of business, since they could not compete with the prices.

On another group trip, earlier in college, I met a family in the Mixteca Alta living in a town with only fifty people left. We were in Oaxaca to study migration, and we saw its effects everywhere. It is mountainous land, full of caves, sweeping vistas, and little plots of corn and beans that had been grown in the region for generations. In the little town we visited, there was no longer a school because there were no children left. One of our hosts gave us a tour of part of the town, stopping at the little church that only held services a few times a year. "We were here," said Don Gregorio, sweeping his hand over the landscape, "before the time of Christ." Most of Oaxaca is Indigenous.

When he introduced us to his daughter and her husband, she showed us pictures of her children on the walls of their little home with a tin roof. "They all left," she told us, except her youngest, who told us he was torn, unsure he would be able to stay in the small agricultural community that could no longer make a living after NAFTA. He was part of an effort to create a farming cooperative in the region, a last-ditch effort to stay on the land he so clearly loved, land his family has stewarded from time immemorial.

Having come from a farming family in the United States, where I knew small farms could no longer make a living due to corporate agriculture, this family's struggle resonated with me. I knew Oaxacan migrants were fleeing to western Washington, recruited by companies who needed their labor for secondary forestry products or to work in canneries along the coast. People who had lived in a place since before the time of Christ were being forced to become wage laborers without documentation, always fearing a US Immigration and Customs Enforcement (ICE) raid and deportation.

As I talked with people in Oaxaca, I saw that, unlike a lot of people in the information bubbles in which I was raised—ones filled by a steady narrative of American exceptionalism—residents of Mexican communities in Oaxaca or on the border understood *why* they were poor and what forces were at play to keep them in their place. They understood that free trade agreements were the latest innovation of neoliberal capitalism to push Indigenous people off their own land, make way for capital investments, and provide cheap labor for US farmers through undocumented labor. They understood that US imperialism, from wars in Columbia to interference in Chile to imposed economic policy in Mexico, kept them poor and maintained US economic dominance in the region.

Learning from Indigenous communities who had been organizing against their own oppression for centuries was perhaps the most worthwhile time I had spent in my life as a poor white person. They taught me about the importance of land, of community resistance, of poor people educating themselves about their own oppression, and of the power of people rising up together to build their own communities and resist state and corporate efforts to end their way of life. Much of what I have been able to learn in my own community I owe to the amazing people I met south of the border, those who taught me to think in terms of material liberation.

Meeting people in other poor communities around the world—people who understood their own oppression and had honed resistance over centuries—taught me concepts to which few poor white people are exposed. Our news media, textbooks, and popular culture are not designed to teach poor white people how systems work to oppress them. Over and over, we believe the lies of white supremacy, blame ourselves for our own poverty and lack of success, and sacrifice everyone around us for a shot at work and land.

As I learned, I began to ask myself if there could be a future in which poor people could work together and organize together across race and national borders. Could the people I come from find a path toward material liberation in solidarity with communities doing so around the globe?

Experiences like this allowed me to analyze and learn why we were poor. Even though graduate school offered an escape from that analysis, I refused to see myself as separate from the people I came from. In retrospect, I wonder if it was pure spite that made me pack up and return to the place I was raised. Yet if I'm honest, it was also my own poverty that led me home. Many poor white millennials have found out just how untrue the assumption that we "move up" in the world with an education is, because in twenty-first-century America, even an advanced degree does not automatically buy a ticket to success. So it was that, with a tapped-out bank account and newly acquired student debt, I returned to the place I was raised.

⊰ **6** ⊱

THE BEGINNING

IT WAS RAINING gently that morning as we stood under the bridge. I had been gone for a week, flying to Los Angeles on plastic money to attend my grandfather's funeral. My grandpa—the first man to teach me anything about racism, the first person to introduce me to the civil rights movement—had worked his entire life at his local grocery store and supported his succession of wives in little trailer parks in the eastern suburbs of LA. His own father had died in an alcoholic binge, in a live-in hotel, where they found his body three days later.

My grandpa had never touched alcohol, and he had done everything right. But his insurance left him a single hospital to treat his esophageal cancer. The final surgery was so poorly executed, and his post-op care so poor, that he died of sepsis a week later. His death certificate names "medical neglect" as cause of death. A year later his ex-wife, my grandmother, would die of medical neglect as well.

The cloudy skies and pissing rain matched my mood. "You okay?" Chubbs, a Native elder from the Chehalis Tribe, asked me.

I told him about my grandfather's death. There were about a dozen people gathered under the Chehalis River bridge, where we always gathered Wednesday morning, myself and a few volunteers, to hand out sandwiches and coffee and chat with people. We were not far from the needle exchange van. The River was just yards away.

Chubbs waved over three or four other Native men. Some were local, and one or two were Alaska Natives from Alaskan Indigenous nations. "We are going to pray for your grandpa, okay?"

They gathered around me in a semicircle and raised their hands. Chubbs and Leonard led the song, a song for my dead, a song to sing my grandpa's soul to rest.

I had come back home with no promises and even less money, and a year of couch surfing had used up much of my social capital. I was ordained a deacon in the Episcopal Church, but my bishop was hesitant to take the next step and ordain me as a priest. I was assigned to St. Andrew's Episcopal Church in Aberdeen, Washington, where my decision to meet and get to know people living on the street of my home county was met with tolerant but open skepticism. I got a part-time job working for minimum wage at a library a few towns away, but I couldn't make rent for the first year of my work.

The only thing I knew how to do was to be present. Present in a place saturated by grief. I had grown up here, just miles from the ragged rocks that formed the far west coastline, in the middle of what was the largest temperate rainforest in the world, with its near-constant rain. I had once run away as quickly as I could from its narrow, isolated fold. And I was back.

The first people I met were Indigenous. That moment of being prayed for under the bridge was one I would not forget. The church and the town were not sure what to do with me, but these Native elders knew exactly how to form community.

⊥ ⊤ ⊿

This history of this region is one of violent conquest, just like everywhere else on Turtle Island.* The Doctrine of Discovery, based on papal bulls issued between 1452 and 1514 and then encoded in US law by the Supreme Court in 1823, says that white Christian Europeans had the right to the land lived on by non-Christian "savages" and the right to their lives and labor as well. This legal fiction became the basis for seizure of Indigenous land by the United States and Canada.

In the middle of the nineteenth century, the US government turned its eyes on the land that is now western Washington State. Settlers had trickled in, but the real draw was the miles and miles of old-growth forest, the towering fir and spruce and hemlock and cedar. Timber companies on the Great Lakes had cut most of the hardwood timber of the upper Midwest and were ready to expand their operations westward. The US government entered into

---

*Indigenous nations frequently use Turtle Island to refer to North America.

negotiation with tribes who had, over the past hundred years, already been decimated. Pandemic after pandemic had reduced the Indigenous population by up to 92 percent in some areas.

From 1855 to 1856, the US government entered into open war with Puget Sound Indigenous people, as Native nations made their last desperate stand for the land they had stewarded from time immemorial. The Treaty of Quinault and the Treaty of Medicine Creek forced nations on the Olympic Penninsula and the Puget Sound into reservations. Some tribes, like those that became the Confederated Tribes of the Chehalis and Shoalwater Bay Tribe, refused to enter into treaty agreements and refused to cede most of what became Grays Harbor County. They were forced onto tiny reservations of a few hundred acres instead.

Now in possession of millions of acres of ancient forest, the US government, in its colonial and capitalist wisdom, sold 900,000 acres of land in 1900 to Weyerhaeuser—the timber company that would dominate Grays Harbor's economy for more than a hundred years—for $6 an acre. For the next century, Native people would struggle in deep poverty on reservations, while Weyerhaeuser and other timber barons would cut the trees that built the cities and towns of the US West Coast and accumulate vast wealth. White settlers, most from Appalachia or Scandinavia, would flock to the region in desperate search for work. Here they would take up the most dangerous job in the United States, felling the forests and changing the landscape forever.

⋆ ⋆ ⋆

Scientists verify what Indigenous people have always claimed: that the social and economic systems of the people who lived in the Pacific Northwest were well organized. At one time, whole food systems were cultivated on the land, creating a thriving local and sustainable economy of people living in balance with the land and accumulating thousands of years of knowledge, traditions, and culture. Agricultural systems were vast and landscape-scale. White people did not recognize Indigenous agriculture, because it did not look like European farming systems that were beginning to make so much money.

Just north of Aberdeen sits the Quinault Indian Nation. Negotiated by the Treaty of Quinault in 1855, Quinault is a huge reservation in terms of land area, taking up a large part of the county. But the Dawes Act of

1887 divided all reservation land into plots, as part of an effort to force
Native people to adopt Western agriculture and as a way to transform even
reservation land into private property that could then be bought and sold
on the open market. This move ensured that much of the land of the reservation ended up in private hands and timber companies. By the 1960s,
only 3 percent of the reservation was actually owned by the Quinault
Nation.

Private property was a tool for the US government to attempt to assimilate
Native people and, eventually, terminate tribal relationships with the federal
government. In a continued quest for real sovereignty and self-determination,
however, over the last forty years the tribe has bought back up to 40 percent
of that land. But poverty and lack of employment on reservations in western
Washington remains dire. The federal government has consistently refused the
necessary resources for people to thrive. Many of the poorest from Quinault
and other reservations end up on the streets of Aberdeen, especially if they also
suffer from addiction. In Grays Harbor, Native Americans are disproportionately represented on the streets: only 5.6 percent of the county's population is
Indigenous, but I would estimate that a third of the people I met on the street
in Grays Harbor were Native—maybe more.

It is a common assumption that rural areas in the United States are
white. It is even common to conflate the ubiquitous "white working class"
with "rural America." Yet even in Grays Harbor County, where the majority of people are white, this is a false equivalency. Most of the rural West is
deeply influenced by the presence of Indigenous nations. And across the
rural US, Indigenous and mestizo immigrants from Mexico and further
south are deeply re-forming culture and identity.

While relationships between Indigenous and white people are common,
we live side by side somewhat uneasily. The history of genocide and land theft
loom large. Timber companies, cities, and farms now occupy most of the
usable land. Native people are left in intense poverty and vulnerable to widespread violence and harm. Here, as all over this continent, missing and murdered Indigenous women leave immense, horrific gaps in every family. The
federally funded Indian boarding school system and cultural repression have
left the Salish languages of the coast near extinction. Native people have suffered hundreds of years of attempts to destroy their cultures, languages, and

identities, and their families and bodies too. Yet they have survived. Not only that; they continue to live into cultural values of reciprocity and generosity.

➤ ⊤ ⌁

At one time, the Northwest coast was a region where, in the words of Roxanne Dunbar Ortiz, "great seafaring and fishing people flourished, linked by culture, common ceremonies, and extensive trade. These were a wealthy people living in a comparative paradise of natural resources, including the sacred salmon. They invented the potlatch, the ceremonial distribution or destruction of accumulated goods, creating a culture of reciprocity." This culture of reciprocity, which once dominated this continent before land-hungry capitalists arrived, is still evident in potlatches, paddle ceremonies, and public services of tribes around this country, despite the US government's long efforts to extinguish it.

I remember driving with a young white homeless man who often worked on boats during the Westport fishing season. He was complaining about Native fishing rights, upheld by what came to be known as the Boldt Decision in 1974, which affirmed tribal treaty rights to half of the fish harvest of the region. The young man was repeating the time-worn arguments of his bosses, who made a killing in the fishing industry. I explained how important it was for Indigenous people to have access to their traditions and traditional food sources.

He commented on how unfair he thought it was that tribal members sometimes receive cash payments from their tribe. While this is not true for most tribal governments in the region, I decided to press in another direction. "I wonder what it would be like to be part of a culture that valued sharing wealth instead of accumulating it all," I mused. "I wonder what it would be like for you to get what you needed, just because you were alive and deserved to be cared for." After all, he was homeless now that the fishing season was over.

He stopped short, and we were both quiet for a moment. "Yeah," he said. "That would be cool."

When I returned home to Grays Harbor, one of the first things I attended was the Tribal Canoe Journey landing, hosted that year by the Quinaults. Every year since 1989, Indigenous nations from the Pacific Northwest revive the tradition of traveling by waterway throughout the region, with different tribes around the region hosting the gathering each year. In 2013, Quinault was the destination of the Tribal Canoe Journey. Tribes from around the Northwest and even farther afield gathered in canoes and paddled from their lands to the Quinault Indian Nation. One observer wrote, "One by one the canoes were welcomed ashore by Quinault Nation leaders, dancers, and singers as they rode the Pacific waves in, completing their journey. Sixty-nine canoes landed on Thursday, August 1 on the Quinault Tribal Beach."

They were welcomed with a potlatch, a tradition among the once-wealthy Salish tribes, where hospitality was on full display. Robin Wall Kimmerer argues in *Braiding Sweetgrass,* her groundbreaking book on Indigenous worldview, that Indigenous people on Turtle Island depended on a culture of reciprocity, a culture in which the land and all life was a gift and that we as humans were called to return gifts in kind. In this region of the Coast Salish, full of forests and rich seas, the wealth of a tribe was demonstrated not by hoarding, as is normalized under capitalism today, but by generosity and hospitality.

In keeping with that hospitality, the entire community was invited to the landing, including those of us who were not Indigenous. There was abundant food for everyone. Each tribe who came was named and honored, and ceremonies to honor Native veterans and each group who came were held.

The Quinault Indian Nation (QIN) and dozens of other tribes in the region, through bold legal action and consistent lobbying at local, state, and federal levels, have fought for environmental measures that will restore local salmon populations. They have successfully prevented oil trains from transporting crude oil into our port. The QIN has also been one of the first communities to take seriously the rising sea levels and the risk of tsunami to the Washington coast. They have drawn up plans to relocate their villages. Meanwhile, places like Aberdeen are losing time as we fight over the future of abandoned buildings on a flood plain.

Many stopgap social services available in Grays Harbor are run by tribes, and most are open to anyone living in the county, including poor whites. Currently, the only inpatient treatment center open to Medicaid in the county, Northwest Indian Treatment, is run by the Squaxin Island Tribe. The Quinault Indian Nation just opened a wraparound treatment and health service. While white business owners and politicians call for the elimination of harm-reduction measures and block efforts to bring in more social services, poorly funded tribes already struggling with mass poverty often provide the stopgap measures that the county needs.

The QIN bypassed the city governement of Aberdeen altogether when they purchased a site and completely self-funded a treatment center, open to anyone who could walk in, providing wraparound services for mental health, addiction, and medical care. While the city had long opposed adding more services, they could not prevent the Nation from funding one themselves. Again, tribal leadership was showing its commitment to and wisdom in offering paths toward healing.

The leadership of Indigenous people may well be the only thing that saves this place.

🕊 🕊 🕊

But the presence of racism and racial hatred is still a real force. In 2018, Quinault tribal member Jimmy Smith-Kramer was celebrating his eighteenth birthday at a campground north of Aberdeen and Hoquiam with his friends. James Walker, a white man camping with his girlfriend, began taunting the group with racial slurs and "war whoops." The argument that ensued left Jimmy dead and his friend gravely injured. James Walker had thrown his truck in reverse, backing into the two young men and killing Jimmy. Although the Quinault Nation believed that the act was a hate crime, Grays Harbor County declined to prosecute it as such, handing down a charge of manslaughter.

Jimmy's death sent shock waves through the local Native community. While local whites wanted to see the incident as a tragic accident, it was clear that racism was alive and well in the poor white community. It was clear the system that pits white people against Indigenous and brown and Black people was still playing a central role in our lives.

Chubbs, who prayed for me under the bridge that day, was once attacked by a group of white young men with swastikas. They broke his leg, an injury leading to its eventual amputation. For years, Chubbs remained a fixture on the streets of Aberdeen, in his wheelchair, catcalling women and offering sage advice to anyone who would listen.

Pandemics, seizure of land, centuries of poverty and oppression, the collusion of poor white people with corporations and the federal government: none of this has kept Indigenous people from fighting for their sovereignty, in this region or on this continent. From slowly recovering control over their own reservation land, to spearheading efforts to restore the salmon population of the West Coast, to planning for sea-level rise, to recovering their languages, the tribes and nations of western Washington have never stopped their struggle to again steward these lands.

The men who generously sang over my dead grandfather's memory were mostly members of the Indian Shaker tradition. It is a beautiful faith, a blending of Christian tradition and Native tradition, a faith closed to non-Native people. There are specific rites and songs for the dead in this tradition, designed to release the person's soul into the afterlife.

Each of the men who stood around me that day had experienced cruel racism. That day, each of them shared the most precious traditions of their people. Since then, I have attended or presided over every single one of their funerals.

Part Two

SURVIVAL

THE RIVER

CLUNK. CLUNK. CLUNK.

At first it sounded like a BB gun, its metallic ring splitting open the silence. As I walked back from the dirt and gravel road by the railroad tracks, through the brush I saw a woman standing on the beach, swinging a metal baseball bat. Clunk. Clunk. The sound was coming from rocks hitting the bat. A sturdy white woman with purple streaks in her hair swung the bat again, sending rocks flying into the wide mouth of the Chehalis River. She saw me, then waved and walked toward me. "It's my stress reliever," she said, indicating the bat.

Spring was just giving way to summer, and the constant rain of the coast was holding off that day, the sun hitting the beach and the dirty water slugging past the foundations of old mills that still lined the banks. "The River" was about a mile-long stretch of land starting at the Chehalis River bridge, where the north and south banks of Aberdeen were connected. This narrow strip of land was bounded by water on one side and a railroad track and yard on the other, with a gravel road running its length along the train tracks. Between the bridge on the west and the eastern business' fence lined with razor wire, encampments came and went.

"You have good aim. People better watch out," I joked, eyeing the bat.

"Aw, I never hit anyone with it. I just threaten to," she laughed.

Misty and her boyfriend, Shawn, came and went from the River depending on whether they had housing or not. So did many others. Some people put up tents. Others lived in cars or RVs. Still others built shacks, some quite incredibly built and even developing, over time, into multiroom homes. One couple, the man out of work after a union job working a pontoon project ended, dug a cave into the embankment, shored it up with pallets, and then covered it with dirt and rotting leaves, making their camp warm for the winter and nearly invisible.

On that day, since it was so nice, many people were out walking, running errands, going to appointments. As we walked back down the main gravel road that ran parallel to the River the full length of the camps, Angie approached us.

She walked faster than anyone I knew, always with a sense of over-whelming purpose. Maybe five feet tall, Angie was one of many Native people to take refuge on the shores of the Chehalis, where the Quinault had treaty fishing rights. She was a force to be reckoned with.

"Hi, Pastor," she yelled. "Love you." She never broke her stride, swinging her own bat and quickly disappearing under the bridge and into Aberdeen's back alleys.

The River was a happening place, especially at night. It was a place you could buy and sell drugs. It was sometimes a haven for stolen goods, although a succession of River residents would take it upon themselves to patrol and evict anyone who would bring unwanted police attention.

Often it was the women who would set up the patrols. While the men dominated the hustling world of the River, it was the women who often kept the peace. Misty and Angie would patrol often, swinging those metal bats and trudging up and down the potholed and gravel "River Street" that ran along the railway yard, which was often full of tanker cars or empty grain cars. They'd stop at trails leading into the brush, hollering at people making needless messes and intervening when a domestic dispute broke out.

In my early years as a chaplain, I attended a training designed by the Episcopal Church for church planters and new ministers. The trainers gave us a checklist for who we should talk to when we started to work in a new town or place. We might want to meet with the Rotary Club, for example, or visit business owners, or talk with the mayor and police chief. Nonprofit and movement-building organizations often suggest similar strategies: if you are starting something new, meet with the socially and economically important people in a place. Go to the places they hang out.

I did precisely the opposite. If there was any single place in the county that respectable people avoided, it was the River. The River was where addicts and sex workers hung out. Even in jail, if you admitted you lived at the River, people would turn up their noses.

When I began meeting people under the Chehalis River bridge, just on the other side of the tracks from the River, I quickly became acquainted with the people who came and went on the narrow stretch of land. Later, I would learn that wealthy business owners called it "Hobo Beach" and that unemployed men were rumored to have camped there for well over a century. To us, though, it was simply the River: the self-designation of a camp of anywhere from ten to two hundred people, depending on the season and the economic reality in town.

The River ruled its own. Every year or two the city would issue eviction notices, and police or property owners would destroy the structures on the banks. But people would always come back. One year, it is rumored, police set the camps all on fire and burned them to the ground, but no one knows for sure. If you ran out of places to couch surf, if there were no hotel rooms you could trade for, or if your house or a hotel were condemned by code enforcement, you went to the River. It was the last place.

🐦 🐦 🐦

It was always about the land. At its core, the River was land. It was physical space people could build a shack on, make a home on, find some sense of self-sufficiency and stability. It was sometimes a family, sometimes a tight-knit community, bound together by survival in a world that had abandoned its inhabitants.

It was also dangerous. Beat downs and robberies, rape and violence could happen there, away from the public eye. You could find the River to be a place of fear, especially if you did not have the protection of people who lived there. Although some people worked hard to chase off dangerous people, particularly predatory men, it didn't always work. The natural landscape was dangerous too. If there were flash floods and you were too close to the beach, you could wake up under water. Winter was a dangerous time, when the cold got into your bones and open flames could take out a whole campsite or a whole hand. Rats were huge, and they were hungry. Infection could be rampant in the mud and in the raw sewage, which was inevitable without any sanitation system beyond buckets and dirty water.

What bothered the townspeople the most, however, was the trash. Online forums were full of complaints about piles of garbage at the River, and about the people who never picked up after themselves. The River saved its garbage, salvaging all sorts of things that may or may not be useful in the future. One resident, who everyone called River Rick, collected cans and driftwood, as well as piles of metal and plastic trash. It looked a mess, but he could often be found in the middle of his piles, building archways of driftwood and art out of bent metal.

There was no place for garbage to go, either. Unlike the townspeople who had garbage collection that removed trash from sight and dumped it in landfills, there was no garbage pickup at the River. Someone would go to jail and their campsite would become a soggy, wet mess of garbage no one else had the time or energy to fix. Often women like Misty and Angie would put together work teams to clean up. But it was discouraging work, and survival was always more important.

When I moved back home, I simply showed up. I ate with people, and I sat in tents in the mud. I walked from camp to camp, checking in on people and talking with them. Sometimes I would bring tarps or tents or supplies. Often I would drive people to the hospital or pick someone up for an appointment for food stamps or drug treatment.

In this place so near and yet so far from town, so much more like a refugee camp than the TV version of twenty-first-century America, I didn't find the Rotary Club. But I found leaders. It was clear, here, that capitalism was a death-dealing system, in which one out of sixteen people in a town could end up living in conditions that would be deemed uninhabitable by any government in the world. It was also clear that here, forged in the housing and economic crises of America's poor, were leaders: leaders who knew how to survive the worst that the world threw at them, who knew how to make something out of nothing, who knew how to salvage their dignity in a world that tossed them aside. There were leaders who knew how to keep up courage when there was nothing left.

In this human crucible, I stood in awe. Misty and Angie, swinging their bats, had found a path through intense hardship, holding on to courage and hope, even when the world abandoned them to their fate.

🕊 🕊 🕊

The last great wave of homelessness in the United States happened during the Great Depression and led to some sweeping political changes through the New Deal. The New Deal introduced measures that sought to regulate and control capitalism's rampage of death—at least for white communities. Homelessness became, for the middle of the twentieth century, a less common condition. The 1960s brought a political will to wage a war on poverty, and public housing expanded across the country. For a brief moment, capitalism in the United States looked like it could become a kinder and gentler animal. Civil rights movements saw increased civil rights for Black and brown communities, and for women, and eventually for queer people. Programs of social uplift provided housing, medical care, education, and food for poor people.

But the 1980s saw a sweeping political effort to deregulate the economy and roll back social service programs at federal and state levels. Unbridled capitalism, through the rise of neoliberal economic policies fully backed by both Republicans and Democrats, began to regain strength. During the Reagan era, new public housing projects were fully defunded. During the Clinton era, welfare reform destroyed most of the social safety net, juvenile delinquency laws criminalized poor and especially Black children, border security and immigration policy became more repressive, and prisons became the new warehouses for surplus labor.

Homelessness began rising exponentially over each decade, and by the second decade of the twenty-first century, it was a full-blown crisis. City after city declared a state of emergency. On the East Coast, vast homeless shelters crammed people together using a lottery system for entry. Farther west, shelters were smaller and less adequate, and tent cities, sometimes even organized by nonprofits or cities themselves, became more and more common.

In a 2018 study, the Poor People's Campaign concluded, "Today's US military budget stands at $716 billion, outpacing the next seven countries combined. That spending accounts for 54 percent of the discretionary budget, while antipoverty spending in the discretionary budget is at only $190 billion." Most of the meager money allocated for housing by federal and state agencies is earmarked for temporary shelter or case management. This has given rise to a nonprofit industrial complex that can pay case managers but cannot build housing.

The two most common forms of welfare money are housing vouchers and food stamps. Housing vouchers shore up the real estate market, providing private landlords with consistent rents. Food stamps provide agribusiness with corporate subsidies, ensuring that they can turn a profit when food prices are out of reach for the average person. Because both function to support the market, these still fall incredibly short of providing actual relief. So people resort to selling food stamps for a couch to sleep on and waiting for months or years to qualify for a housing voucher—only to wait more months or years to find an open unit.

Even as homelessness soars, and even after a crippling pandemic, state and federal governments refuse to seriously consider building more public housing or expanding social services. Instead, local and state governments increase spending for policing and homeless sweeps and focus on openly blaming drug addiction on people's poor choices. The federal government has devolved into a single-minded focus on political one-upmanship between two ineffective parties. While chaos reigns, the market reigns supreme, making record profits while people suffer and die.

In such times, places like the River become important and contested sites. At the River, homelessness was in full view of a town who did not want to see it. At its core, the River was the last place for poor people—white and Native, Black and brown—to pitch a fight for survival.

❧ 8 ❧

"THE AMERICAN DREAM" AND ITS SIGNS

ON THE EDGE of the River's boundaries, near a razor wire fence, stood a neat wooden shack. Pieced together with driftwood and old bits of plywood and pallets, the shack was so nice one might actually call it a small house. It had a wood stove inside, and wood smoke would drift up lazily on cold mornings. A neat pile of chopped wood sat just outside the door.

If you went inside, you'd see the floors were made of brick. In front of the house stood an archway built out of driftwood. Stuck to its side was a plastic orange mailbox marked "The Daily World," as if the delivery guy just drove down the gravel road every morning to deliver the daily newspaper.

Michael, a young white man, had spent much of his adult life on the River, preferring the quiet of self-sufficiency to the roar of the modern world. He was quiet, happier chopping wood than holding a conversation, but I always stopped to at least say hello.

That particular day was warm, probably mid-summer. "How are you?" I hollered, noticing that he and a friend were stripped to the waist, hard at work.

"Oh, we're all right," he yelled back. "Just livin' the American Dream." He stopped and swept his hand dramatically along his handiwork. "See, I even have a white picket fence!"

So he did. Someone had left a white picket fence in a dump pile somewhere, and now here it was, taking shape around his driftwood shack. Michael smiled wryly, enjoying his turn of phrase. When he did talk, he had a way with words.

Another afternoon in mid-spring, as the sun peeked through a sheet of raindrops, I drove up in my red Ford Ranger and saw a sign posted next to the newspaper mailbox. It read: "NOTICE TO VACATE. Do Not Enter. Unsafe to Occupy."

I went up for a closer look. Michael saw me and gestured to his own sign, hanging above the arch: NO TRESPASSING.

The city did eventually bulldoze his home. Michael ferried what he could of his belongings on a homemade raft across the river. He rebuilt, again and again. Again and again, the landowner or city would demolish his creations.

A few years after the first bulldozers, in the middle of another eviction of yet another rendition of his river home, we were loading my truck with a few of his valuables—primarily a one-hundred-pound wooden trunk with his tools. Frustrated and sweating, pressured to leave by police, Michael stopped to wipe his face. Leaning over to me, he said, "I have this poem that keeps going around and around in my head." He recited his poem for me:

> *They may take my home*
> *They may scatter my belongings*
> *But they will surely burn in hell.*
> *For whoever is no man's keeper*
> *Is no man at all*
> *But a beast, a tool of the devil.*

⸙

People will do whatever it takes to survive. No matter who they are or what their moral inclinations may be, people usually instinctively make the best decision that they can under the circumstances, the decision that will allow them to survive. I do not mean this as a sweeping statement on human decision-making; I mean that, when faced with the struggle for survival, people will usually do whatever it takes to meet their material needs. They will make a way out of no way, and they will make decisions that are often judged by outsiders who have not had to face life-and-death decisions on a daily basis. Often, when I talk about the choices faced by people on the street, case managers or housed people will express judgment about people's decision-making, whether judging sex work, drug use or involvement, or breaking the law. As if people are not faced with a whole list of bad choices. As if people are not just trying to choose the one that helps them survive best.

We do not talk nearly enough about how much humans need each other and a sense of community to survive. So while people absolutely do things for which they hate themselves, they also often end up helping each other in ways you find in few other communities. Sometimes that means you see so much beauty in the middle of pain. Michael's beautiful little homes, crafted with all the love he had to offer, were, at least some of the time, sanctuaries. People still talk about them. Many a person with nowhere to go one night had slept in one of Michael's houses. Sometimes he had to tell people to leave him alone. Sometimes he lost himself in his own struggle for survival. But he took what life offered him and made the best choice that he could. Knowing he could go to jail for doing it. Knowing he could be swept by police at any moment.

On the streets, the absurdity of leaving people to die in the middle of staggering wealth becomes stunningly obvious. It is perfectly legal for an eight-month pregnant mom to have nowhere to stay. It is also perfectly legal, and frighteningly common, for police to tell her to move on, knowing perfectly well there is nowhere for her to go. There may or may not be resources available to her, but no law or policy says she deserves anything better. If she walks into a store and leaves with a piece of chicken and does not pay, however, she will be criminally charged for getting her needs met, even though she has no money or means to get money. If she does it enough times, or is trespassed from the store and returns, she can get a felony and go to prison. Walmart will win, every time. Capitalism will literally pay thousands of dollars to prosecute someone for stealing while hungry. Meanwhile, you have to fight tooth and nail to find money to feed that person in the first place—and even then, there is no constitutional right to have food or shelter, no law that says it must be provided; it is considered a concern for voluntary charity.

It was perfectly legal for Michael to die of starvation or hunger or cold. No one would be arrested or prosecuted if he did. Yet by building a home for himself on someone else's abandoned and unused property, he was breaking the law. Police had not only the choice but the duty to destroy that home and drive him away. It did not matter that no one had done anything with that piece of property for decades, or that the city had no feasible plan to develop the site. It was private property, the most inviolable and sacred values of capitalism. It always comes down to the land.

🐦 🐦 🐦

Capitalism relies on dispossession. Dispossession of land, resources, and the means to make a living. Dispossession of everything except your body, which you must sell for labor.

Private property is fundamental to this system. For most of human history, people have lived on the same land for generation upon generation. For most of human history, even as empires rise and fall, people have belonged to a place, even though war and disaster sometimes drive people to migrate. Here, on the banks of the Chehalis, Indigenous people have lived and fished and hunted from time immemorial.* These rivers along the coast had provided abundantly and were home to vibrant and ancient life systems, as well as to an incredible Salish culture that spanned the rainforests of the Northwest coastline.

In many parts of the world, empires have fought for control of land, but they did not always dispossess the people who had lived there since memory began. Even in Europe, under feudalism, most people lived on land their ancestors had lived on for many generations and had access to common land, even while kings and empires fought over who controlled what boundaries. Capitalism, however, put land in the hands of private, wealthy individuals, who had sole right to the land and whatever resources it generated.

Unlike what most Americans believe, "private property" does not refer to a individual's ability to own their own home or possessions; most economic systems provide for this. As this chapter shows, many people are prevented from having a home under a system of private property because under capitalism one person or corporation can acquire title to vast amounts of land and completely control it, strip it of resources, profit off it, and prevent anyone else from benefiting from it. In the last five hundred years, this has put entire ecosystems and even human survival in peril.

Private property reduces the land to a commodity that is bought and sold on an open market, and usually accumulated by the wealthiest corporations and individuals. Nearly 40 percent of the land area in Grays Harbor is owned by five or six timber companies, the largest of which is Weyerhaeuser. It is perfectly legal for Weyerhaeuser—after cutting all the timber on their lands multiple times, after employing people in the most dangerous

---

*This phrase, "from time immemorial," is used by Indigenous scholars to refer to their historic and continuous connection to the land before conquest and colonization. It also challenges the Western assumption that Native communities have a relatively short history in the Americas. I will use this phrase often, as an acknowledgment of Indigenous history and sovereignty.

job in the world, after turning their sights to easier markets and laying off those workers, and after making a killing off the resources of this county—to simply sit on close to 200,000 acres.

On the other hand, if you accidentally cut down a tree on this property that is marked for profit and profit alone, you can go to prison, even if you only used it for firewood. It is entirely illegal for Michael to build a shack on a piece of land no one is using.

I often explain homelessness like this: homelessness is not having any legal access to space. This is what made the River so important, and such a point of contention in the community. People must have space to live and, increasingly, they have no legal access to it. So they squat.

Squatting is what poor people have done ever since this country was founded. It is what people without homes are forced to do every day, whether in doorways, in tents along highways or riverbanks, or in abandoned buildings. Every single one of those survival tactics is usually illegal. Most towns and cities have ordinances forbidding people to sleep in doorways and allowing police to move people along or arrest them if they do not. Police routinely sweep tent encampments, rounding up people and throwing away their belongings. Towns spend thousands, sometimes millions, on cleanup and fencing. Getting caught in an abandoned building in Washington State is a felony, and you will spend jail time for it. It does not matter that the house is sitting vacant and unused.

The insanity of private property laws demonstrates more clearly than anything else that we live in a system that cares for capital and property more than life itself. People are always free to die, just so long as they do not trespass or steal.

Of course, because humans are wired for survival, they trespass, steal, and squat anyway. These acts of survival are in themselves acts of resistance against a system that has marked poor people for death. Survival is resistance. In the twenty-first-century United States, building a home from scraps and trash on a riverbank becomes a supreme act of resistance.

≼ 9 ≽

BAPTISM ON THE EDGE OF LOSS

POVERTY IS PARTICULARLY devastating for children. We live in a culture that already has very little regard for the health, well-being, or rights of children. Parents and guardians, unless there is government intervention, have exclusive control over a child's life, leaving them particularly vulnerable to abuse. The desperation that poverty brings can make children even more vulnerable.

From birth to death, poor people's lives are regulated and controlled by a variety of institutions. Capitalism is upheld by a state bureaucracy (and war machine) that functions both to control poor people and to maintain a base of unemployed workers as a sort of reserve labor force. As increased mechanization replaces human labor, and as globalization has allowed corporations to put factories in whichever countries have the cheapest labor, this surplus labor force has grown significantly, especially in rural areas.

The first of the institutions to enter poor people's lives is often Child Protective Services (CPS). This sometimes happens at birth, as at the first birth I attended as a chaplain. Aaron, a chaplain and organizer alongside me from the beginning, accompanied me to visit Christina, who had been living off and on at the River and then at a church-sponsored tent city. Christina, who was very young, had dropped off the radar for a while, but she called me when she was admitted to the local hospital to give birth.

Her little boy was so tiny and so perfect. She sat in the hospital bed, with the curtains drawn, holding her little one for dear life.

A nurse came in. "We are watching Baby right now," she said. "He might start withdrawing and, if he does, we will need to transfer him to the NICU in Tacoma." Christina nodded.

The nurse left the room, and together Aaron and I sat with her and her boyfriend, Johnny, for a while. Heavy in the air between us was the knowledge that CPS had been notified by hospital staff, and that it was only a matter of time before social workers arrived.

"Do you want to name him and baptize him?" I asked.

Christina and Johnny nodded. "Let's baptize him," she said.

"What do you want to name him?" I asked. They had chosen Dakota.

It is easy to judge young mothers like Christina: for their addictions, for their inability to adequately care for their babies. Children deserve love and care and they deserve safety, and sometimes that means intervention is necessary. Yet it is easy to forget the stories behind that reality. Christina had been on the streets since she was fifteen, and she had experienced her own deep trauma as a child. For the past six years, she had been simply trying to survive, striving to find a place to stay or food or security each day, every day. What the statistics about her life do not tell you is that she was kind, she wanted to go to college, and she struggled with a learning disability. The community and the system never bothered to measure her strength or her courage, only her mistakes.

Aaron found some water in a plastic bottle, and I grabbed the little glass container of holy oil I always carried in my truck. Aaron stood with the young parents as Christina held her son. He was so tiny, so perfect, his tiny fist balled outside the blanket. So innocent, to be born into such a world, so undeserving of the trauma that had been part of his and his mother's life since before he was born.

Soon the nurse would come and take the baby back to the NICU. For now, we gathered in a small circle in the room. "You are sealed by the Holy Spirit in baptism and marked as Christ's own forever," I said, after the baptism, as I carefully traced the sign of the cross in oil over his tiny forehead.

A police officer and CPS social workers arrived the next day and took custody of Dakota. Three days later, I attended the family planning meeting with Christina. The social worker drew out a long history, highlighting all her mistakes. It was indeed a grim picture. But it was also one that never acknowledged her own trauma or strength.

Over time, I would learn how the system worked and how to help mothers navigate it. That was not the first time I realized that social safety nets are not necessarily designed to help poor people or foster healing for anyone involved. When children's lives are reduced to their value as future workers, little effort or care is made to ensure that they have all the things they need for health and healing.

In Grays Harbor, one in fifteen kids have been accepted to a CPS referral and become wards of the state. In many families, children have been raised for generations by the state, by foster families, or given out for adoption when parental rights are terminated, robbing an entire culture of any knowledge of how to raise children.

Poverty is an ugly thing, something that breeds despair, as generation after generation of families grow up without their basic needs being met, with the constant death that poverty brings, and with the trauma and violence that surrounds them. Drug use looms large in Grays Harbor. Babies are born addicted, sometimes spending weeks detoxing in NICUs. It is not uncommon for children to start using at age thirteen or fourteen with their parents, or to run away from abusive situations and end up using on the street at the same age. Those young people then have children, and it is tragically common for babies to be born exposed to drugs. Most of the time, the young parents lose custody.

It is a painful cycle. Abused children and foster children grow up, have their own babies, and then lose them to the state when they cannot meet requirements for stability and health. Many young men and women are deep in their addiction, living on the street, with no clear path out. Nothing is more terrifying than coming across toddlers living in a van while their parents shoot up, or a seven-year-old living in a tent with an addicted mom. Some mothers choose to find homes or family members who can care for their children adequately. Others hope against hope that something in their life will fall into place before they give birth, allowing them to mother their children.

Many times, addiction, mental health, and disability make young mothers less likely to be able to safely and adequately parent their children. Many of the moms I work with would agree that they do not have what they need to take care of their babies. Some mothers decide to not fight their cases, knowing that another family could give them a much better shot at life than they can. Others are fortunate enough to have family members who can care for their children when they cannot. Many grandparents and aunts and uncles are raising a second generation of children, offering love and support when the parent can't. The rest, however, end up in foster care or, if they are older, in group homes.

Many people become social workers out of an earnest desire to make a difference and help people. But they often end up working for agencies like CPS, which are also designed to monitor people's behavior. They end up functioning as gatekeepers in poor people's lives. That does not mean that every parent is fit to raise their child, nor that intervention is not necessary in community life. I grew up in deeply abusive systems, and I have wished many times that authorities would have intervened in the abusive homes around me (and I've also wondered why agencies like CPS do not more thoroughly investigate Christian homeschool families). I have nothing but support and gratitude for the many foster and adoptive parents who take children and treat them well. Yet it is still important to understand the larger system that has made this whole apparatus necessary.

What if, instead of immediately removing children, CPS could put a strong system of community support in place for poor parents? So many young parents need treatment, housing, stability, and income. They are not abusive or cruel; they love their children and want the best for them. They simply do not have the material resources to live that out. What if we supported mothers instead of punishing them? What if poor babies got to heal with their parents instead of undergo the trauma of separation? What if we designed policies to end poverty and promote the health of the whole community? This does not mean removal is not necessary in cases of abuse, or if a parent is not in a place to be able to heal. It just means that poor communities need so much more support to find paths toward healing.

The trauma of losing a child can tear a person apart. I have seen parents rally and find a decent case manager who can help them get into treatment and find housing, with the hope and prospect of reuniting with their children as a motivation. Unfortunately, I have seen many more dive deeper into their addiction, self-medicating for the pain of loss.

↳ ⼂ ⼅

Like many other racialized policies in the United States, policies around child protection that were actually designed to control people of color are often extended to poor white people. The roots of child removal in this country run deep, stretching into our history of Indigenous genocide and racialized slavery. In the early nineteenth century, as the United States cast a greedy eye on the land inhabited by Indigenous people in the West, the US and Canadian governments opened Indian boarding schools. One way to destroy a culture and break their will is to gain control of the children, and the residential schooling system was designed to do just that. The stated goal was to "kill the Indian, save the man." Indigenous families were forced to place their children in these residential schools, where they were punished for speaking their languages and for maintaining Indigenous customs and clothing, and where they were taught to be wage laborers. If they survived. The abuse that children endured in these schools is extensively documented in both the United States and Canada. As the vast graveyards discovered over the past few years show, thousands of children never made it home, falling victim to disease and abuse. Secretary of Interior Deb Haaland initiated the first report of Indian boarding schools in the United States, beginning a long process of federal acknowledgment of the incredible harm and loss perpetrated on generations of children and their families and communities.

Black children have systematically faced forced separation and generational abuse, beginning with forced separation of family members under the slave economy. In the South, Du Bois discusses the ways that "child-bearing was a profitable occupation" for enslavers, who could then use Black children as enslaved workers. Child removal in the United States after slavery has continued to disproportionately remove Black children, with a staggering one in ten Black children removed from their parents in the United States in 2022.

These policies of child removal now form the basis for agencies like CPS. These policies are rooted in capitalism's need for a future labor force, and in the white supremacy of policies designed to remove children from Black, brown, and Indigenous parents and into white schools or homes for assimilation. When many boarding schools were finally closed in the middle and late parts of the twentieth century, removing Native children and placing them in white foster and adoptive homes became a new way to continue cultural genocide. This also happened in Black and other communities of color around the country. While Native advocates successfully lobbied for the Indian Child Welfare Act to ensure that Native children remain in Native homes, the rates of child removal are still very high in Indian Country. At the time of writing, this act is currently under review by the conservative US Supreme Court as they consider overturning this protection.

These policies, rooted in the genocide of Indigenous people and the enslavement of Black people, have extended to many poor white communities. Ultimately, failed white people are also seen as incapable of properly raising their children. Poor children across race are removed generationally from communities like Grays Harbor, furthering a sense of communal despair and loss of a future. And those children, including those who need to be removed for their safety, are often seen as problems of the state, going to group homes and foster care unable to meet their needs, furthering the communal trauma as they age out of the system and end up right where their parents were a few decades before.

The demoralizing and traumatizing effects of child removal reverberates through poor Black, Native, and white communities. On the street, young women and men like Christina and Johnny talk constantly about their children. Children often search for and find their birth family after foster care ends, only to get caught up in the world of addiction and the streets, with little else to turn to. These broken families fragment and fracture the larger community, sapping our will to survive, demonstrating more clearly than anything that we have no future. If children are the future of any people, the deadly interplay of addiction with the policy of child removal demonstrates just how closely death stalks our community.

10

CHILDHOOD NIGHTMARES

YOU MIGHT THINK that a community so eager to remove children from parental care would find ways to value its youth. But until 2021, when the laws changed, Washington State had the highest rate of youth incarceration for noncriminal offenses in the country. In 2015, Grays Harbor led the state on this count, with 77.2 percent of their arrested children incarcerated for truancy charges. That year, they incarcerated 541 children for truancy. Meanwhile King County, an urban county with a population over two million, incarcerated only 180. We live in a country that affords children no human rights—the United States is the only country that has refused to ratify the UN Convention on the Rights of a Child—and this is particularly true if they are poor.

No institution is more infamous among poor Grays Harborites than juvenile hall. The Honorable Gordon Godfrey sat on the bench and heard most juvenile court cases from 1992 to 2014. While many in town enjoyed his cutting sarcasm and rogue methods, he garnered very little respect from the youth who stood before him. Judge Godfrey pioneered the enforcement of Washington State's already severe truancy laws. This system is particularly supported by the school system, where teachers with problem or absent students would refer them to the courts and the school itself would open a case against the child. In this way, institutions whose stated goal is the education and nurture of children become instead their prosecutor, actively putting children as young as eight years old in jail for truancy or misbehavior. Every child who grew up in the county for about four decades remembers being threatened if they missed school even for a sick day with Judge Godfrey.

I was raised in a community that threw away their children. As I visited young adults in county jail, they told me chilling stories about their experiences in juvenile hall, before they ended up in jail as adults. I had experienced my own share of abuse and witnessed my own share of violence as a child. But I was shocked at the stories I heard from struggling young people:

of violence and abuse perpetrated in institutions that were widely assumed by the community to be supports for them.

These stories reverberate in my head. A young white women told me how her dad, who struggled with blindness and deep poverty, tried to navigate an "at-risk youth" program the court put her in when she was thirteen. Frustrated by his daughter's truancy and feeling like he had no other option, her dad had called and reported her. The judge had sternly lectured him the last time he stood in the family courtroom to report his daughter's noncompliance. Now the tall, male officer who came to his front door had grabbed the girl, crying and trying to run away, wrenching her arm as he slammed her against the side of the police car. Her arm broke in a sickening crunch.

A young Black woman in jail, one of the few Black kids in the school district, recounted to me how she had stood before the judge in family court. Harsh fluorescent lights shone down on her in the windowless room that smelled of old upholstered chairs. Her eyes were swollen, one almost shut, and visible bruises bloomed across her face and arms. She raised defiant eyes to the judge. "What happened to her?" the judge demanded.

The officer in the courtroom shifted. "They slammed me against the wall," she shot, still defiant, to the judge.

"Get her to a hospital," he ordered. "Now."

In 2017, the American Civil Liberties Union (ACLU) met with the local League of Women Voters, informing the local community about a lawsuit the ACLU was filing against the Grays Harbor Youth Detention Center. They described the conditions in the jail, including the center's use of a small room for punishment, a room where children would be minimally fed and were expected to relieve themselves in a grate in the middle of the floor. A young guy, a student at Grays Harbor Community College, said in the meeting, "Oh, I remember that room. I was left in there for days as a kid."

The skinny white boy, maybe fourteen then and in his midtwenties when he spoke to me, talked about what a defiant kid he was. Most working-class families in Grays Harbor are historically what we refer to as "blue dog Democrats"; that is, they are pro-union, and, until the 2016 election, this county was one of the most consistently blue county in the country. "Why are you playing this bullshit?" he told me he said one time, to one of the juvie guards was playing conservative talk radio.

"Hey, you don't agree with it, huh?" the guard jeered. "Don't want to hear it? You know what, you are gonna listen," he hissed, grabbing him and shoving him down hard in the restraining chair. The boy struggled as he strapped him down. The guard flipped up the radio volume. "Now you are gonna listen to it!" he said, his angry red face close to the boy's. "Fuck you," the boy spit back. The guard turned on his heels and left him, strapped down, for hours, conservative talk radio bouncing off the walls around him.

Statistics began to turn a corner in 2017, when a family sued Grays Harbor Juvenile Detention for child torture. They alleged that their then sixteen-year-old son had been placed in solitary confinement for extended periods while detained for petty theft, and that he had been placed in solitary confinement forty times over a three-year period. The ACLU wrote, "During that time, MD spent a total of about seventy-five days locked in a room or in a padded cell with little human interaction or access to his mother, for minor infractions like talking back, leaving a glob of toothpaste on the door to his room, passing notes, spilling water, 'being rude,' and cursing. During one 8-day stretch, he was locked in a room that was spattered with food and blood, with a feces-covered grate over a hole in the ground to use for a toilet." Outdoor exercise was nearly nonexistent. The lawsuit was settled out of court, with the family receiving a sizable settlement and the detention center promising change.

It is too glib to say hurt people hurt people. But it is true that traumatized communities often revisit trauma and abuse on their own children. Poor parents often fear for their children's futures in a harsh world, and they try to prepare them for it. By enrolling them in court programs. By creating cultish groups to control their behavior. By teaching them to learn to take a beating.

What is worse is that parents are taught to do so not just by their own pasts but by the courts, by judges, by teachers, by religious leaders and churches, and by police and social workers. I know CPS workers who have required parents to spank their children. Poor children are meant to be broken early, to be taught their place early. From nearly the moment we are born, we are born into the trauma and hurt of a system bent on breaking our wills and hearts.

In Grays Harbor, for decades, all the institutions that serve children—schools, CPS, and corrections—were heavily invested in youth incarceration. After Godfrey, Judge Edwards presided over family court. He told the newspapers, in his defense of widespread youth incarceration: "I always come back to the same point, and that is, 'How can I help these kids become successful if I can't teach them that there are consequences attached to their actions?'"

For decades, this was the single most important tool in the arsenal of Grays Harbor schools, where teachers could recommend incarceration and the school itself would bring the charges. Incarceration has been billed as the solution to juvenile misbehavior, and many people, teachers and parents included, have a hard time imagining an alternative. When I have publicly criticized this practice, I always hear from parents and teachers who insist that there is simply no other way to control wayward children, that locking them in jail is the only answer.

Juvenile incarceration often becomes young people's first step into the prison system. Over and over, the young people I visited in jail talk about their first time in jail. For most of them, it was between the ages of eight and fifteen, for skipping school or petty theft or mouthing off to a teacher. Thrown away before they even reach adulthood, these young people end up on drugs and committing more serious offenses as their struggles increase in early adulthood.

Poor white people are so often urged to participate in hurting their children. Many poor white parents resist and refuse to participate in systems of harm, like the family who sued the detention center or the father who just refused to report on his daughter. Even so, the culture we live in pushes us on every side to engage in "tough love" and abusive tactics, and these become generationally acceptable and normalized in many families.

We have no internal analysis that says that we do not deserve this. We are desperate to prove ourselves worthy of whiteness. And so we sometimes hurt our own children, inflicting the same pain that was inflicted on us. So often our self-hatred comes out as harm to our children. I recall, vividly, sitting down with parents who were accused of child abuse. The desperately poor white woman in front of me, a woman who struggled with such severe trauma that she could not leave her house, said, "Hitting a kid doesn't hurt them. They need discipline. I got hit and I turned out okay." The painful irony of that statement was utterly lost on her. White people, including poor white people, have too often normalized generational violence, and it begins in childhood.

Because of that, many poor neighborhoods have "street moms," usually white or Latina, who provide a haven for struggling children and teens. These surrogate parents are rarely official foster parents, but they often open their homes to hurting kids for a meal, for a shower, or just for a safe place to be to do homework or escape the chaos of their home lives.

Thankfully, the laws in Washington State are changing. Child incarceration is becoming a less available option. But the damage that has been done will be felt for years to come.

⚜ 11 ⚜

THE THEATRICS OF TERROR

ONE SUNDAY AFTERNOON, I noticed there were a lot more people than usual on the street when I rolled up in my little red Ford Ranger to open the church for our regular Sunday afternoon drop-in and dinner.

"You really should go down to the River," someone told me, panting from running. "They are telling everyone they have to leave. They are looking for someone."

I left the church and drove down to the other side of the tracks, where I would have a semi-clear view of what was happening. Police cars barred all entrances to the River camp. The scanner reported that a suspect had driven a vehicle at high speeds through the camp and abandoned the vehicle.

At this point, several hundred people were living there, pitching tents in all corners of the brush and building numerous wooden structures with pallets and tarps and blankets. People were streaming out of the camp.

I stood with a group of people from the camp, watching. Many melted into the side streets, afraid of arrest. There was a police boat on the river, and police cars were parked everywhere. Before we knew it, city police had showed up with an armored tank. In many small towns across the United States, weapons of war from surplus military equipment are repurposed for use on the streets against civilian populations. The tank started rolling through the camp, an officer broadcasting a warning to any residents still there to leave immediately. Officers with assault rifles combed the area, going from tent to tent.

I heard a scream as the tank rolled farther through the camp, and my heart sank. Several women with severe mental illness were staying in the camp at the time, and I could see one of them now, yelling at officers as they turned toward her with their rifles. She had no idea what was happening. Every fiber of my being wanted to go to her, to intervene, but an armored vehicle and police cars blocked any way forward.

The brutality of the state's systems of control continues well past child-hood and adolescence and into adulthood, particularly (and especially) if you are poor. And now that brutality was being literalized before our eyes. I took out my phone and took some photographs of what was unfolding in front of us—a small, desperate act against the powerlessness of the moment.

The October wind bit deep and darkness came early. It was hours before things cleared up and the police left, never having found the guy they were looking for. As I walked back into the camp with people who lived there, we looked for the woman, but she was hiding and would not let any-one near her. "Ah shit, my tent's all slashed up," another young woman said as she came out of hiding, cautiously. "Yeah, I was hiding the whole time."

Some people had stayed, hidden in holes under the riverbank or under their tents, listening to what sounded like a war zone outside. What I noticed most was the sense of violation. "They would never have done this in a residential neighborhood in town," someone said. "They could only do this because we are homeless."

I posted my pictures to social media and expressed my outrage. My posts drew the ire of the young mayor, who responded in length to my post. The city would end up agreeing to replace the slashed tents, which was a small comfort. The sense of unease remained.

♣ ♠ ♦

Policing in the United States exists as "theatrics of terror," writes theologian Mark Lewis Taylor. He argues that policing is designed to strike terror in the hearts of the people who are targeted—usually poor communities and com-munities of color. Working with communities of people who are homeless, I have seen this firsthand. The goal seems clear: keep people off their game, keep them on alert, keep them scared. Show up with force on occasion, and strike terror in people's hearts.

People on the street feel particularly vulnerable. Most survival plans, such as camping on public or private land or sleeping in doorways, are illegal or penalized. No matter where they set up a camp or roll out a sleeping bag, it's all but guaranteed they will be asked to move. If they set up large camps, they are subject to sweeps. Whether they are alone or in groups, in cities and in rural areas, police threaten them, toss their belongings, or ticket them.

This sweep of the River reminded people that nothing was secure, that everything could be taken away at a moment's notice. It reminded people that they were illegal squatters on someone else's land, that their fellow community members thought little of them, and that the city could do whatever they wanted with their belongings and even bodies.

If you are housed, you have a lease or at least a verbal agreement to live somewhere, or you have a deed or a mortgage attached to a deed. If you have money, you can pay to be in most places: coffee shops, stores, places of business. But if you are homeless, you might sleep on the couch of a friend, who can kick you out in a moment. You might sleep in your car, but there is no legal place to park it. You might pitch a tent, but there is no legal place in most cities to pitch a tent. You might sleep in a doorway, but most cities have ordinances forbidding it. You cannot sit long in a café without money. You are not welcome in stores if you cannot buy anything. In towns and cities across the nation, churches and libraries may be the only free public spaces where people can exist without breaking a law.

In 2016, the city of Seattle spent $1 million to clear out "the Jungle," a large network of encampments along the I-5 corridor. It was the largest sweep in the Northwest in a decade. Throughout the country, where encampments along highways and rivers are becoming the norm, cities organize regular sweeps, hauling off tents or shacks, often along with everything a person owns. Many times, cities will fence off areas frequently used for camping, forcing people to go elsewhere. I have visited camps in Seattle, Portland, Salinas, and Olympia, and the stories are all the same. The cry from homeless people everywhere is, "Where do we go? Move on to where?"

Enforcement became even more brutal during the COVID-19 pandemic. Two women I know were roused by police kicking them in the head in the early morning. They told the women to move on. "Where do you want us to go?" they asked. The response: "Anywhere but here."

"We cause no harm to that area but just want to sleep or rest, yet some of you people just can't let us be," Melissa Hill, who had survived homelessness off and on in Aberdeen for some time, wrote in a letter to the editor to Aberdeen's *Daily World*. "If you refuse to help or even smile our way, then don't hinder or hurt us by bullying or throwing explosives at our camps. . . . How would you feel to think your life could potentially be in danger because of a person or persons who didn't like you just because of who you are, what you look like, how you dress or what you do?"

This constant state of terror is exhausting. For people on the streets, every day involves looking for a place to go that is inconspicuous, out of the way of police sweeps. Every time you get settled, you are moved again. Back on the River, after that afternoon, people felt uneasy. They were waiting for the next shoe to drop: waiting for a new eviction order or a new police action, any of which could happen at any moment and completely disrupt their already wrecked lives.

☙ 12 ❧

ON THE RUN

I FOUND PARKING on a side street, as cars were lining around the block of the funeral home in Hoquiam, one of Aberdeen's neighboring and adjoining cities. The day was warm, and I knew it would be warmer inside. I had driven a young man there, and we had parked across the street. Before he got out of the car, Levi glanced around and then hurried across the street and toward the chapel. He threw one more glance over his shoulder before ducking into the funeral home.

Levi had an active warrant, as did most of the young men with whom I worked. Most had warrants issued by the Department of Corrections (DOC) for failing to report to a probation officer. When people are sentenced for felony convictions, they usually spend some part of that time on probation after serving time in prison: released from jail, free to live in the community, but bound by a behavioral contract and regular check-ins with a supervising officer. If you are able to get your life on track, get off drugs, and get housed, this is not a huge burden. DOC officers can be a great source of support for offenders trying to reenter society. For people who end up back on the street, however, this system just means more jail time. Each violation—failure to check in, failure to pass a clean drug test (perhaps the most common reason people don't check in in the first place), living in an unapproved home—can earn you up to thirty days in jail.

Small city jails in Washington State can make a lot of money through contracts with the DOC to hold offenders for these jail stays, and several jails in the region had those contracts. Their officers would assist DOC in locating and arresting people who were violating probation, and DOC would pay them—per person, per night—to hold them.

Levi was anxious being in public, knowing that his warrant put him at risk of pursuit. I followed him into the small chapel in the funeral home and found a seat. The pastor doing the funeral spoke for a bit. Sitting next to Levi, I could tell he was dressed in the best clothes he had. Tear after tear rolled down his cheeks as the speakers played "In the Arms of an Angel" to a slideshow of his friend's life.

Not far from the funeral home, flowers and candles lined the river where Levi's friend had died at age thirty-five. Stopped by police, also with a DOC warrant, Levi's friend had jumped in the river during the chase that ensued. His body was found days later. Levi had been one of the last of his friends to see him alive.

While the small crowd of family and friends told stories of this young man's life, little was said at the funeral about his death and how he had died. One awkward young man, shaking uncontrollably, simply said, "It's a shame how he had to go." His younger brother wept as he said, "The best thing he and my dad did for me is get me out of Grays Harbor, where I could make a living and raise a family."

There were reasons Levi looked warily across the street before going to his friend's funeral. Only a few months before, Levi had been beaten down in a church parking lot. The parking lot was home to the tent city in which he had been staying. Three officers, looking to arrest him on his DOC warrant, entered the camp early in the morning, barged into his tent, and slammed him into the ground. He was hauled out in handcuffs, bruised, his eye streaming blood.

> ⟁ ⟁ ⟁

Police violence in the United States is largely associated with violence against Black communities. While police killings are the sixth leading cause of death for young men ages twenty-five to twenty-nine across race, the rates are much higher for young Black men. By race, 7.9 out of a million Black people are killed by police. That's more than double that of whites, who were killed at a rate of 3.3 out of a million.

The People's Policy Project did a study that attempted to account for the intersections of race and class by analyzing the poverty rates in the neighborhoods where people were killed. Researchers divided communities in which people had been shot into five levels of socioeconomic status and found that experiences of police violence differ significantly between rich and poor white communities. They also showed how egregious police violence was in Black communities regardless of class. At the lowest socioeconomic level, police killings were 7.9 out of a million for poor whites, as compared to 2.2 in the wealthiest neighborhoods. For Black people, rates were 12.3 in the poorest neighborhoods and still a whopping 6.7 in the wealthiest neighborhoods.

Statistically, the racial group most likely to be killed by police are Native Americans. Young Indigenous men and women in our community, who are often brutalized in police chases and shakedowns, are targeted with less mercy than the white kids. Because Grays Harbor is majority white, all police-related deaths I know of in this community have been white, except for a Native man who was struck and killed crossing the street by a corrections officer driving to work. But I cannot recall the number of scars I have seen on young Native bodies as I visited jails and hospitals around the county. One young Native woman has bruises and scars from every police encounter she has had—including a deep scar across her head when police slammed her head into the pavement. I have seen the scars after police threw a young Native man down flights of concrete stairs. Deep wounds on another from being ripped up by police dogs.

When I spoke to a white court-appointed attorney of a Native young man about his injuries during arrest, he shook his head at me. "Yeah, those Native kids just always run and provoke the police. I wish they would be taught better." The prevalence of racism in a small white-controlled community runs deep and informs the biases of police, prosecutor, and defense attorney alike.

A few years later, I was in a courtroom in Aberdeen. Kevin was in his early twenties, but he didn't look much older than sixteen. Kevin was a short Native guy with a quirky smile and soft voice, and I had met him at the River. In the courtroom, I sat on the hard wood bench in the back as an observer. When they brought in inmates charged with misdemeanors to be heard before the city judge, my mouth dropped. Chained to the group, Kevin was unrecognizable. As the proceedings wore on, he sat in a daze, and when he was called up, he could not form a coherent sentence. His eyes were swollen shut, and his face was purple and swollen with bruises. It looked like his nose was shattered. He kept slumping forward. He was arraigned and assigned an attorney, everything proceeding as if nothing was the matter, as if the young man before the court was not nearly comatose.

As the chain of inmates was led out of the courtroom, the judge asked me who I was there for. I told her, and I asked her if Kevin had received any medical care or if she would ensure that he would. She shrugged. "That is up to the jail," she said, closing the courtroom for recess.

Kevin's picture appeared in the newspaper that day. A young reporter had heard on the scanner that there was a police chase at the River camp and had rushed to get documentation. I am always grateful for the rare reporters who seek to document actions like this. Kevin had been reported by Safeway for stealing, and police had seen him and given chase. He made it to the River camp, to the side his family camped on. Whatever they had done to him, it had been enough to break his face open.

The reporter caught a photograph as two officers hauled up Kevin, his face swollen and streaming blood, his clothes bloodied. Later Kevin would tell me that he remembered nothing about what had happened.

Police are on the front lines of enforcing the value of private property over human life. Poor white men and women join both the military and police force for survival, for a way out of poverty, and to join something bigger than themselves. While they, too, are trying to survive in a world with few job options, they often end up hurting the communities they signed up to protect.

Many scholars point to a correlation between the early formation of slave patrols in the Carolinas and throughout the South in the early 1700s—where mostly poor white men hunted and controlled Black people—and the formation of municipal police forces in the early 1900s, which, in the South, immediately began enforcing Jim Crow laws. This brutality against Black people forms the foundation of modern-day policing. Today, police, prison guards, and other law enforcement often represent ways that poor people, searching for respectability, enforce the status quo on other poor people, often in their own communities.

A brutalized population of poor people is a controlled one. Police have little training, most of the time, and have almost complete free rein to threaten, intimidate, and assault people deemed to be breaking the law.

And because the criminal justice system has no way of actually processing or housing the number of people arrested and charged, there are always high numbers of warrants out for people's arrest. Many are for misdemeanor offenses, driving offenses, and petty theft, and, when people don't show up to court after a citation, bench warrants are issued. Felony warrants, for court appearances on felony charges, are more serious, as are DOC warrants. In practice, this means that large numbers of people in communities like mine are looking over their shoulder much of the time, until the day comes they are arrested.

Like most people from working-class families, I have personal ties with officers of the law. Most of the men and a few of the women in my family have served in the military. Both my grandfathers served in the police force, one in the Los Angeles Police Department's reserve unit. He left the force during the Rodney King rebellion, openly opposed to police violence against the Black community.

My dad may have been raised by a police officer, but I grew up with working-class rules: no snitching. When I was a child, my father would handle many situations himself, intervening in domestic violence disputes of neighbors and such. I never knew him to call the police. Ever. If police came to our door, there was a strict no-talking policy. My dad even broke off friendships if he knew someone reported on anyone else. There's plenty of cognitive dissonance in growing up poor and white, and attitudes toward police are no exception.

As a poor white person with some nostalgia about police officers and small towns, I had hoped to find less brutality in a small town than I had witnessed in larger cities. I had hoped to find more compassion, and occasionally I did. I met many police officers who have genuine concern for people, who often go out of their way to check on people or keep them safe. I met several young officers who shared with me how difficult it is to arrest people they had graduated from high school with only a few years earlier. Yet well-meaning people can be part of a deadly system, regardless of their intentions, and young people who want to serve their community can end up shooting unarmed people, without consequences.

Violence is pervasive. In 2016, Sarah Palmer was tazed to death. Sarah was living in a group home in Hoquiam to which police were called to mediate a domestic dispute. They got into a tussle with the tiny woman and a Taser was deployed, killing her. The coroner ruled her cause of death as natural: a "sudden unexpected death due to excited delirium and schizophrenia, paranoid type."

Patrick West was shot to death in nearby Montesano, a sleepy little town, when crisis services called for backup during a mental health crisis. Local police called for backup, and two other departments, Aberdeen and Hoquiam, showed up as part of a critical response unit. Officers said he was waving a "makeshift sword" in his backyard, behind a fence. For them, that justified their move to eventually end negotiations, break into the house, and shoot him. He had a wife and parents, who were begging police to leave him alone, as well as a nine-year-old daughter. The Grays Harbor County prosecutor ruled his death justified.

The family came forward later with a civil lawsuit, giving a more complete story and forcing the three cities involved to settle for $3 million. The lawsuit said, "They seized Pat's home and property, surrounding it with armed officers, positioning snipers on nearby rooftops and driving an armored vehicle into Pat's front yard . . . And finally—despite hearing from their own negotiators that Pat was 'coming down' from his agitated state—they approached the house with a heavily armed team to breach the door to Pat's basement workshop with a battering ram." This heavily militarized response—to a man in the middle of a mental health crisis, with no criminal record—ended with a Hoquiam officer firing seven shots into his arm and back.

Kristopher Fitzpatrick, known on the street and to his family as "Pillsy," after the Pillsbury Doughboy, was shot on the streets of Aberdeen, also likely in the middle of a mental health crisis. A neighboring business caught much of the standoff on their security cameras, including the shooting, and that video was widely circulated in the community and on social media, drawing widespread outrage. Kristopher was well loved by many, and, in the video, it does not appear that he has a weapon. Police, on the other hand, claim he did have and brandish a gun, and they released a picture to that effect. The prosecutor ruled that deadly force was justified, and there was no further investigation.

In a society built around the protection of property and capital at all costs, the bodies of poor people bear the brunt of the violence required to maintain that system.

⚘ **13** ⚘

THE VALUE OF PUNISHMENT

FROM THE JUVENILE justice system in childhood to the streets and prison in adulthood, many poor people around the nation in find themselves constantly in and out of the prison system. Grays Harbor County is no exception. According to the Prison Policy Project in 2022, Grays Harbor County "has the highest county [incarceration] rate in the state, with 470 people imprisoned per 100,000 residents." Nearby reservations, such as the Squaxin Island Reservation, experience staggering incarceration rates, with more than 1,000 of 100,000 people incarcerated.

As I began to get to know people experiencing homelessness in Grays Harbor, I started visiting them in jail and then corresponding with them when they went to prison. Some of the most powerful conversations I have had have been in jail. I felt honored to share some part of people's lives and listen to their stories.

Bobby's laugh is infectious. A young white man who loves poetry and Tupac, he had accumulated multiple charges in multiple counties by the time I first met him in Grays Harbor County Jail. His stint in county jail lasted the better part of a year as he fought his case.

Some people are better than others at tolerating lockup. People who are sometimes called "institutionalized" have been in and out of jail and prison since childhood, and they often know how to "do time." Natural extroverts and team players can sometimes find their place in the jail and prison system well. And then there are people like Bobby, who just simply cannot tolerate being caged.

Human beings did not evolve with the capacity to be locked in tiny rooms for long periods of time, any more than any other animal, and it seriously affects our nervous system. Some people adapt, often at great cost to their souls and bodies. Other people react by raging and destroying themselves and everyone around them. It is as if the trauma freeze response, so important to navigating incarceration, isn't possible for them, and they are stuck in a constant fight-and-flight response. Bobby's rage and terror and pain exploded all around him at regular intervals. I met with him and advocated on his behalf as often as I could. He was often "in the hole" (in solitary confinement), beating his head against the walls, demanding what he needed. One day he slit his wrists. I saw him a few days later, his wrist heavily bandaged, with a wry smile on his face.

We exchanged letters and phone calls during his longer stint in the Washington State prison system. Bobby struggled deeply with depression and loneliness. As the months turned to years and he was moved from prison to prison, he found employment inside the prison. In the prison system, a major incentive for good behavior is the privilege to break the endless monotony of prison life and be given a job, either in the jail system itself or in prison industry labor. At first, he learned woodshop. He crafted beautiful wooden boxes, several of which he donated for fundraising for people who were homeless.

When he was moved out to a different prison, Bobby was trained as a firefighter. His team would be first responders to major fires in Washington State. With minimal protective equipment, Bobby would push through rattlesnake-infested brush to the front lines of wildfires. Doing the most dangerous jobs in fire containment, his team would dig trenches, fell trees, and clear brush. They'd be close enough to the fires to feel the intense heat. They'd always be one step away from being trapped.

Bobby was thrilled: thrilled to be outside, to be working with a team, to be doing valuable and useful work, and most of all, to be making money. Many people assume that prisoners get all of their needs met in prison, but nothing could be further from the truth. If you want hygiene supplies or food to supplement meager prison rations, you pay exorbitant rates through the commissary system, where, when I was helping buy items in 2020, a packet of ramen might cost a dollar each. You could get a single pair of socks for $1.75 and 1.8 ounces of deodorant for $3. The most coveted items in prison are electronic players that cost $70 and allow inmates to play music, watch movies, and email their loved ones—for about sixteen cents per email.

Bobby was paid a few dollars a day, including hazard pay. The DOC would take almost half his pay for his court fines and fees. It was a good deal for him, however; he got to be outside, doing important work, and he could buy the things he needed to make his stay easier. His days passed more quickly and, as fire season drew to a close, realized he would be out by Christmas.

⯅ ⯈ ⯆

The story we tell ourselves as a society is that when people do bad things, they pay the consequences of their choices. The reality is much more muddled. In the United States, incarceration is heavily racialized, with Black communities and other communities of color incarcerated at much higher rates than white communities. The prison system is a continuation of a slave economy. Incarceration is a way to both lock up the parts of the population not needed for regular employment and to force them to work for nearly free.

Incarceration is big business. As working-class jobs decreased in the 1980s, incarceration increased. The war on drugs populated prisons quickly, but so did the overpolicing of poor communities. There are so many ways to end up in prison as a poor person: dealing or using drugs (depending on state law), breaking into an abandoned home to sleep, stealing to survive or pay your dealer or pay for a couch for the night, or getting involved in the drug trade and all the violence that economy engenders.

Corporate labor is often farmed out to state prisons. The *Seattle Times* reported in 2014, "Today, some 1,600 incarcerated men and women in prison factories produce everything from dorm furniture to school lunches. Washington Correctional Industries (CI) generates up to $70 million in sales a year, ranking as the nation's fourth-largest prison labor program." Prisoners in Washington State, however, make between 65 cents and $2.70 an hour.

State prisons—which warehouse people whose fathers often worked union factory jobs that are no longer available—can produce all sorts of items needed in the global market for a fraction of the cost, because labor is just about free. While factory workers were once paid union wages and made $60,000 a year to produce needed parts, their incarcerated sons and daughters often make a few dollars a day to do similar work within the prison-industrial complex.

The US Constitution actually allows for forced labor, right there in the Thirteenth Amendment. It says, "Neither slavery nor involuntary servitude, except as a punishment for crime whereof the party shall have been duly convicted, shall exist within the United States, or any place subject to their jurisdiction." This justification for Southern states to jail and imprison Black people after the end of slavery continues to be used today to provide nearly free labor to a variety of industries.

This loophole in the Constitution provides states with cost-effective ways to cut corners on producing things like license plates. In the 1980s and 1990s, when trade agreements allowed corporations in the United States to seek cheaper and cheaper labor abroad, crime bills opened up a source of cheap labor domestically: prisoners. The 2.3 million people incarcerated in the United States (about 1 percent of the population) provide a perfect solution to companies no longer willing to pay a living wage.

A growing number of retail outlets are also using prison labor. In Washington State, in an effort to reduce overcrowding in prisons, work-release programs loan the labor of some inmates to corporations. The state provides a group home and oversight and rents out their labor to restaurant chains and other outlet stores.

Black men are more likely to end up in jail and are far more likely to have longer sentences than white men. In Black, Indigenous, and brown communities, mass incarceration has been a continuation of a slave economy and a racialized way to control communities of color and rob their labor.

In white communities, the reality is different by—and sharply dependent upon—class. If you are respectable, you may be afraid of the police, but you are not in serious danger of incarceration. If you are poor, however, incarceration often becomes a generational reality. A People's Policy Project study found that, for the poorest economic group, 43 percent of white men and 47 percent of Black men had been to jail.

This does not contradict the reality that Black people are incarcerated at a much higher rate than whites: overall, Black men are five times more likely than white men to be in prison. But like all other systems, policies that targeted Black, Indigenous, and brown people in this country are also employed against poor white people, punishing them for their failure to thrive. The policies that have roots in US racism and colonialism are then used to abuse and punish poor whites who fail white supremacy.

Prison is the last and most powerful of state systems to control workers, and it leaves the most lasting scars on poor communities. Nearly everyone in poor communities knows someone in jail or prison. Families are separated. Incarcerated people are barred from voting through their sentence and probation. In many states, felons cannot ever vote again, although Washington State has now dropped that tactic and allows voting after the terms of probation are fulfilled. Landlords and employers regularly discriminate against people fresh out of prison. Not only does caging human beings take a heavy toll on their minds and bodies; it also cripples poor communities.

From birth to death, poor people in this country are policed and punished. From child removal and child incarceration to the prison industrial complex, poor life is marked by failure to succeed in a system rigged against them.

Part Three

DEATH

DEATH ON THE RIVER

IF YOU ARE looking for despair, you will find it in every corner of the world of the poor. The overdoses, the violence, the drugs, the rates of suicide: all these demonstrate the suffering and despair of poor communities. From the moment we are born, we are targets in a world that was not built for our survival or thriving. When greed is the endgame and we exist solely as a possible labor market, we die of medical neglect, we die of self-inflicted injury, we die of drug overdoses, and we die of violence. Liberation theologian Gustavo Gutierrez says that poverty is defined as "early and unjust death." This phrase defines poverty in the United States today. In his groundbreaking book, *A Theology of Liberation*, Gutierrez expounds further: "In the final analysis, poverty means death: lack of food and housing, the inability to attend properly to health and education needs, the exploitation of workers, permanent unemployment, the lack of respect for one's human dignity, and unjust limitations placed on personal freedom in the areas of self-expression, politics, and religion."

Yet in the middle of the great suffering that marks the lives of poor people from the moment they are born, the human spirit somehow demonstrates its resilience. In a world where life matters so little that no one even counts the number of people who die of medical neglect, holding a funeral and naming the dead is an act of resistance. In a world where getting adequate medical care is often a distant dream, demanding the care you need is an act of resistance. In a world where death stalks your every step, laughter itself is resistance. In a world that has worked to destroy Indigenous lifeways, singing the songs of your people under a bridge is an act of resistance. Survival itself is an act of resistance.

You cannot understand poverty in the United States without understanding this. It is normative across professions—from clergy to social workers, from teachers to lawyers—to judge the decisions other people make for their own survival through the lens of their own security and their own morality. This is a stubborn aspect of white supremacy: blaming poor people for the mistakes they make while enforcing and upholding the systems that continue to kill them.

⋆ ⋆ ⋆

The man who lived on the River the longest, at least in living memory, was Shawn. He'd lived there off and on since he was fifteen years old. A runaway, he would drink with friends there, camp there, and over the three decades since, he always came back to the place he once took refuge.

Shawn was a fixture in the community that always formed on that little stretch of land. Sometimes he ruled it, his temper vibrating through the entire area. At other times he was the protector of the outcasts. More than a few people felt his fists, especially in his younger years; others found in his presence a refuge from angry boyfriends or the relentless fear of the streets.

Shawn's health had been failing for some time. He was growing morbidly obese, driving around in his ancient, battered Tahoe. It was under his protection that I began visiting the camp along the River.

From there, he began renting a room in the Thunderbird, a tattered motel. On oxygen and then off it again, he fretted that he preferred the River to the ugly, dirty, roach-filled hotel. The city moved in and shut down the Thunderbird, displacing dozens of people and dumping Shawn right back on the street. His girlfriend, Misty, worried about him incessantly, alternately doing all she could to care for him and leaving him alone in his bouts of rage.

Later he was placed in slum apartments, in no better living conditions than the Thunderbird, in units that were periodically without running water or working appliances. But he needed oxygen more and more. Again came evictions, when the city declared the building unfit for habitation. The water was off for days, and I would lug water room to room, hauling it in buckets in my truck from a church down the street. Shawn wanted to fight the eviction, and we thought about how to do a public protest. But as is often the case, people were thrown into a struggle for survival, and a protest never happened.

Shawn was in and out of the hospital, but no real effort seemed to be made to support his failing health. This was partly due to his own stubbornness and partly because hospitals often put very little effort into the health needs of people who are addicted. Lack of health care means that poor people live every day in the constant, brutal face of unjust death.

Shortly before he died, Shawn moved back to the River, a place that, though difficult to live in, was his heart's home. He once told me that the River was where he wanted to die. There, where over a hundred others also ended up, he took people under his protection and let them camp in the area that was known as "Shawn's Camp." He kept the peace as best he could and he doled out favors like a drug kingpin.

The entire time I knew Shawn, he knew he was dying young. He never begged, and in those final few weeks, he seemed to be quietly waiting for the end. No one really believed, though, that he would go so soon. He was only nine years older than me, growing up during the fall of the timber empire and the rise of the drug economy. He always seemed older. To me, he was always respectful and kind. He expressed his appreciation to me for every little thing, and he was never eager to ask for help. Always demanding respect, he was a failing, strong, powerful, dying man.

The last conversation I had with him, he was advocating for the people who lived at the River. He wanted sanitation along the riverbanks, a demand of residents there for decades, and I promised I would do what I could.

One day I got a series of phone calls saying that EMTs were attempting to revive him at his campsite. I arrived just a bit before they called the time of death, and I watched with Misty as they did chest compressions and tried to revive him. They finally called it, Misty weeping in my arms.

All around the campsite, groups of folks—his drinking buddies from a bygone time, the kids he took under his wing, the men and women who knew and respected him—gathered, openly weeping. As police arrived to assess the scene, some of the grievers, knowing they had warrants, melted away into the brush around the River. Others, so young, so serious, so sad, resolutely sat with their friends, squirming under the gaze of the cops who knew they were on the run. Shawn's son, in his twenties, recently homeless and in the camp with his dad, stood close, his face a mask of rage and grief.

They covered his body with a sheet. The patriarch of the River, the protector of so many, loved and feared, was dead, his immense frame spread eagle in the dirt.

People clustered everywhere, some collapsing in sobs and others stand-ing in lonely grief. Some community members from town came down to show support, though some angered family and friends by laughing and talking among themselves, openly and obliviously disrespectful of a community in stunned grief. One police officer tried to crack as many jokes as possible, since Shawn was well-known to him and to the police force. It was well meaning, for the most part, but power dynamics sizzled in the air as Shawn's son struggled to keep his temper under control.

When they finally moved in to take pictures and then to transport the body to the morgue, everyone stepped back for a moment. I knelt down into the dirt and prayed over his body, laying my hands on his forehead, saying, "May the road rise up to meet you, may the wind always be at your back, and may God hold you in the palm of his hand forever." I traced the sign of the cross on his forehead and drew the sheet back over him, then stood back with Misty as they rolled the body into a body bag, zipped it up, and loaded him on a stretcher.

He was gone. Tomorrow we would go the morgue and talk about arrangements. But today was for grieving at the River. His son put up a giant wood cross for his dad, in preparation for the traditional bonfire that marked every death at the River. For the rest of the afternoon, Shawn's son-in-law hauled gravel and rocks and built a monument around the cross along with a huge fire pit, sweat mingling with misty rain as he toiled in memory of the man who had once been his patron. His grief was palpable, but he managed to skillfully construct a huge memorial and light an enormous fire. Men from all over the campsite hauled a ton of wood, chopping it, stacking it, preparing for an all-night vigil in the only place Shawn ever truly called home.

They invited me to come to this great fire in honor of the man who had found refuge and home here, on the riverbank of the Chehalis. The fire was huge. You could hear the river moving in front of us in the darkness, carrying their memories forever. People gathered, came in and out to pay their respects, argued with each other, and played music. By now, I knew them all, loved them all. As I shook hands and exchanged hugs before leaving, Misty asked us to gather for a prayer circle and candle lighting around the memorial cross. About thirty of us joined hands and lit tea light candles, laying them in the care-fully constructed gravel base of the memorial cross. I spoke about remembering

Shawn, how we missed him, how shit like this was hard, but that we knew he was looking down on us. "Rest in peace, Shawn," I concluded. "Rise in power."

There was a whisper of wind through the campsite as he passed by. His spirit seemed to rest on the place that had been his refuge in life, here at the edge of the world.

⋆ ⋆ ⋆

We held Shawn's funeral at the local Methodist church. At least two hundred people came, gathering to listen to his favorite music and share their favorite stories. His seven-year-old daughter, who was there with her mother, was still reeling from her brother's (Shawn's stepson's) suicide at eighteen.

We learn to practice remembering our dead. Not only are poor people consigned to death; they are often consigned to death without a name, especially in communities that feel great deal of shame around how their loved one died. One of the first things that I noticed in my work, as I watched young people die around me, is that so often no one holds funerals for them or names their dead. There are few formal structures to either name or mourn the lost. Often, if families can't afford or do not want the remains, people are cremated and their ashes left in a vault. When one funeral home in our town closed, the local news reported that hundreds of human remains had been found there, unmarked and unclaimed. Poor people often have no formal way to remember or reclaim their dead.

One of the most important practices of my ministry was to reverse the process of erasure and hold funerals and memorials for our dead. I often tracked down the only photographs of them in existence to give to their friends and loved ones. In borrowed churches, we said their names. As Salvadoran liberation theologian Jon Sobrino says, "Just by mentioning the names of the tortured, dead, and disappeared, we recognize their fundamental dignity as human beings who deserve to be remembered as such."

Every year, some of us do an All Saints service near November 1 and put up the photographs and names of all the people we know who have died in the past year. We pray and light candles and leave the sanctuary of whatever borrowed church we are using open for several hours. People drift in and out to remember and toast and pray with the saints, with our lost ones, with our dead.

The most notable feature of this service is always two things: there are always frames left blank, because no one has photographs of the person who died; and most people are young, under fifty. Setting up before the service each year, I am always overwhelmed by the number of young faces represented, dead before their time. By 2019, we had put up fifty-two pictures.

As a tribute to those I have buried, so young and so often, I have a tattoo on my arm. It's a tattoo of La Virgen de Guadalupe, her arms outstretched. Under her image are the initials of our lost ones. In this way she becomes a Pietà, of sorts: the sorrowful Mother holding the bodies of her dying children. This, too, is a memorial, a tribute to the fact that people indeed lived and were full persons.

By the time I stepped down from ministry, the tattoo on my arm had become an entire sleeve, with forty sets of initials engraved on my skin. It is a holy rosary twisting around my left arm from top to bottom, recording many of the people I have buried and only a fraction of those I have known among the dead. Recording in ink some of the staggering losses of one poor community, it is a memorial. It etches the memory of early and unjust death on my skin.

🌿 **15** 🌿

SHAKER FUNERAL

I HAVE OFTEN attended funerals in the Shaker tradition, a church within Indigenous Salish tribes in the Northwest that practices a closed tradition. I have felt deeply privileged to witness these celebrations of life. In white communities, families are often ashamed of their loved ones' drug abuse or cannot afford to collect remains, and so they simply allow death to pass by without public acknowledgment. But this is almost never the case in Native communities. No matter the family's relationship, no matter how fraught, and no matter the conditions of death, the dead are always honored and celebrated.

Leona was alternately the sweetest and the stubbornest woman I ever met. Leona's older sisters were among the many missing Indigenous women and girls of this country, and she didn't even meet them until she was five and they were back in their mother's care. As an adult, after she lost her mother, Leona drank herself to the streets.

I first met Leona under the bridge where we handed out sandwiches every week. Every week she would show up and ask, "You got any tuna?" We always tried to have tuna, just for her.

Sometimes she would be shooting off jokes, laughing at the world in her ubiquitous sense of humor. Other times she would start sobbing quietly. "My auntie, my cousin, my nephew, just died," she'd say. Sometimes they were people she had lost long ago, sometimes they were people she had lost only in her mind, and sometimes there was a funeral planned that week. When her drinking was at its worst, it was her mother she missed most.

One minute vulnerable and tender, and the next in a screaming fight, Leona self-medicated her own immense pain. With a string of sometimes abusive and sometimes kind boyfriends, she somehow coped with her own deteriorating mental health.

Her sisters and brothers loved her. Each of them had their own struggles, and her older sisters, Jean and Francheska, took her in time and time again.

Jean, a Quinault elder, started Tribal Sovereign NDN Tea in 2015, harvesting Bog Labrador and selling Indian Tea. "Native Americans are the original sustainable society," she told one interviewer. "That's why I chose Labrador tea. We take some and we leave some." Jean is one of a growing group of Indigenous women starting small businesses and offering healing to a place deeply fractured by genocide, poverty, racism, and environmental destruction. She sells the tea online and at events around the region, offering leaves for free during the recent coronavirus epidemic.

Leona always knew she could go find her family when she needed them. Her family always tracked down where she was, always brought her care packages, and panicked on social media when they could not find her. Every time they eventually did.

Until they didn't. Leona had taken off to live with a boyfriend in a shack without running water or electricity several hours south. By all reports she was trying to get clean. Far away from adequate medical care, resistant to mental health care, she had dropped off the radar for months. After a frantic weeks-long search by her family, the boyfriend showed up at Francheska's house with the news that Leona had died alone, during a seizure, and that paramedics had been unable to revive her.

Her memorial service was long, an evening vigil followed by a larger funeral and then a reception the next day. Her body lay as if in state, as people told their stories and walked up to hug each of her family members.

The Shaker pastor celebrated her life and told stories, and each person reminded the family that Leona was loved and that they were loved. Unlike some white Christian pastors I have heard, the Shaker pastor did not castigate Leona for her failings. He simply stated the reality and said that each of them was doing the best that they could.

Candles were lit and bells were rung and songs were sung by the elders of the Shaker tradition. Together they guided Leona's soul to the afterlife in the language and ceremonies of her people.

I felt privileged to have known her, and to know her family. I sat there with my wife and with Bonnie, another pastor with whom I worked. We were some of the few white people there. I felt privileged, and humbled, too, to witness and observe traditions that belonged to the place much more than I did.

Before the service, Francheska gathered a group to make hundreds of tuna sandwiches in Leona's honor. Afterward, wearing t-shirts with Leona's picture, family and friends caravanned to a large encampment with a van full of food. In Shaker tradition, a "last supper" is always held for the dead. While family gathered in a rented hall, it was important to them that Leona's street family also took part in her last supper. People who knew her in life had the opportunity to eat together and honor her in death. Within a culture of reciprocity, they both offered their condolences to the family and accepted a final meal.

🦃 🪶 🦃

Despite colonization's best efforts, the traditions indigenous to this part of Turtle Island—the rituals native to this land of cedar trees and waterways— still survive. One of the ways they have survived is in the Indian Shaker Church. (There is no relation to the Shaker tradition among white people on the Eastern coast of the United States, the United Society of Believers in Christ's Second Appearing.) Founded by a Native man by the name of John Slocum, who died and met Jesus before returning to his people, it is a unique and beautiful syncretization of Christian and Native traditions. I have developed a deep respect for this tradition and have been honored to be invited to take part in these funerals.

For a very long time, the Indian Shaker Church was banned in the United States, along with all Indigenous religious practice. The Squaxin Island Tribe notes, in a description of the faith, that "some members of the Squaxin Island Tribe were even put in chains and jailed for practicing their belief in Jesus through the Indian Shaker Church." It was not until 1978 that President Carter signed the American Indian Religious Freedom Act, allowing Native people to freely practice their own traditions and religions.

The fact that Leona was buried in the traditions of her people: it is nothing short of a miracle. It is a monument to the strength and resilience of the people who have been here since time immemorial.

At the same time, the fact that she was dead at the age of fifty-two was testament to the continuing genocide of her people. There was the continued lack of health care, the continued lack of resources, the continued deep poverty of Native communities. On March 1, 2022, Fawn Sharp, president of the National Congress of American Indians and vice president of the Quinault Indian Nation, testified before Congress. "For far too long, Indian Country's needs—particularly in the areas of health and infrastructure—have been neglected or, in some cases, completely ignored," she said. "Because of this, our communities suffered from poor access to health services, broken or non-existent infrastructure, and above-average rates of immunocompromising diseases."

The First Peoples of this place continue to walk down the valley of the shadow of death. Despite the best efforts of the United States, they continue to survive, and they keep finding ways to preserve the traditions and lifeways that formed this region for thousands of years.

❧ 16 ❧

HOSPITAL VISITS

MY PHONE DINGED. Phones rarely last long outside, and people never have minutes for calling and texting, so Facebook Messenger is the easiest way to stay in touch, since you only need Wi-Fi to access it. Nearly everyone got in touch with me through Messenger. I looked at my screen and found a message from Garrett: "Can u take me to the hospital."

I had heard he had been hit by a car not long before, in a hit and run. When Garrett was high, he did the craziest things. Once when he was fleeing the police on a bike, a second vehicle pulled out in front of him and he vaulted over the handlebars, landing on the windshield.

He lived in a church-sponsored tent city for a while, until he was kicked out for his behavior. Having nowhere else to go, he used to sneak back into the camp and lie quietly under his girlfriend's blankets for days at a time. His grandma told me once that she used to do that for him when he was a teenager and his dad would throw him out in a rage: she would sneak him back into the house, put him under her blankets, and hide him so he could sleep.

I had some free time, so I arranged to meet Garrett at the library. He limped into the truck and I told him, "Look, I have a meeting in an hour. So I can drop you off at the hospital, but I'm gonna have to leave you there." He rolled his eyes but agreed.

I left him after check-in and drove to a church vestry meeting. I was due to give an update about my work on the streets, and so I gave it, to what ended up being a rather surly crowd. After the meeting, I went back to the hospital to check on him.

Walking through the parking lot, I squinted when I saw a man who looked like Garrett, in a hospital wheelchair, on the driver's side of a parked car. Sure enough, as I came closer, I could tell it was him. Wielding a wire coat hanger, he was madly trying to open the lock. I raised my eyebrows as he raised his hands in the air. "Yes!" he yelled, falling back on the chair as it rolled back wildly.

Apparently an older woman had locked her keys in the car while dropping off her husband in the ER. She had walked into the waiting room and bellowed, "Anyone in here got any carjacking experience?" Garrett and another man were only too eager to raise their hands, and so now there they were, competing for who could break in the fastest.

The streets and poor communities of the United States are places of brutality and unending death and heartache. They are also places of unending laughter and humor. I have never laughed so often nor so hard as I have on the street.

Most people I met on the street are young. Abuse, drugs, joblessness, and mental illness have pushed them to the streets. But even in a tent, young women will carefully do their makeup. Even sleeping on a sidewalk, young people will beg, barter, or steal whatever trendy jeans and Jordans they can find. No matter where they find themselves, they try to help each other when they can and where vendettas allow, and they find ways to celebrate and laugh and live.

All the facade of mainstream culture melts away and things become, in their words, "real." Emotions are raw: anger and anxiety, but love and joy as well. People carry their burdens and their past and their trauma as well as they can, and often laughter rings as the real-est sound of them all.

Garrett never got the medical care he needed that night, nor most of the other times he sought it. He was labeled "drug seeking"—and perhaps he was. However, he was certainly seeking all the things the rest of us seek too: love and community, health and wholeness, and, most importantly in that moment, adequate medical care for his mental and physical health needs. When people are dismissed as drug seeking, they rarely get treatment for their infections, their wounds, their developing chronic health issues, or their mental health needs.

He also never lost his ability to laugh, even as, eventually, he confronted a long prison sentence. His grandma continued to support him through it all: talking to him on the phone, buying him a player when she could, and staying in touch with his girlfriend.

🡇 🡆 🡇

I was at the meal program we ran in Aberdeen when someone asked me, "Can you go check on Mimi? She really needs to go to the hospital." I nodded, hands full, and tossed off kitchen duties to a volunteer.

Apartment buildings across the alley from the church are always full of low-income renters, who sometimes have water and power and sometimes do not. People were clustered at the bottom of the stairs, smoking. More people were clustered upstairs, most high or getting high. It was dark and dingy. I knocked on Mimi's door and someone called out, "Give us a minute." I always appreciate that people rarely shoot up in front of me. It's a small and profound mark of respect that always moves me.

Mimi's boyfriend came out. "I told her I'd take her to the hospital. But I don't got no gas."

"I can fill up your tank," I told him.

"She won't go." He gestured to the bedroom. "Go talk to her."

One of her legs was swollen twice the size of the leg next to it. She was huddled in shorts and a t-shirt, rocking on a chair rhythmically. I knelt down next to her.

"I ain't going to that Aberdeen hospital," she told me. "I was there last week. They were awful to me." The local hospital was consistently underfunded and understaffed, and staff were notoriously curt with drug-addicted clients. They also rarely provided medical withdrawal for opiate-addicted clients who came in for other complaints.

"Okay," I told her. "I understand. What about Elma? Or Olympia?"

Our conversation came and went as she drifted in and out of consciousness. I spoke to her boyfriend, and it was clear he wasn't going to be able to drive her anytime soon. The streets were a hard taskmaster, and he had errands first.

Finally, I turned to her. "You are going to die here if you don't go. Will you let me take you?" Finally, tears running down her face, Mimi nodded. Before she could change her mind, I turned to her boyfriend. "Can you carry her down these stairs? I'll bring my truck to the front."

It was an hour's drive to St. Peter's Hospital, the nearest trauma hospital. I knew leaving her at a closer hospital would only mean she would be transferred and might slip between the cracks. Infections like this one were particularly bad that year, sweeping through flophouses and hotels and encampments, leaving people without fingers or toes or even whole limbs, sometimes leading to death when infection spread quickly.

Mercifully, the emergency room at St. Pete's was almost empty, and the nurses were kind. Mimi was triaged immediately, and the nurse rushed her to a room. I stayed through the doctor's visit, only leaving when I knew she would be admitted, placed on withdrawal support, and had agreed to stay through a heavy and immediate round of antibiotics.

Much later, Mimi would write me a letter from prison. "I wasn't sure then that I wanted to be saved, but thank you for saving my life."

★ ➤ ✦

The barriers to medical care in poor communities are many. Hospitals are usually underfunded and overburdened. Drug use complicates medical care, both because of the prejudice of medical providers and the reluctance of people in addiction to admit their use by seeking medical care. Dirty needles, bad drugs, and injecting yourself with substances with who knows what in it: all of this creates a medical nightmare. Add to that the trauma and resulting mental health crises many people find themselves in, and it's no wonder that our premature death rates are so high.

Even when people do decide to seek care, the next steps can be hard. I once walked a half mile with a guy in a wheelbarrow to load him into my truck and take him to the hospital. Transportation is always difficult, even to a local hospital, but becomes even harder if you need a better hospital. In Grays Harbor, most of the time, people refuse to go to the local hospital and insist they would rather die than go there again because of how they have been treated.

This means that people usually wait far too long before seeking care. I have driven semi-conscious people to the hospital often. I have sat through hours with people, gently convincing them to stay as their anxiety becomes too much to manage, as they start withdrawing, as they deal with a harried and overwhelmed nursing staff.

Often it is too late. Or too late to save a limb. I know several elders who are now in wheelchairs, often still on the street, because they lost limbs to infection. Usually they were treated too late and then could not keep their wounds clean. By the time they return to an ER, the limb is beyond saving. I always carried a first aid kit, and perhaps the thing I did most often in my work was clean wounds and rebandage them. Nothing is more terrifying than finding an elder in a corner of a flophouse, comatose, with a rotting limb.

Sometimes people are lucky enough that they only lose fingers. Other times deep, ugly wounds reaching to the bone slowly heal and close over. The streets are dirty, and it is impossible to stay clean. Shared bedding and clothing spread infection. People reuse needles or use other people's needles as they shoot up drugs, and of course that spreads infection. Some people wonder if the drugs themselves contain infectious bacteria.

Drug use is complicated and devastating to any community. Often, when political conversations drift to extreme poverty in the United States, I have noticed that progressive antipoverty activists sometimes gloss over the messiness, and prevalence, of drugs in poor communities. I believe they do this partly to make the important point that many poor people do not, in fact, use drugs, but also because media narratives seem to continually demand perfect victims.

There are no perfect poor people. Certainly, many poor people never touch drugs. Just as certain is the fact that drugs absolutely contribute to the high rates of premature death in poor communities.

Fentanyl and methamphetamines come to Grays Harbor through a vast, global network of drug distribution. The United States has engaged in a four-decades-long "war on drugs," criminalizing their manufacture and distribution. But this effort has only created a more impoverished and more heavily criminalized poor population, putting no dent in the use of drugs themselves. Drugs tear apart poor communities, leaving them less likely to organize for change and less able to understand their own suffering. Whether on purpose or by accident, capitalism greatly benefits by keeping poor communities drugged and self-loathing, reducing the likelihood that these communities will have the resources or desire to fight back.

Mimi survived, whether she wanted to or not. She would go on to play her part in fighting back, even when all the forces around her were pushing her toward death.

⚜ **17** ⚜

KNEELING IN CHAINS

NOT EVERYONE SURVIVES.

The borrowed Episcopal church was packed again. It had been a year of back-to-back funerals. This one was for "Mama Milk," a woman in her fifties who was everyone's street mother. Legend had it that she once rode with the Hells Angels.

The streets knew her as Mama. She had raised her own family, and many other children in my age group, in the chaotic and violent years of the 1980s and 90s, when drug manufacturing in Grays Harbor was at its peak. White gangs ran the streets and ruled the white side of the prisons. She raised the generation that never had a chance in this county: the kids who were almost destined to take part in the growing underground drug empire as gainful employment waned in timber country.

In all the pictures of her, Mama Milk is wearing bright colors and laughing. She was a bright spot in a dark time, a flower child at the heart of the drug war. I knew her only briefly, but I saw her kindness and intensity. Once, on a particularly busy day at one of our feeding programs, she grabbed my wrists, looked me in the eye, and told me to keep on keeping on.

While I did not know her well, the hundreds of young people whose lives she had touched showed up for her funeral. It nearly took an act of God to bring her family together under that church roof the day of her memorial service. She had two daughters who did most of the planning, both incredible women who had put their lives back together after an incredibly traumatic early life. They had both gotten clean and were raising adorable little families. Bringing her four sons together was a miracle that barely happened. I spent an entire morning the day before waiting to see if her youngest son, being held on a probation violation, could be released from jail. Two other sons were in prison, and it cost over two thousand dollars to get them there. I raised half that money, and their family and friends raised the rest.

When the day finally came, it was standing room only in the church. Two of her sons, wearing orange and flanked by DOC officers, were sitting in the front pew. One of them wrote to me later: "This day seems so surreal to me. I left my prison at 7 A.M.. Drove shackled, chained, and naked, save for shoes and jumpsuit, 300 miles. When I arrived at your church, I was enveloped in love by friends and family. It was truly overwhelming to come from this environment to that."

We delayed the service nearly an hour waiting for the last son to get there. He was pulled over by police just blocks away, his car full of the flower arrangements he had made himself, and ticketed for driving without a license. At least he didn't go to jail.

A broad array of faith traditions were represented. Some of her family had been raised Catholic, and she herself had been a regular attender at Catholic mass at one time. Her grandson, an adorable four-year-old, came up and sang a Native chant from his father's people. Many others subscribed to Ásatrú, or Norse heathenism.

I spoke the traditional Christian words: *We must all go down to the dust, but even at the grave, we make our song: Alleluia, Alleluia, Alleluia.*

At the end of every funeral, I set up a table in the front, with a photograph and the ashes of the person we are commemorating, if the family could afford to obtain them. Then I ask people to line up and light candles as a way to say goodbye.

Mama's children came up first, and the sight is burned into my memory forever. Her two sons from prison were in orange jumpsuits, their wrists and ankles chained to their waists. As they struggled to kneel, in chains, in front of their mother's photograph, there was a collective intake of breath in the sanctuary. Their sisters gathered around to help them light candles. Time froze there, for a moment, as children who had not been under the same roof since childhood knelt, some in chains, to say goodbye to their mother.

🕊 🕊 🕊

As a chaplain, you learn to meet people where they are, without judgment. I had learned to be present to people who were able to pull themselves out of addiction and just desperately wanted everyone else they loved to survive too. And I was present to people who could barely keep their head up from drug use, who were usually masking intense physical and emotional pain.

Knowing and loving all these people meant that, along with the community, I mourned loss after loss after loss. Overdose deaths, in 2017, were at an all-time high. From 2012 to 2016, there were thirty-eight unintentional overdose deaths in the county. In 2016, EMS services had administered naloxone, a drug that reverses an opiate overdose, seventy-seven times; in 2017, sixty-three times. Up until 2016, public health officials refused to consider making naloxone available to the community, even though most other counties at the time had public distribution programs. When I met with the head of the county health department at the time, she told me it was too politically difficult and she did not want to take up the fight. At the time, I could not even get my doctor to prescribe it. I had to go to a different county just to have a dose available to carry with me as I visited camps and flop houses and hosted meals and gatherings.

In mid-2016, I got a call from a public health official who told me that they had finally partnered with the University of Washington, in a five-year study, to distributed naloxone as widely as they could. I happened to pick up the call while I was driving to the coroner's office. With me was the girlfriend of a young man who had just died of an overdose. We were on our way to pick up his things. It was a cruel irony. Around that same time, in a tent city on a church parking lot, another man was found dead of an overdose. After the crime scene was cleared I prayed over his body, lying there on the asphalt, before the coroner took him away.

There is so much shame in drug use, and it is crippling. That very shame often drives people deeper and deeper into self-medication and eventual death. But while there is intense shaming by the wider community and even people's families, people on the streets have a strange love and acceptance of each other, in the mess of it all. When no one else will, they listen to each other. People make a strange family, bound together by trauma and loss, shame and addiction.

"The opposite of addiction isn't sobriety. It's connection," writes Johann Hari in *Chasing the Scream*. "It's all I can offer. It's all that will help him in the end. If you are alone, you cannot escape addiction. If you are loved, you have a chance. For a hundred years we have been singing war songs about addicts. All along, we should have been singing love songs to them."

At that funeral, we sang Mama Milk a love song, and we sang a love song to her friends and family. As the DOC officers shepherded her two sons out of the sanctuary and back to the prison van, people gathered around them outside, tearful and wrapping their arms around them. Her daughters headed back into the church afterward, before going back to the homes they had built for themselves with such determination and courage. There, in the room hushed and dark and lit only by candles, they collected their mother's pictures and her ashes.

⚜ 18 ⚜

SEEKING REDEMPTION

WE LIVE IN the shadow of all this death. Here in its shadow, the legacy of white supremacy and colonialism drives wedges between poor people, redirecting legitimate anger at the conditions in which people live toward other poor people. Instead of raging at the system that extracts our labor and destroys the land and our spirits, we rage at each other. The most effective way to drive this wedge is to offer one group an advantage—however slight—over others.

The Grays Harbor electorate swung red in 2016 for the first time in ninety years. Since then, the Grays Harbor Republican Party and affiliate groups have grown, as has the agitation of a group of very loud and angry business owners and citizens. Over the past five years, they have galvanized and put forward candidates for all local seats on city councils, on the county commission, and as mayors. They regularly swing majorities on city councils and have two out of three seats on the county commission. Clearly well-funded, they have taken the local political class and replaced it with something new and much more openly vitriolic.

The rallying point of these groups has been ridding the town of people who are addicted or homeless, issues that can be easily sensationalized. Citizen groups picketed the public health department for months on end to protest the county's site for the distribution of naloxone as well as the needle exchange, a harm-reduction measure that has been proven to reduce blood-borne disease and save lives. Protesters would congregate at the needle exchange site under the Chehalis bridge, where public health workers would distribute naloxone and clean needles, filming people and screaming at them. At one point someone brought along a gun.

The work I did, alongside many others, also attracted a lot of vitriol, partly because we regularly engaged local politics. We attended public health meetings, city council meetings, and sometimes county commissioner meetings, often with people currently homeless who were willing to share their stories. Community pages would fill with rants about my work, and sometimes I would be followed when driving around town.

It was frustrating work. City council members were often openly hostile and fed on the hostility of those in the community who stood up to say how much they hated seeing homeless people, how afraid they felt of panhandlers, and how Aberdeen would never recover so long as they had a visible "homeless problem." One downtown property owner said, "They just all need to die out." In a city council meeting, an elected official once approached me once, saying, "I'm watching you."

🐦 🐦 🐦

Curses were echoing off the muddy banks of the Chehalis when I got out of the truck. A small excavator and a large truck and trailer were parked at one end of the River, and I saw the excavator stopped up against what used to be someone's shack. The wood- and tarp-covered structure was splintered, and all its contents spilled out in the mud. A tall woman, Shawna, was holding a steel bar in the middle of the wreckage and screaming, "Get the fuck out of my face!"

It took me a moment to figure out what was happening. At that point, the property that people camped on at the River was owned by a local man who also owned a trailer park. Every year or so, the city would send him a letter, asking him to remove the "public nuisances" from his property. And every year or so, he would tell people at the River they had to leave or else take his little excavator down to clear camps out himself. He would claim the city was fining him, the city would deny it, and on and on the cycle would go.

That day he had gone down there himself, bellowing loudly at anyone who would listen about the "lazy druggies" on his property. He had also paid some of the residents of his trailer park to help him clear out people and their belongings.

Facing Shawna, who was standing over the remains of her cabin, was a shorter, older woman, who for a few moments was matching Shawna cuss word for cuss word. The older woman lived in the trailer park and was here with the group tasked with clearing out River residents and their things. I walked over, careful to stay neutral and calm, just as the older woman burst out: "Do you think I *want* to fucking be here? My cousin lives down here too. I didn't have a choice."

The tension broke for a moment and the steel bar dropped. Both women walked away.

I did not know the older woman from the trailer park, but I know a lot of people like her. So many poor people hang on to housing by a thread, in trailer parks, in run-down apartments, in substandard housing. Working jobs at McDonalds or as caretakers, standing all day, making minimum wage, they often cobble together multiple jobs and side hustles to pay for rent and maybe have enough money left over for food and heat. They work so hard to make it, and they get frustrated by the prevalence of drugs among their loved ones. They get annoyed by the people experiencing homelessness who come into the shops where they work and steal—tents, or alcohol, or candles to stay warm. They are also worried about their own family members in similar situations. So if town leaders and influential business and property owners stir up that frustration, an offer of an opportunity to clear up a homeless camp as a side hustle can seem like a good idea to make a few extra bucks.

Someone had called the police by that time, and the officer who arrived informed the property owner that he could remove trash from the site but could not destroy people's structures or tents or harass the people themselves. Clearly tired of the contentious issue of people camping along the River, the officer pointed out that he was aware that the property owner had given at least some people permission to be there and that the matter actually needed to be settled in the courts.

That day remains in my mind as an example of how poor people are constantly pitted against each other. That day, people paying rent to live in a shitty trailer park on the edge of a tiny town were pitted against people who had lost a place to live and were building shacks on the banks of a river.

                                   ⋏ ⋏ ⋏

Several residents of the River were standing in a circle, and others were standing along the edges. They were facing a group of young men who held donuts in one hand and chains in the other. They had brought food to start with, in the back of their pickups, but residents eyed their donuts warily and just watched. I stood with the folks at the River, slightly in front, every muscle taut. It was clear both sides were angry, and both were likely armed. Out of the corner of my eye, I noticed a few weapons.

The night before, Tyler, the son of a local businessman, had posted a call on social media for citizens of Aberdeen to join him to tow out vehicles and RVs parked at the camp. In an impassioned plea, he said that the encampment at the River was a blight on the town and that he was going to help clear it. The week before, he had towed away a vehicle with someone sleeping in it, damaging their only place to sleep.

Tyler had a rough history. Born to a "respectable" family in town, he had been one of the bad kids and had dabbled in drugs. He had lived on the River at one point himself, and he had spent time in and out of jail. But now he was a few months clean and eager for redemption. He had his own small business by that time, and he had heard the cry of local business owners up in arms about homeless people sleeping in front of businesses or camping in large numbers along the Chehalis. In Facebook rants, he and his followers began savagely attacking advocates as well, including some choice words directed at my sexuality and gender.

That morning, Tyler and his group were clearly filled with righteous indignation. Both sides were nearly silent. One young woman, who only months before had been living at the River but had been able to get into treatment, stepped forward from Tyler's group.

"You want some donuts, guys? We just want to help."

Johnny, Christina's boyfriend, spoke harshly. "You have chosen your side," he snarled. "We don't want your damn donuts."

Tears sprang into her eyes. I walked over to her from where I had been standing and gave her a hug. "I thought these guys just wanted to help," she said, a tear running down her face.

"I know," I told her. I stepped back to the group of River residents as lines were drawn again. The men and women from the River standing next to cars and RVs, tents and cabins, were tense, silent. The men with trucks and chains, frustration growing on their faces, conferred about what to do next.

Someone must have called the police, because some police cars soon arrived. I breathed a sigh of relief when I saw Officer Glaser step out of his cruiser. He was an officer well-known on the street for his fairness and kindness. Everyone's hands went down quickly, and the chains disappeared.

Officer Glaser managed to talk down both sides, de-escalating the tension. Eventually Tyler and his group left, with frustrated muttering.

A few days later, two women from the camp walked into district court and filed antiharassment orders, showing video after video of being harassed by Tyler's group.

After a few court dates, Tyler and his group would fade into the background. But that morning standoff remains for me a clear reminder of the difficulty organizing in white communities. Poor white people have always had a carrot dangled under our nose—an incentive of "improving our station" in life, however slight—that keeps us from fully analyzing the systems of which we are a part. And we are always clearly divided by class. If you can make it—if you can prove yourself to be *just* respectable enough—you are expected to throw your lot in with the ruling class. And you are rewarded for it, some of the time.

It was also a clear reminder of the ways that the drug war has divided our communities and torn them apart. We have been taught that tough love is what is needed to rescue our loved ones. We have been taught to reject people in active addiction, in a vain hope that they will "hit rock bottom" and recover.

Tyler's quest for redemption saddened me deeply. I saw the ghosts of my own upbringing in his eyes: shame for a past we cannot change, hunger for approval and love in a community that had once shunned us. In his eyes I saw the same hunger for redemption that had driven my parents into abusive cults, that drove struggling small business owners to target people who were homeless, that drove respectable white people to terrorize their neighbors.

Redemption under capitalism always means hating yourself. Hating yourself for any mistakes you might have made, hating yourself for not succeeding, hating yourself for being poor. Redemption, then, comes by holding the lines of respectability, by defending private property, and by targeting those deemed outsiders.

Every single town and city I have lived and worked in claims that people who are homeless are shipped in from somewhere else. Some people might actually believe that, but I do not think they care if it is true or not. It is certainly statistically untrue. For example, in Los Angeles, a study showed that 64 percent of unhoused people in Los Angeles County have lived there for more than ten years, and only 18 percent said they had lived elsewhere before becoming homeless. In Aberdeen, most people I know lived in Aberdeen housed before they ever became homeless.

The claim that people come from elsewhere, however, is simply saying this: people who are homeless are outsiders and outcast to the community. It does not matter that you actually went to the same high school. It is simply the declaration that, once you have fallen from grace, you do not belong.

And so, to reinstate his status in a community that had once given up on him, Tyler found a way to distance himself from the outcasts. He found a way to prove himself valuable to the business-owning community, to prove himself one of them.

Weeks after the standoff at the River, I sat in a courtroom with the two women from the River as they filed antiharassment orders against Tyler. I watched Tyler, sitting with a lone friend, as his hands shook with anxiety. And I wanted nothing more than to put my hand on his shoulder and tell him that there was a better way than the one he had found. There is another path, one that leads toward liberation.

Part Four

RESISTANCE

❧ 19 ❧

A RAINBOW COALITION

THE 1960S WERE a time of social upheaval. Uprisings and movement build-ing, across a wide array of communities, was in full swing. People were in the streets protesting war, demanding civil rights, demanding a change to legal sys-tems of oppression against Black people, against queer people, against women. Not all the movements were aligned or were even able to work together in any significant way. Racial barriers loomed large, just as they had during union organizing in the decades before. Clearly, a key strategy of colonialism and capitalism—keeping people divided by race and identity—was still function-ing just as it was designed.

In Chicago, however, something was brewing. In a Methodist church, members of an organization calling themselves the Young Patriots were speak-ing alongside leaders from the Black Panthers. The Young Patriots called themselves an organization by and for hillbillies: the many young white people who had moved to Chicago from Appalachia in the decades follow-ing the Second World War. Both groups, along with the Puerto Rican Young Lords and others, were facing horrific living conditions and police violence in impoverished, working-class Chicago. They also shared a belief in material liberation, demanding more than civil rights but economic rights as well.

The Black Panthers, Young Lords, and Young Patriots slowly, and with difficulty, built an alliance between poor communities across race. Hy Thur-man, a cofounder of the Young Patriots, recalls, "Why would the Black Pan-thers and the Young Lords welcome whites, who have traditionally been their oppressors, into a coalition as equals? . . . We were welcomed into the coalition due to our antiracist politics, and because we were a group that have proven that many members had evolved from street gang members and poor oppressed Southern whites in to community organizers."

The young people of the Young Patriots looked a lot like members of any other white street gang in Chicago. But they saw themselves as hillbillies looking for liberation for their own communities—and, importantly, doing so in solidarity with other oppressed groups. This alliance faced many obstacles, of course, not the least of which was the suspicion that exists between racial groups in the United States. The Young Patriots did a variety of campaigns, including those focused on what the Black Panthers called "projects of survival." Realizing that poor people did not have access to the food and medical care that they needed, they started projects that brought those resources to their people. They also worked to build a larger class consciousness.

The Patriots provided protection at times for members of the Black Panthers. Bobby Lee told the story of how two police officers followed him out of a church meeting and arrested him. When the Patriots leadership saw what was happening, they gathered all the white folks from the meeting—men, women, and children—who then surrounded the police car and demanded Bobby's release. They got it.

The Young Patriots joined many campaigns alongside the Black Panthers, the Young Lords, and Native American activists in Chicago. They were clear that they were hillbillies—white Southerners who wanted to dismantle capitalism—and saw themselves as distinct from educated and middle-class white leftists. Hy Thurman has written extensively about his involvement as a founding member of the Young Patriots in his lovely book, *The Revolutionary Hillbilly*. In rural Oregon, Chuck Armsbury organized a chapter of the Young Patriots. Armsbury was targeted by local whites, who fired on their headquarters. He said, "Back then, there were Minutemen militias who weren't too happy about whites and Blacks in a rural area cooperating with one another." Armsbury would end up spending ten years in prison after he was arrested for carrying a loaded gun and a notebook containing, according to the police report, "revolutionary theory."

In Chicago, the Young Patriots published a newspaper called *The Patriot: People's News Service*. In their March 21, 1970, issue, they had a quote that has stuck with me throughout my work. Under a picture of an older white man, who is visibly poor, holding a baby, it reads: "We are the living reminder that when they threw out their white trash, they didn't burn it."

This quotation neatly summed up the experience of many poor whites, and it gave a glimmer of hope that the racial divide that has been part of the American experiment could be broken. It was a reminder that poor whites were capable of turning on their oppressors and dismantling those systems. It was the opposite of the slur as I had experienced it in liberal white circles. If the ruling class wanted to call us "white trash," well, so be it. We would simply remind them that we were still around, still alive after centuries of poverty and oppression, and still finding common cause with other poor folks.

The FBI, with J. Edgar Hoover at the helm, saw the Black Panthers as a threat. This coalition, which was developing across race, posed a threat in their minds as well. Bobby Lee of the Black Panthers would later observe, "The Rainbow Coalition was their worst nightmare."

🔻 🔺 🔻

So far in this book, we have looked at what life is like in one very poor community in the United States at the beginning of the third millennium. Because any struggle for life and any effort to stay alive is a form of resistance, we have looked at people's efforts to survive in a world that was not meant for their thriving.

In the next chapters, we will look at paths forward—not just for survival but for resistance. It's a resistance that seeks to undermine the systems that oppress us and create a better world. I will also explain some of the strategies that I engaged in over my decade of work in Grays Harbor County, some more effective than others. We will celebrate the many leaders of movements for change and resistance: from leaders of national movements like the Rainbow Coalition and the Poor People's Campaign to individuals fighting for change in their own communities—lawyers and preachers to shelter workers and farmers and families.

Working to end poverty—which means, essentially, the end of capitalism—is an enormous undertaking. It took five hundred years in the Americas to get us where we are at now, living with vast inequality, genocide, poverty, war, and the threat of environmental catastrophe. It took five hundred years to seize land and acquire labor and try to stamp out Indigenous culture. The owning class's hold has always been tenuous, however, which is why violence is so often employed against poor people. There has always been resistance, much of it successful and some of it, over the past several centuries, nearly bringing down the system itself.

As long as there are poor people—as long as the majority of people in the world do not benefit from capitalism—they remain the Achilles' heel of the system. The poverty and struggle of the global poor are linked. As the United States and the West engage in protracted imperial wars and conflicts around the globe, the misery of the global poor may be particular to a place, but it is also bound together at its source. Black people, immigrants, Indigenous people, poor white people: all are suffering, often in different ways and to different degrees. Over the past century, Black and brown people have borne a large part of the burden of work and energy to resist racialized capitalism. Perhaps now is the moment that poor white people can join them and replicate the Rainbow Coalition on a larger scale.

In the end, poor people across the nation and across the globe are the majority. In this lies our power to topple the system that extracts our labor, kills our children, and destroys the earth for profit.

It may take us another five hundred years to fully end this system—if the earth itself does not end it first. But what would happen if larger numbers of poor white people joined in resistance to the system that is killing us all?

❧ 20 ❧

A POOR PEOPLE'S CAMPAIGN, THEN AND NOW

IN MAY 1968, Native American activists from the Puget Sound, just sixty miles east of Grays Harbor, were in the middle of a fight for fishing rights. In Washington State, large fishing corporations were allowed to fish salmon almost to the point of extinction. Yet tribal members were arrested for fishing in waters in which they had treaty rights to fish and were given no rights to participate in fishery management.

Hank Adams, raised on the Quinault Indian Nation, had been organizing "fish-ins" since 1964. He was arrested multiple times in his efforts to gain tribal fishing rights for himself and his people. Adams would become one of the most prominent West Coast voices in the first Poor People's Campaign meeting of 1968. The brainchild of Martin Luther King, Jr., in December 1967, the Poor People's Campaign was an effort to create a national movement to unite poor people across race across the country to address what King called the three evils: racism, materialism, and militarism. In that speech, he said, "The fact is that Capitalism was built on the exploitation and suffering of black slaves and continues to thrive on the exploitation of the poor—both black and white, both here and abroad. . . . The way to end poverty is to end the exploitation of the poor, ensure them a fair share of the government services and the nation's resources."

But Dr. King had been assassinated just the month before the first march was planned. Organizers decided to march anyway, gathering together one of the largest poor people's marches in US history. Rev. Dr. Ralph Abernathy explained that the intention of the Poor People's Campaign was to "dramatize the plight of America's poor of all races and make very clear that they are sick and tired of waiting for a better life." People from all over the country gathered and built Resurrection City in front of the Capitol. Black families from the Deep South who had come by mule train, Indigenous people from the Northwest, caravans from all over the country, organizers and college students, poor people of all ages: all set up tents in the mall in front of the Capitol, posting signs to end poverty in the mud and muck of a rainy early summer. Their efforts climaxed with a Solidarity Day Rally for Jobs, Peace, and Freedom on June 19.

Dr. King and other organizers had a much larger vision for this effort, but it fell short as the nation reeled from his assassination, the Vietnam War, and internal divisions. In the end, Resurrection City dispersed, and the remaining leaders were arrested. Yet it remained a powerful symbol: linking multiple movements, bringing together poor people across race, and uniting for an economic bill of rights. For Hank Adams and other Native leaders, the march allowed them to also protest for Native sovereignty and bring their demands to the halls of power. For Black, Chicano/a, white, and Native poor people, the Poor People's Campaign offered the chance to share their experiences of poverty and injustice and build relationships that would reverberate through the rest of the century.

Almost fifty years later, the Kairos Center at Union Theological Seminary and Rev. Dr. William Barber's Repairers of the Breach discussed reviving the Poor People's Campaign. Would it be possible to pick up the unfinished work of the Poor People's Campaign from 1968 and create a broad-based movement of poor people? I had taken a class from the organization that would become the Kairos Center while in seminary, and I was inspired by their message of uniting poor people across the country. When I moved back to Grays Harbor County, I wondered how to bring that message home.

During my first year as a chaplain, as I was building relationships on the streets of Aberdeen, I met Aaron Scott, who was a graduate of Union Theological Seminary and was trained by the Poverty Initiative. He had moved to Washington State and was also discerning next steps. Together, we wondered how to talk about wider issues facing poor people on a local level, and how to engage in popular organizing and base building in Grays Harbor.

So in the summer of 2014, Aaron and I and friends John and Colleen Wessel-McCoy and their kids went on a camping trip on the coast. We stayed in a yurt on a beach in Westport, and we began talking about what it would mean to bring the Poor People's Campaign to our area. What might it mean to organize in Grays Harbor in context of building a larger movement of poor people?

While we played in the waves of the Pacific, a dream was born. Aaron and I would work together to build a new organization—with few resources and even less money—and call it Chaplains on the Harbor. We wanted to do two things: to engage in projects of survival (giving people access to food, clothing, and shelter), while also educating and organizing poor people to become leaders in a movement to end poverty.

The Episcopal Church had just closed their church building in Westport and was considering what to do with it. We decided to put together a proposal to turn the church into a community center. We envisioned it as a place we could offer meals and support people in meeting their basic needs, while also providing education around poverty in our community. We hoped people—particularly those who were marginalized in other places—could find in this space a kind of home, a kind of belonging.

In February 2015, we opened the space as a community center once a week, organizing lunch, pastoral care, and occasional events. This, coupled with continued street outreach in Aberdeen, became core to our mission and everyday work. Bonnie Campbell, a local Episcopal priest and longtime mentor of mine, joined us as a volunteer from the beginning, bring her skills in crisis work and boundless love and respect for everyone she met.

The quieter work was that of education and narrative building. In a community where people blamed poor people for their poverty and where poor people were grappling with all the realities this book lays out, creating a new narrative was important. Aaron had a unique ability to both meet people where they were and guide them toward crafting a new narrative. He hosted popular education programs in Westport and Aberdeen, calling them the School of Hard Knocks. Poor women from trailer parks, homeless Native men and women, and young people caught in addiction all attended and shared their experiences. Together they began to unpack how capitalism functions and brainstormed about what it might look like to resist.

We hosted State of the Streets events in both towns, inviting local residents, social service providers, and public officials to listen to poor and homeless people share their stories. We heard about how hard it was to get a job, about experiences of losing children to CPS, about how difficult it was to find housing or shelter or even public bathrooms, and about the struggle for survival.

It was a start. Aaron and I took the message we were hearing from the people around us to churches, colleges, and organizations around the state. We brought people from the community with us to share their stories. We preached, and we wrote, and we began the work of shaping a new narrative.

And through it all, we kept connecting to the growing revival of the Poor People's Campaign. Aaron attended events, orchestrated speakers, and developed relationships with communities around the country who were also experiencing poverty. In 2016, Chaplains on the Harbor officially joined the Poor People's Campaign: A National Call for Moral Revival. Much of the work of organizing we have been able to do has been in concert with our connections to a larger movement. Over the years, members of our team have visited teams and organizations around the country, and they have visited us.

Staying connected to a larger narrative and a larger movement is vital to any work on the ground. As we confronted the deadly reality of poverty in our community, we now knew that we were not alone. We knew that we were part of something bigger, that we were part of a fight that had been going on for decades and even centuries. That knowledge kept us going and gave us inspiration.

⚜ 21 ⚜

FACING OFF WITH VIGILANTES

"YOU CAN JUST get out of our town, Reverend!" the gray-haired, weather-beaten man sneered, the word "reverend" spat as a curse.

I was at a city council meeting in Westport, a tiny town of just over two thousand residents on the tip of the coast. It was a hardscrabble town, once the central location for the Chehalis Tribe, who had long since been driven out. Now Westport was the home of hardened fishermen and a handful of retirees.

The town was desperately poor, with 71 percent of its population unemployed, retired, or out of the workforce by my estimation, using collated data. The boat owners, and the fishing industry itself, who sailed the high seas to bring in the nation's fish and seafood, were at the top of the food chain. Even though fishing has been a declining industry for decades, in 2018, Westport was still one of the top five commercial landings on the West Coast. The man spitting in my face was a boat and tavern owner, clearly friends with the mayor, who sat silently and said nothing to stop his tirade.

Less than a month earlier, Chaplains on the Harbor had applied for a permit from the city to host a tent encampment for the allowable three months. We were now using the old Episcopal church building in Westport as a base for our operations, and as a community center for people who were poor or addicted or homeless in Westport. Now it was approaching winter, and one person, then two, then three had asked for permission to pitch tents in the back of the church. By the time this city council meeting took place, about twelve people were staying on the property.

The problem with opening the doors for projects of survival is that the need is always far larger than the resources. Sometimes you get roped into projects for which you did not originally plan.

Now we were standing there, making our case for the permit: Aaron and I, a few supporters, and two people who were staying at the church and who later had to leave the meeting when they could not control their emotions. "We have a long history of vigilantes in this town," the man continued, still in my face, as the crowd of seventy or so murmured their approval or uncertainty. "And if the city council doesn't vote the way we want, we will take care of it!"

At the beginning of the council meeting, a council member had at least tried to keep order. Over the course of the interminable hour or two, however, people expressed their anger and frustration, occasionally their support, and a few made threats. The man got up again, sensing the crowd's frustration, and waved his arms. "I will personally pay $2,000 to whoever will run this pastor and these people out of town, by whatever means necessary," he announced.

The council voted to deny us the permit.

≱ ⊤ ↙

While the townspeople declared victory, we wondered what to do next. We attempted to file a police report regarding the threats made at the meeting and two subsequent run-ins we had with the speaker's son. But the police department refused to issue a no-trespassing order, and the sense of vulnerability among those staying outside the church, already palpable before the meeting, only increased.

When a nineteen-year-old was assaulted on the property, and another older, disabled man was nearly run over by a truck, we decided to remove all tents from the property and open up the inside of the church as shelter.

Thus began a one-hundred-day experiment with running an overnight shelter. It was a season of building trust and relationships that has borne fruit to this day—and one that nearly killed us with exhaustion.

When we opened our doors, we declared sanctuary. Unless we called 911 with a medical emergency, and once or twice for a mental health crisis, we asked police to stay out of the church. We became known for the words printed on the welcome mat at our door: "Come Back with a Warrant." All the young people with bench warrants or who had been kicked out by parents due to drug abuse or mental health started trickling in to stay. We became the only public place these young people—most with felonies, most heavily using drugs, most with deeply abusive and dysfunctional pasts—would come for a meal or a place to rest.

While many in the Westport community did not appreciate our harboring of their least favorite sons and daughters, we developed a kind of community. Guests included a fisherman whose boat was lost in a storm, a family kicked out of their home, a man looking for work, a gaggle of young men and women succumbing to heroin addiction, and several severely disabled women, one of whom had an incredibly irritating habit of asking anyone she walked by for drugs (something that endeared neither her nor us to the neighbors).

When we had first taken over the closed Episcopal church, we had simply opened one day a week: to get to know people and learn from each other and offer worship or prayer to whoever wanted it. But we learned an essential lesson that winter: that one of the most precious things the church could offer in a world where everything was for sale is space. In a society where there is no place you can go without paying for it or breaking the law, the church has unusual power. Churches can, at least in the state of Washington, invoke their constitutional right to religious freedom and to practice their faith by providing service to people who are poor or homeless. So even if a city or a neighborhood refuses to allow a homeless shelter or feeding program—which nearly every neighborhood tends to do, if push comes to shove—churches can do it. It is a lasting legacy of sanctuary: that medieval practice that allowed churches to provide sanctuary to anyone who asked and protect them even from the law itself.

Just before our trial by fire in Westport, Aaron and I had helped a small group of churches organize a tent city in their parking lots in Aberdeen and Hoquiam. When the little camp of twenty-two people moved in, the church's secretary got a letter from one of the most prominent evangelical pastors in town. He complained that the camp was full of people doing drugs who would "degrade the area."

The letter struck me as deeply ironic. Here was a man publicly claiming to follow Jesus of Nazareth, the same man who came under fire for hanging out with tax collectors and sinners, complaining that churches were hanging out with the wrong sort of people.

We quickly learned that small-town America has a very effective system for controlling poor people and that this system works very well. When the law cannot keep poor people under control, extrajudicial punishment can.

★ ⊤ ↙

The man at the Westport City Council meeting was not joking when he said that there is a long history of vigilantism in Grays Harbor. On November 7, 1890, a group of businessmen, looking to take over Chinese small businesses, gathered a mob to drive out the remaining Chinese families who had refused to leave when the Aberdeen City Council passed a resolution banning Chinese people from the city. The twenty remaining Chinese residents were attacked, beaten, and driven out of the city and their property seized. Six men were charged in an attack on one Chinese resident, John Wing, who gave testimony. But two of them were prominent citizens (one a newspaper editor), and all of them were supported by the timber barons of Aberdeen. None were ever convicted.

In 1912, Finnish, Irish, Greek, and other immigrant workers organized the largest strike in Aberdeen history, across lines of race, under the auspices of the International Workers of the World (IWW), also known as the Wobblies. The business community responded not only with police but with a variety of strikebreaking efforts, including the organization of a citizens' committee. At the height of the conflict, the citizens' committee was one thousand members strong. Members would routinely would beat and kidnap striking workers, sometimes driving them out beyond the town's boundaries with a threat to never return. Eleven years later, a hired gun shot and killed striking worker William McKay.

The Wobblies had a deep impact on the history of the Northwest coast. Eventually, most full-time workers unionized. Until 2016, Grays Harbor was a dedicated "blue dog Democrat," union-strong county. The legacy of union organizing reverberated through the twentieth century, but so did the legacy of vigilantism.

In Aberdeen, as in cities across the country, vigilante groups targeting homeless people have become more and more common. Guys in pickup trucks tail people and threaten them in supermarket parking lots. Community groups organize and take pictures of people who are unhoused and stalk them around town. If a person leaves their tent, they might return and find that someone has taken everything they own and disappeared. No one is ever investigated, and no one is ever charged.

Facebook is an ideal forum for small-town discontent, gossip, and vigilantism. People express intention to assault people, to drive their crop dusters full of poison over camps, to burn or slash tents. They gather groups together to target people, posting their intentions on hate-filled community pages.

I learned very early in my time as a chaplain to stay off community Facebook pages. Everything that people may not have the courage to say to your face ends up there. Anytime I stood up with poor people—launching projects of survival or making public statements about homelessness—I would end up with a rash of hatred directed my way. I kept my social media pages free of that by shutting off comments, blocking angry stalkers, and keeping settings private. But the community Facebook pages would go to town, and I eventually learned to simply stop reading. But I still managed to collect a whole file of nasty comments and open threats.

"I hope you know how much you are hated," one guy texted me. "You are an apostate priest," another commented, and often. Slurs, hateful comments about my sexuality: nothing was off limits. I ignored it all as best I could. Except the direct threats. In one thread, a one-time friend posted: "People who didn't like what she did in Westport threatened her with violence. It worked back then, maybe it will work now."

🐦 🐦 🐦

I learned to live with the unknown. I watched my back. I made sure I had a locked door at home at all times, and a loaded gun. Just in case.

Members of the recently formed tent city in Aberdeen offered to come stay overnight with Aaron and me in Westport to protect us. Scotty was one of those. He stayed at tent city, and, at one point, an angry local tossed a forty-pound rock into his tent. It just missed his head.

"Edgar! E-D-G-A-R!" You could always hear Scotty's voice as he walked up the street at dawn. Scotty was never without his little black Chihuahua—unless the little dog got a mind of his own, that is, and went trotting off down the street. Every neighborhood Scotty lived in got used to hearing him walk down the street calling for Edgar. He always found him.

Scotty was a natural leader. He grew up in Los Angeles in an interracial neighborhood during the Watts Rebellion. He talked often about how that experience formed him, how he as a white kid would do the talking to the police for his Black friends, how deeply he was formed by Black music and by the history of Black resistance to oppression. He had a keen sense of justice and a deep understanding of how poor people in the United States were screwed. He also mentored young people on the street, warning them of the dangers of white supremacy and white power groups.

Scotty moved north to Oregon and Washington with family. He landed in Grays Harbor for a significant portion of his adult life, working a string of temp jobs in the logging industry. At some point, heroin had gotten the better of him, and in the years I knew him, he would swing between active addiction and methadone treatment.

This particular day Scotty was in Westport, staying overnight in the shelter we opened up after we received so many threats. I had shared with him what happened at the city council meeting, and, immediately, he and a few others said, "We are coming to stay out there with you as your body-guards." Thankfully, the job of bodyguard ended up being a relatively boring one, as we only had a few angry people show up at our doors. But Scotty was always ready to jump in and help keep our doors open during that one-hundred-day stretch of sanctuary.

At the same time, a cold weather shelter was opening in Aberdeen, in the basement of the local Methodist church, and Scotty jumped into that work with gusto as well. If there was no one else to help volunteers keep order and cook a meal, he was there, a leader ready to serve his community.

But after a friend died in his tent of an overdose, at the church-sponsored tent city, Scotty retreated further into himself. I'll never forget the day: sensing the grim specter of death in the parking lot, hearing the story, kneeling at the man's head and saying a prayer over his cold body. After that, even though the hosting church at the time was gracious and extended their stay as long as possible, no other church would take the little tent city. Most of the little band of people experimenting with community in a church parking lot went back to the River.

After that, Scotty's health worsened. His few visits to the local hospital always yielded uncertain results, with no clear diagnosis and no support for withdrawal. It became harder and harder for him to breathe. One night, he told a friend in his final shack at the river, "I don't want to die down here." They called his daughter, who rushed him out of town to a hospital in Olympia, where he had a heart attack while waiting in the ER. The doctors said his body was failing, the effects of long-term medical neglect, and intubated him. Luckily, he woke up one last time, breathed on his own, and got to see his entire family and all his grandkids. For the first time, he was getting adequate medical care, but it was too late.

When I met Scotty's mother, a tenacious frail white woman, I understood her son. "No one cares if people are dying unless they are middle-class white people," she told me, sitting at Scotty's bedside. "I learned that in LA. If you are Black, if you are poor, no one cares."

I decided to go up to the hospital one last time to see Scotty, and it turned out that it was the last night he was alive. It was a Catholic hospital, so they had people coming in to sit with him, in keeping with their policy that no one dies alone. My wife and I stayed with him most of the night. We sang, over and over, his favorite spiritual: "Swing low, sweet chariot. Comin' for to carry me home . . ."

He died the next day.

⚔ 22 ⚔

PROJECTS OF SURVIVAL, ABERDEEN STYLE

SCOTTY WAS NOT the only leader to develop out of the tent city in Aberdeen. Tracy joined the camp when the house she was staying in was condemned and demolished. She and her boyfriend were given twenty-four hours to vacate, and they made it out with a fraction of their belongings and set up a tent in the church parking lot next door. In her late forties, Tracy carpooled with her daughter to work every day, cleaning hotels in Ocean Shores, sleeping every night in a tent. One night someone threw a Molotov cocktail over the fence around the church camp and set her tent on fire. Thankfully no one was hurt, although the tent had to be replaced.

In the middle of her own struggle for survival, she joined a group of volunteers who set up an ad hoc winter shelter in the basement of the United Methodist Church in Aberdeen. Just like our little ad hoc shelter in Westport, they were open to anyone who needed it.

Anyone who has stayed or volunteered in a low-barrier shelter can attest to the drama that often attends it. In Aberdeen, there would be up to fifty people staying the night, from young sex workers looking for a break to older women who could no longer care for themselves to young gang members running from the police. It makes for busy, colorful nights and stressful mornings.

One morning at the Methodist church, volunteers were making breakfast and waking up residents to prepare for closing. One woman, one of the sweetest and most difficult people I have ever met, decided to make her last stand against leaving.

One moment, everything was going fine. The next, she was standing, completely naked, on top of a chair, holding a picture of Jesus in one hand and an American flag in the other. Both were property of the church that the group of volunteers was borrowing for the shelter.

"Honey, you can't take those things," Tracy told her.

"It's mine," she shouted, hoisting high the picture of Jesus. "He's my dad!"

"Yes, honey, he's all of our dad," Tracy said calmly, helping the woman step down off the chair. "But we still need to put those back."

No one could talk someone down quite like Tracy could. That winter, she found her passion. While that particular shelter only lasted two seasons, she continued to find ways to volunteer and give back to the community she loved. She was eager to learn, eager to make connections, and eager to help people survive.

She got clean, kicking several addictions, and over several years, she found housing. When Aaron and I, exhausted by ad hoc shelter management, finally were able to find grant funding to support a formal winter shelter in Westport, we asked Tracy to lead it. We also hired her daughter, Skye.

Together they made an unstoppable team. They ran outreach in Aberdeen and winter shelter in Westport. They built relationships with people struggling on the edge and had a gift for connecting to people in active addiction without judgment and also bringing their own experiences of survival and recovery.

Skye had grown up with her mom's addiction and in the shadow of her pain and poverty. She was tough as nails, but with a rare compassion for people whom society rejected. Skye had built a whole life for herself, with a home and a gaggle of dogs and a husband who had taken up carpentry once out of prison, and she took pride in her work. She had keen insight into the struggles of poor people in the United States and brought a measured thoughtfulness to our work.

Skye and Tracy built a strong shelter project over the years, and eventually we won county funding to support it. I'm not sure there is any harder work in the world than to bring together a bunch of people who have only homelessness in common, to house them in an open church space, and to prevent them from killing each other. Shelters all over the country can be dangerous places, and supervising them can be too. Drug use, domestic violence, spats over a million things, and the mental illness that inevitably accompanies all that struggle—all of these things make temporary shelter hard.

We were never more sure that housing was what people needed. Temporary shelters represent a project of survival, an important emergency response. But people without homes needed guaranteed housing, the one thing the US government seems dead set against giving them, at least anywhere close to the scale of need. Since it was deadly clear that the country had no intention of doing so, this project of survival blossomed and built relationships.

Tracy and Skye prided themselves on keeping the peace every winter and treating people with respect and dignity. Their team grew to include more people in recovery and more people dedicated to making their community a better place.

⤩ ⤒ ⤪

"Hey, you have a cigarette?" the man asked.

"Aw, we're out," Tracy told him. We hand out cigarettes often in street outreach, as a way to strike up a conversation with people who are not likely to talk to strangers. It's also a gesture of nonjudgment to people who are judged for everything they do, and because, like most poor people in Grays Harbor, a lot of us on staff smoked.

The man looked crestfallen. "Oh, fine. You can have one of mine. Here." Tracy dug her pack out of her sweatshirt pocket, her purple hair glinting in the sun. He brightened in an instant and she held out her light.

I always loved doing outreach with Tracy. A steady stream of people would come up to get sandwiches out of the Chaplains van, and a similarly steady stream of people would come up to Tracy to talk. Some just wanted a cigarette. Others wanted to chat about their day.

"I've just got diagnosed with liver cancer," one older man told her, tears in his eyes. "I don't know how long I've got. I stopped drinking, though."

Tracy would listen to each person in turn, shooting the breeze or stepping aside so people could talk about more serious matters. She'd play with a young woman's dog and ask where she was camping.

"Can I have four sandwiches?" someone would ask. "I've got a few other people in my tent."

"Maybe," Tracy would say. "Wait until more people come up and if we have extra, you can have them." She always did give extra sandwiches.

That day, as people flocked to the van for sandwiches, things were calm. Tracy was present, with people right where they were, no judgment, fully herself. It was the perfect picture of a wounded healer.

At Chaplains on the Harbor, a team of women hold together the outreach programming. All of them have come out of the deep trauma that poor women experience in the United States, from drug abuse and homelessness to personal violence. Perhaps one of the deepest joys of my ministry has been seeing them take positions of leadership and grow into a sense of their own power. Most of them are older than I am, with a great deal more experience in the world, but we also share stories of personal pain and struggle. Perhaps it is fair to say we have mentored each other.

A working-class mom of four adult sons with special needs who can cook like no other. A woman taking care of her husband who was injured at work but was refused worker's compensation because the company he worked for did not want to take responsibility. Mothers of kids on the street. Survivors of so much loss. Women with so much to give the world—and give they do, out of their own abundant love and personal healing.

All of them have been ostracized by the community or even their churches for their work, accused of loving drug addicts too much, accused of enabling people who are unhoused too much. Every time, they respond that they are following their calling to serve their community, enabling people to stay alive. They keep showing up to cook the best food they can on the tightest budget, to make people as comfortable as they can in the middle of so much want, to dry people's clothes, to counsel people in tears when life gets too much. They show up to tell the guy who had too much to drink that he cannot use racial slurs, and to tell the police that no, they cannot enter the building.

They insist that their own lives are worth saving, and, if theirs, so is everyone else's. They insist that, no matter how broken people are by the cold and hunger and pain of the streets, life is precious. They insist that abandonment is not an option. They hold their own hands against the hemorrhaging wounds of poverty-stricken America. And they have marched into the halls of power, in protests, in meetings with legislators, in city council meetings— every place they can find—to demand that it end.

The beauty of their love has graced their community; the strength of their commitment gives us hope for the future. If anyone can build a better world, it is these women who have transformed their personal pain into healing for their world.

In 2021, Aaron took this team to visit Jackson, Mississippi, to visit with the Poor People's Campaign committee doing work and outreach there. They made sandwiches together with leaders from Jackson, handed out food, visited civil rights sites, and learned about the realities of poverty and racism in the Deep South. Tracy, raised on a steady diet of anti-Blackness and redneck bravado, like so many of us were, told me, "I never knew all that the Black community faced. I didn't know the history of the civil rights movement. When I saw where Emmett Till died, I felt the hairs on my arm stand up. The people who organize there are fricking amazing."

The two groups shared what they had learned in two very different places: Jackson, Mississippi, majority Black and intensely poor, and Aberdeen, Washington, majority white and intensely poor. People who were raised to hate each other met each other instead. And worked together. Organizers in Jackson dubbed them the "trailer park brigade."

It's just as the Young Patriots said: when they took their white trash out, they really did forget to burn it.

23

RAISING THE FLAG

"HEY, HOW ARE ya?" A young Black man walked into the church feeding program.

"Just being Black in Aberdeen," Sasha shot back.

"I feel ya." He nodded as he walked toward the coffee pot.

We were sitting together before our regular Sunday meal, discussing yet another eviction at the River. A group of people living there had decided to gather before the meal to talk with me and talk about what they could do in response to the eviction order issued by the property owner. They had just a few days to comply.

The deadline day dawned bright and sunny, and a dozen or so people were still scrambling to move their belongings. Members of the community were there to support residents, as police were expected to enforce this eviction.

Tempers ran high and frayed often. A lesbian couple were frantically gathering all their valuables from their tarped four-person tent. Johnny, Christina's boyfriend, was snarling at everything in his path as he mulled his options. Should they go to the other side of the river? Should they go to a logging road? Could they camp in someone's yard? Would they only be able to carry what they could on their back, or was there a truck that could move more? Eviction from a tent might be less work than eviction from a house, but the anxiety and fear are much the same.

Sasha had been camping there for a few months. She was the only Black woman in the camp, staying on the Native side of camp.

"I'm not leaving," several people said solidly. "They are just going to have to arrest me."

I told folks I would help however I could. If they wanted help moving, I had my truck. If they wanted to make a stand, I would get arrested with them.

Resolve started to wear down as six police cars came down the dusty gravel road toward the camp. Many people already had warrants and did not particularly care to risk longer jail stays. A few people simply disappeared into the brush. Others returned to their tents to pack.

"You need to leave by the end of the day," the officers told them. People fidgeted, restless, eyeing the row of police along the tracks.

Sasha, however, did no such thing. She was staying in an old SUV, and she drove that car smack into the middle of the camp. With her white boyfriend hiding inside, she found a large American flag and crawled up to the top of her SUV. She sat there atop the vehicle, the flag fluttering from her hand. It was her stand.

Suddenly all the folks hiding in their tents came out. A white kid with a swastika across his chest stood next to her, his head held high.

The tension nearly buzzed in the air as police formed a line along the road and people camping at the River gathered around Sasha, her flag held high. One officer came forward and talked to her in low overtones, but she shook her head vigorously. "No, sir," she said loudly. "I am NOT leaving." I moved to stand next to her.

The officer stood back, and we watched the police officers talking with each other.

Without any words, campers stood with their heads held high, together, in a line, with Sasha and her flag waving high above them. Today, they were people. Today, this moment, they had their dignity. They made their stand.

The police officers got back in their vehicles and drove away.

All but a few people left the River that night, and that stand really lasted only a few hours. But the story of Sasha's stand became a rallying point for people for years to come. For a moment, white, Black, and Native people, gay and straight, young and old, all stood together under a flag waved by one courageous Black woman, staking their claim to some space, some right to exist in a land that has rarely been free despite the bravery of its most oppressed.

On the River that day, for a short moment in time, a group of poor and landless people across race united around a tiny, rough piece of land where each of them had found a temporary and fragile and often dangerous home. We knew that change would come slowly; the evils of poverty, militarism, and racism won't get toppled overnight. But the small moments are important too: moments in which people can see themselves as fully human, see their own lives as worth defending, see their rights against a system that is killing them, and begin to stand up. It is in crucibles like this that leaders are formed. It is in crucibles like this that chinks have been formed in the systems that have oppressed us for five centuries. Together, slowly but steadily, we can erode their power.

$$\textbf{\textit{h}} \quad \textbf{r} \quad \textbf{\textit{d}}$$

The image of a white man who had joined a white power gang in prison taking orders from a Black woman has stayed with me through my work. For many young men, there is little choice inside a strictly racially segregated prison system but to throw their lot with their own racial group for survival. Mexican gangs in prison are now often accepting white kids, meaning that, increasingly, white young men can opt out of white gangs, with all their ideology of supremacy. But my generation of millennials joined white power gangs, and there is no real way out on the streets or in prison.

The Fourteen Words: if you do any prison outreach among white men, you will hear about them. Coined by a white man in prison for hate crimes against Jewish people, it makes an all too popular prison tattoo today. These are the Fourteen Words: "We must secure the existence of our people and a future for white children."

If that sentence sounds like Hitler, it's because it was inspired by him. It is hard to put into words how deeply disturbing it is to live and work in a poor white community, where people have so little access to any of the things they need, and hear these words. This is the response of white nationalists to the struggle of their own community: keep having white babies and fight for the supremacy of white people in the United States.

People like Stephen McNallen, who founded the Asatru Folk Assembly (AFA), a version of Norse paganism popular with white prison groups, openly propagate theories of white nationalism and exclusivity. Most practitioners of Ásatrú throughout the United States and Europe are antiracist, and influential Hilmar Örn Hilmarsson of Iceland's Ásatrú Fellowship has condemned the racism of groups like AFA. Leaders like McNallen, however, use Norse paganism to claim that maintaining white purity is crucial. The AFA's website includes in their statement of ethics: "We in Asatru support strong, healthy white family relationships. We want our children to grow up to be mothers and fathers to white children of their own." It is a variation of the same ideology in which I was raised: specific roles for men and women, a belief that white people should control this continent, and a divine justification for subjugation and violence.

The struggle of poor white people is real, and it can be desperate. But too often all the anger and rage of young people, legitimate anger at the suffering of their lives, gets turned on Black and brown bodies, in prison and out. Poor white people become weapons wielded with deadly intent and impact. Prison inmates have a hard time uniting against poor conditions across race when they are constantly fighting each other. People in Ferguson, Missouri, and Aberdeen, Washington, cannot unite against police violence if they see each other as enemies. Workers cannot unionize effectively if they hate each other.

There is a certain obscenity to baiting people to fight other poor people in defense of their abusers, to turning broken bodies into weapons to protect the continued accumulation of profit. But it has happened from the beginning. From the day that Black people were declared chattel slaves and white indentured servants were freed, from the day white people could be police officers and hunt Black people for the masters, from the day white people were told Black people would be competition for finite jobs, from the day the Ku Klux Klan recruited poor whites to lynch poor Black people, from the day white workers were given better opportunities than Black people, poor whites have grasped at the straws white supremacy has offered them.

A central goal of any serious effort toward organizing poor white people should be addressing the ideology of groups in prison and recovery groups, like the Asatru Folk Assembly and the Klan. So many of my conversations with young white men in prison centered around questioning the white supremacy they were surrounded with and how they might find a different path, one of solidarity across race.

≛ ⸙ ⸘

Sometimes poor white people have rejected the empty promises of white supremacy and stood in opposition to a camp eviction. Or pitched whole battles against the slave economy.

Shortly before the Civil War, a poor white man led a ragtag army—composed of Black men who had escaped from slavery and poor white men—against Southern planters, with the stated objective of ending slavery. In 1859, John Brown led his small group of men on a raid of Harpers Ferry, West Virginia, taking several planters hostage and taking over the armory and several other buildings.

In 1837, Brown had made this vow at a funeral for an abolitionist: "Here before God, in the presence of these witnesses, I consecrate my life to the destruction of slavery." Later, he met Harriet Tubman, whom he always called "the General." He raised money for arms, believing that slavery could only be ended by armed conflict (an assertion that would prove prophetic), aware that enslavement was a heinous act of violence and contrary to God himself. His little army engaged in efforts to free enslaved people and retaliate against masters.

Harpers Ferry was his last stand. Eventually, his men were either killed or captured and charged with treason, murder, and "conspiring with Negroes to produce insurrection." Only a few years later, soldiers would be singing, "John Brown's body lies moldering in the grave, but his spirit goes marching on."

John Brown was a poor white man who broke through the lies that divide us by race and who insisted that no one was free unless all of us are free. He realized that his own liberation was bound up in the liberation of his Black brothers and sisters. To this day, his story inspires poor white people to consider their place in the systems that oppress us and to work across race for true liberation.

Aaron Scott preached these words in a Seattle church: "We, now, in 2015, have other abolitions to secure. Poverty and racism endure—protected and perpetuated by law, by culture, by economics, by theology just as slavery was. In the work of tearing down this wall, we stand on some of the biggest shoulders history has on offer. And we also stand side by side with saints, from Felony Flats in Aberdeen to Seattle's South End."

Because poor white and poor Black people have been pitted against each other for so long, such an alliance can seem shaky at best and highly risky at worst. Poor whites still have the protection that their whiteness gives them. James Cone was not wrong when he wrote: "Whenever black people have entered into a mutual relation with white people, with rare exception, the relationship has always worked to the detriment of our struggle."

Only time will tell if a new coalition of poor people like the Poor People's Campaign might prove to be an exception. If capitalism's goal of pitting people against each other by race is to maintain economic wealth and power, to keep land and production centralized among powerful elites and corporate interests, and to keep poor people poor, then uniting across race would be a powerful tool in ending it. There are 140 million poor people in this country, 66 million of whom are white. There are many obstacles in the way of such a union across the carefully crafted lines of division.

There are also moments of hope. On a riverbank in Aberdeen. In a desperate last stand at Harpers Ferry. We will need more than moments to build cross-racial alliances that last.

⚜ **24** ⚜

HEALING IS REVOLUTIONARY

THE EPISCOPAL DIOCESE of Olympia, the body that sponsored our work, decided to make a short film about our work at Chaplains on the Harbor. One rainy day, they brought cameras down to the tent encampments and to the church where we hosted meals.

Unsurprisingly, not many people on the street wanted to be interviewed, but two young men agreed to come to the church as long as they could come together. Randy and Nate showed up very late, both visibly high and camera shy, despite their agreement to the interview.

They spoke about their lives: about undergoing harrowing experiences on the street, and about living with addiction. At the end, the cameraperson asked them, "If you could say one thing to the city you live in, to your community, what would you say?"

They were restless at that point, and they paused. "A chance," Randy finally said. "I'd ask them to give us a chance."

I've never forgotten that interview. In time, they fought for their chance. Randy was arrested and faced a considerable prison system, but he lucked out when he was offered diversion in the form of long-term treatment, just as the county was changing their policies. He stuck with it and I visited him in treatment, where he got clean and then found long-term work.

Nate also got clean a bit later and went to work. Years later, he invited me out for a meal at Denny's. For years, I had bought people meals at Denny's as a way to check in with them. This time, however, Nate invited me. He wanted me to meet his family as they built a new life.

While much of our work at Chaplains on the Harbor centered on supporting and listening to people in crisis, and often in active addiction, we were increasingly aware of the importance of supporting people in healing from addiction and from the trauma and mental health realities that result. Building leadership in communities meant that people had to find ways to heal.

When we first started, jail and prison were the county's only response to addiction. As you know by now, Grays Harbor has high incarceration rates, both adult and juvenile. Beginning seriously in 2018, the county was pressured to come up with better solutions. A persistent superior court justice, Judge Steven Brown, pushed the county to start diversion programs that offered treatment instead of jail time, and eventually, to set up a drug court. I will be forever grateful for his efforts.

Up until that time, access to drug treatment was sporadic and limited. It required someone struggling with addiction to meet several appointments and wait for bed dates. Meanwhile, they would often fall deeper into addiction or even die before that day came. Some people managed it, but others died with dates for appointments in their pocket.

A drug court began allowing qualifying participants (usually only nonviolent offenders) to enter an intense wraparound treatment program that provided housing, mental health and substance abuse treatment, accountability, and eventually employment. Instead of people serving their sentence only to end up back on the streets with no support, some had the option to try for treatment. Drug court also supported medication-assisted treatment like methadone and Suboxone. Although many in the community are critical of harm-reduction measures like these, medication-assisted treatment is an evidence-based treatment that has worked incredibly well for many people addicted to heroin.

A drug court is not particularly revolutionary, but services like this are critical for poor communities who have been robbed of resources for so long. It gives people hope. It brings in new options for healing. It saves lives. And I have seen incredible leaders come out of programs like these, people with a passion for healing their communities and changing the world.

🕊 🕊 🕊

I heard voices raised in the brush before I found the campsite. Their voices echoed down the River as I made my way through the trails in the brush to Simon and Sandra's campsite. It sounded like they were arguing, again.

There were probably two hundred people staying at the River at that point. It was warm and sticky, just the kind of weather that stirs up arguments.

I checked on Sandra, a Native woman, and her young white boyfriend, Simon, as often as I could. Both of them were disabled; Sandra was recovering from a stroke and Simon from a street fight that had left his leg shattered. Both were also heavily addicted. I had known them both for some time, as they had lived on sidewalks, in the church tent city, and now on the banks of the Chehalis River.

They stopped arguing when I called out.

"Hey, Pastor." Simon was so thin, his cheeks sunken with drugs and hunger.

"How is the search for housing going?" I asked them.

Sandra shook her head. Six months earlier, they had received a housing voucher: full funding to pay rent and get them settled. But there was no apartment in Aberdeen to be found. They had called the list of landlords the agency had given them, and they had followed up multiple times, but still no luck.

A year later, I saw Sandra and Simon at the River again. They waved me down. "We have some water and food for people," Sandra told me, leaning out of the window of their new car.

It had been an eight-month wait, but they had finally gotten housing. Best of all, they were clean. Both their faces shone with health. Simon had landed a job at the casino, and Sandra had finally won her disability claim.

I continued to stay in touch with them. For the last several years, Simon and Sandra have worked with their church to offer support to the people they know and love on the street. Sandra wrote an article about her experience for the Quinault Indian Nation's newspaper, the *Nugguam*, recounting her experience:

> *I experienced a stroke three years ago as a result of using meth
> and then this led to me becoming homeless. I was even living in a
> tent city by the Chehalis River. That was hard, being surrounded
> by heroin, alcohol and meth users. I heard gunshots, and bombs
> being set off. Overdoses were common, approximately average of
> 12 overdoses in one week and a lot of violence. While we lived there
> the Aberdeen police harassed us, they slashed our tents, knocked all
> our belongings over . . . This experience has also given me and my
> husband a heart for the homeless people and we make it a habit of
> helping them and volunteering to bring them supplies, food and
> give them rides to the laundromat.*

Recovery from drug addiction is a revolutionary act. It is often the first step toward healing from collective and personal trauma. Addiction is both a medical condition that needs to be addressed as a public health concern, and an escape, a way to manage ongoing trauma, which often feels like it will never end. To face that pain is an act of extraordinary courage. To find the courage to heal, in the broken wreckage of our communities in the present, is an act of rebellion against the current order of things.

Sandra and Simon were able to find a way out. For them, finally landing the lottery for housing was critical, and something within them made them grab for healing and hold it tight. They found the support they needed. They finally started to believe they had value and worth.

On one hand, they got lucky. On the other, they grabbed freedom and healing. In their own path out, they reached back, throwing a lifeline to the people they had been in community with for so long. One of the greatest honors of my work over the past decade has been watching hundreds of people get clean and then reach back through various community efforts and organizations, reach back to people dealing with homelessness and addiction, reach back into prisons, reach back to their old haunts, bringing hope against hope. These are the true, unsung heroes of Grays Harbor. While too many business people and politicians bemoan "the undesirables," these brave souls fight for the soul of their community and pour out love and care in the forgotten alleys and flophouses of a struggling community. "Blessed are the meek," Jesus says, "for they shall inherit the earth."

The towns teetering on the edge of destruction might yet be saved. If that happens, it will be due in part to the brave souls who show love to each other and who have called each other back from the pit of despair.

25

MUSTARD SEED MOVEMENT

MOVEMENTS THAT BEGIN to shift the tide are often sparked by small moments.

In the early summer of 2017, April Obi, a local Native woman, reached out to the community to plan a vigil. She had multiple family members on the street and living at the River. Many people had died that year. She had started attending city council meetings, and she was following some of the cruel comments people were making. Many of her friends also had people they loved who were living on the street. She decided to organize a vigil for the homeless.

It was a beautiful evening that started at Zelasco Park, a central green space at the entrance into downtown Aberdeen. April set up a table with the pictures of people who had died. She invited Native drummers to sing and chant. And she had buckets of candles, real and battery operated, for people to take, light, and then carry through the downtown corridor, following the drummers.

Her Facebook event page, in the days leading up to the evening, had turned ugly. People threatened to break up the vigil. One of the city council members was a local store owner, and her husband taunted April for her Native identity, making racist, mocking comments.

April was not to be deterred, however, and the vigil went ahead as planned, and it was beautiful. Many community supporters, as well as people who were homeless, attended. We chatted and carried candles. And before we all left, we provided wound care to a few people who needed it.

But the pre-vigil online harassment was not the end of April's troubles. Afterward, someone threw bags of garbage in her yard, then broken glass. She continued receiving threats via Facebook and then by phone. She had to involve local police for her own protection. People knew where she lived and stalked her. It was clear that vigilantes in the community were more than happy to try and drive out a Native woman who had dared speak up.

A few months later, we received news that Bishop Michael Curry, the first Black presiding bishop of the Episcopal Church, was touring the Diocese of Olympia and planned to stop in Aberdeen to visit with Chaplains on the Harbor. We decided to use that visit as an opportunity to stage a protest, and we joined with a variety of local activists and groups to plan an event to demand housing and drug treatment services for the community.

Over that spring, we had participated in the Poor People's Campaign's "40 Days of Action," centered in Washington State in the capital of Olympia. Using that momentum, we decided to ask the Washington Poor People's Campaign and its committee, local activists like April, and people experiencing poverty locally to join us. For the first time, Chaplains on the Harbor joined in a coalition to organize a public march and protest that would highlight the suffering in the town and demand housing and treatment for its people. We named the protest "Harbor Rising."

Aberdeen hadn't seen many protests since the days when mills were open full force and unionized loggers were demanding fair labor practices. But that was decades ago. I was nervous.

🖢 𝕋 🖢

We started in a vacant parking lot, outside the old union offices of the IWW, where radical labor organizers had held their meetings a century before. We drew around one hundred people: local supporters, church people who just wanted to see the presiding bishop, members of the Washington State Poor People's Campaign, clergy from around the diocese, and local homeless activists. April had assembled a group of Native drummers, who led us in prayer and song to open and then lead our march.

Carrying our banner with the words "HARBOR RISING" carefully painted on it in front, we marched first to the River, where several hundred people were camping that summer. I had warned our marchers to be respectful and to stay away from people's camps to protect their privacy, but a few residents of the River had planned to join the group. They spoke about the difficulties they faced, living in the numerous shacks lining the riverbank. They spoke about how they were hated by city residents. A former resident, now in a wheelchair due to an infection that took one of his legs, spoke about his life there.

Our numbers swelling, we marched back into the center of town, stopping at empty building after empty building. We held signs that said "Future Detox Center" and "Future Housing Site." We knew that city leaders often discouraged treatment centers in town, and we knew that the county had estimated that nearly two thousand units of housing were needed to meet the current demand.

Unhoused people who were riding bicycles escorted us across traffic as we made our way to city hall. On the front steps that Saturday afternoon, we set up a memorial to our dead. Thirty pictures with candles were spread across the steps, the names and faces of each person we had lost on the street on display. I read their names as we opened the gathering.

Native drummers again opened our time, singing songs of healing and hope. Several people shared their stories. Then Bishop Michael Curry gave a rousing speech on the steps of city hall. Comparing April's experience to that of Rosa Parks, he told us that we were building a "mustard seed movement." He called us to follow Jesus's way of love, and he called on any city council members who considered themselves followers of Jesus to open their eyes to the suffering of their homeless citizens.

"What I hope for is an awakening of awareness of the need to care for the homeless in ways that are just and loving," Bishop Curry said to the local press. When he called us a mustard seed movement—that is, the small beginnings of a much larger fight for justice—we could see ourselves in the biblical story. We could see ourselves as part of a larger faith story. We were part of a long faith tradition of "praying with our feet": marching in public, nonviolently, for material change and liberation.

We then announced our intention to camp in front of city hall that night. Twelve of us, including Christina, who was living at the River at the time, pitched our tents in front of the pictures of our dead. We were unsure of how the town would receive our symbolic actions of protest. Given the level of threats we had faced in the community, we had hired security for our march. People muttered on Facebook but left us alone. Police circled the block, but we stayed peaceful, and they left us alone too.

The next day as we were dispersing, however, the town exploded in rage. The local radio heard from outraged local businesses who felt targeted by the protest. Several members of our coalition had agreed to stop specifically in front of the local business who had been involved in harassing April and whose owner sat on city council. In the filmed encounter, several people asked her if she would support housing and treatment in the city. She ordered them out of her business and they left, but she posted a video all over the internet, claiming she would file charges for harassment. Commentators suggested that the venerable bishop must have been hoodwinked into participating in such an event. More harassment, and more concern about possible retaliation became a part of life for many of us.

Many of the people venting their anger against people who were unhoused were themselves only a paycheck away from homelessness. Poverty rates are high in Aberdeen, with half of the population accessing at least food stamps to make ends meet. Even people with jobs are struggling to keep their families afloat, and so are most small business owners. Many people who were barely housed or struggling to make ends meet joined us, as did a few small business owners, and we wanted to reach more. While popular narratives make "the homeless" their own class of people, the reality is that they are simply the part of the working class: those unfortunate enough to not have a place to sell their labor or otherwise unable to work. They are us. We are all in this together.

Our own coalition seemed fragile at times. It is difficult to maintain coalitions between people organizing for change, as disagreements flare and people crumble under pressure. Even so, work for change continued and leaders were born. April continued to agitate and advocate for her homeless neighbors, as did most of the local leaders present that day. Those who made their home at the River were reminded that people all over the country were on their side in their struggle for housing and safety.

It was a mustard seed moment. Only time would tell what would grow from that small seed.

⚜ **26** ⚜

AN ODE TO JOY

IT WAS A beautiful summer day at Sam Benn Park in Aberdeen. The park is on a hill, so the land dips gently and was dappled with sunlight through the red cedar trees.

I had started my ministry single. When I resolved to stay in Grays Harbor, everyone I knew was sure I would never find a relationship. I had been single for eight years when I met Emily.

Her smile lit up my life. She met my quiet seriousness with laughter and adventure. She was a crisis counselor in town, freshly returned from college, also from Grays Harbor, and eager to serve the community. We dated for months without realizing it, both working full time and keeping two shelters open in our spare time before we officially started dating. Emily worked with Tracy in Aberdeen.

Two years later, I found myself at Sam Benn Park for our wedding. Her large family had planned it, and it was perfect. We had red checkered picnic blankets, her mom grew strawberries for flowers, and her aunts and cousins catered corn and hot dogs for the reception.

Emily's dad had died of a rare form of cancer, one the family believes was related to the toxic waste runoff from a mill, but her stepdad built us a cedar arbor. Bonnie, who was my colleague and, by coincidence, also Emily's longtime pastor, was our officiant. Like always, Bonnie's constant loving presence made life better for us all.

We invited folks from the streets, and, just before the ceremony was supposed to start, people streamed from the homeless camps around town to join us. My parents refused to attend, but both my sisters were there and so was my aunt. For the first time anyone there had ever seen, I wore a suit in lieu of jeans.

I walked "down the aisle" of sand and grass to the arbor first, flanked by my aunt and sisters and surrounded by the young men and women from the streets. Some were in recovery, some were not, but all were so dear to me, and all were excited to walk me down the aisle. Somehow, being surrounded by so many people I loved mitigated the pain of absent parents. They all said that they would be my dad.

Emily came next, flanked by her mom and stepdad.

"In sickness and in health, as long as we both shall live," we said. As we kissed, the hundred or so people sitting on the lawn around the arbor cheered.

We danced afterward to all our favorite music: country, pop, and rap, joined by the community we had formed, all feeling a little awkward together, all finding ways to eat and celebrate.

Emily's family, my sisters and aunt, Chaplains on the Harbor apprentices just recently in recovery, and the men and women of Aberdeen and Westport's streets all danced together. Shirley was there in her best black dress, Pixie with her painted nails, Christina with her hand on my shoulder down the aisle. Misty and Ang came, and John, and Greg, nodding out, but still there in time with Jamie and his dog, Jackson.

We took pictures afterward. I still treasure the picture of Greg and me, as I would lead his funeral a few years later. And Emily still complains that in our wedding photographs I was clowning too much. In almost all of the pictures from that jubilant, exhausting day, I am either flying my middle finger or making a peace sign.

🔻 🔺 🔻

Early in my ministry, I attended a local pastors' group for the first time. I was nervous. I had grown up in this county, and I knew just how conservative some of the churches were. I also was hesitant to reacquaint myself with pastors from my past who had done a great deal of harm in my life. A local liberal pastor went with me, however, and I worked up my courage to attend.

I was the only queer person there. That month, they had a special presentation they were very excited about: a local Baptist church had supported the education and training of a young white man who was now heavily involved in Republican politics. The kid looked like he was about nineteen, and he was excited to share what he had learned. He proceeded to pull up a slideshow: "Why the Gay Agenda Is a Threat to Religious Freedom."

In retrospect, I should have just left. But I stayed. The Pentecostal husband and wife pastor team next to me were clearly uncomfortable with my queerness, so maybe I stayed to watch them squirm. This clean-cut, fresh-faced kid also looked like all the kids I knew growing up in the Quiverfull movement. He reminded me of the young men who were raised on a mission to take back America for Jesus, who were raised to see liberals and gays as the enemy, who were raised to believe they were warriors for Christ in a sinful world that must be subjugated to the truth of the fundamentalist gospel. And I felt cold sweat on the back of my neck, realizing that I embodied the threat they had been taught to target.

Instead of becoming who my parents and church wanted me to become, I had cut my losses, and my hair, and decided to live life on my own terms.

And I never went back to that pastor's group.

🕊 🕊 🕊

Later, as my work drew more and more fire, one of the most prominent local pastors referred to me as a "self-appointed lesbian pastor." As the wider community increasingly opposed my work, as I got more and more threats against my safety, most of them also subtly or not so subtly referenced my queerness.

The streets were a different story. Certainly, some people got huffy that I was gay, but for the most part, I found ready acceptance. I met people where they were at, and they met me. The streets are funny that way. Violence is a real and present danger for queer people. But when people are forced to survive, there is also a camaraderie, one that no longer expects respectability.

Even on the streets, where gay, trans, and queer young people often face great risk, there can be a culture of acceptance. I do not say this to mitigate the danger queer young people face: from parents who throw them out of the house, from hostile men on the street or from pimps, from the jail system, and from unaccepting case managers who do not prioritize their needs. But when people are thrown together for survival, an uneasy solidarity forms. A majority of young people I knew on the streets considered themselves queer and would often partner in multiple ways, in queer or polyamorous relationships. Queer young people are far more likely than their straight counterparts to end up on the street or to be kicked out of home at young ages. In a recent study in the United States, 20 percent of young people in juvenile justice systems identify as queer or gender nonconforming, and 40 percent of homeless youth identify as queer or gender non-conforming.

My queerness forced me to see that the world we lived in was toxic to human thriving. I sometimes wonder whether if I weren't queer I might have missed it.

My parents tried to pretend I was not gay for as long as possible, and although they refused to come to the wedding, they could pretend no longer. When I told my aunt or my sisters I was gay, they shrugged and said, "I just want you to be happy." Emily's grandpa gave her a lecture on how to preserve her credit in a relationship when she came out to him, saying; "I don't care if you like men or women; just make sure you take care of your own finances!" Small-town folks can have a pragmatic approach to personal identity, interested more in maintaining a relationship with people they care about than imposing the moral code they may hear from conservative pastors.

Even when people voted for Trump or held different political views, we were still defined in relationship to each other. The people who came to our wedding were from across political spectrums. They were also from many different worlds: working people who held jobs at Walmart or prisons, people on Social Security barely hanging on, people in the throes of addiction, people in recovery and struggling to find stability, Native folks from the Quinault Nation, priest friends from Seattle, people who lived in a shack or tent by the river. Our guests were people who, in other times and places, might hate each other or abuse each other. People who may have never met otherwise. My college professor with my uncle-in-law. People living on the street with a small business owner. People living in deep poverty with people who are unquestionably respectable. Queer elders with queer street kids.

For one short moment, our love brought them together in an outpouring of joy. Finding moments of joy is essential to any work for change. We also have learned to hold on to laughter and joy. When you might lose everything at any minute, you learn to dance every moment you can.

Part Five

BUILDING

ANNIVERSARY OF THE BLACK PANTHERS

IT WAS A sunny day in Seattle as we all gathered in the Central District. Having piled into several cars for the two-and-a-half-hour drive through I-5 northbound traffic, a group of young people from Grays Harbor had arrived to meet with some of the elders of the movement to abolish poverty: the founders of the Young Patriots and the Black Panthers.

The year before, Aaron and I had launched multiple fundraisers in order to start a supportive employment and apprenticeship program. Our vision was to hire young people coming off the street and out of jail, paying them enough to allow them to stabilize their life: get housing, stay in recovery, do the work to reinstate their driver's licenses, address court issues. We were deeply committed to building leaders in a movement to end poverty, and it was clear to us that leaders needed enough stability in life to find their own way and their own healing.

We were doing what no other agency we knew of was doing. There were supportive employment programs around the country such as Homeboy Industries, the largest gang intervention program in the world, and Thistle Farms, offering housing and jobs to women leaving the sex industry and streets. There were also plenty of activist organizations offering leadership development. But they mostly targeted college students who had the means and support to delve into justice work.

We wanted to bring those two things together: developing leaders to build a movement and offering supportive employment. We wanted to allow poor and homeless people to take leadership in ways that were meaningful and powerful, both in local and national organizing to end poverty.

Over the course of eight months, we had hired five apprentices, most working on a small leased piece of land to grow vegetables to sell as a kind of social enterprise. James was a white kid who had landed on the street at nineteen. He was now housed and working on getting his two kids back after a long CPS case. He was here in Seattle with his wife Dalia, a shy Latina woman with a winning smile. Danny was there, by far the tallest of us all, clowning by posing on top of every street barrier he could find. Shyla, getting her life on track after having a baby, and several others joined us.

Together we entered the cool lobby of the Langston Hughes Performing Arts Institute, where shirts and buttons were on table displays, emblazoned with the words "Black Panthers Seattle, 50th Anniversary." As we were ushered in the back, Aaron introduced us to Hy Thurman, founding member of the Young Patriot's Party in Chicago. Decades before, as we saw in Chapter 19, poor whites and Puerto Ricans had formed the Rainbow Coalition with the Black Panthers, organizing against police violence and for community resources. Next to him was Chuck Armsbury, who worked as a Young Patriot in Eugene, Oregon, and spent some time in prison for it.

Not long before we left for Seattle, our group had watched some grainy black-and-white footage of one of the first meetings between the Young Patriots and Bobby Lee of the Black Panthers. Young white men and women were detailing their experiences with poor wages, police violence, and bad housing conditions. Watching the footage of poor white Chicagoans learning to organize themselves and learning from Black Panther leaders, we found a story that resonated deeply with our crew.

Now, fifty years later, we had been invited to speak with Hy Thurman and Chuck Armsbury. As a group of young people who were working to organize our own community around our shared needs, we were trying to root ourselves in a tradition that already existed—one of cross-racial organizing for material liberation and an end to the poverty that plagued our communities.

We all crowded into the front row seats, everyone trying to stay quiet. It was the first time some of our group had been to a speaking event like this. First, Hy and Chuck spoke about what it was like to organize poor white people in concert with the Black Panthers in the 1960s. When it came time for us to speak, Aaron took the lead. He explained our mission and how we were developing projects of survival in Aberdeen and Westport, places that were once the center of radical union organizing before most of the union jobs disappeared.

In our work in Grays Harbor, we have specifically patterned our work on the model of the Young Patriots, working in concert with the Black

Panthers. The Black Panthers were highly disciplined, and most of their work was out of the public eye. Perhaps their greatest legacy was the clinics and feeding programs established in poor urban neighborhoods, many of which are still operating. Their response to police brutality, widespread poverty, and desperate circumstances was to start feeding programs, arm themselves and form police watch groups, organize education programs, and bring in medical clinics.

They did very little marching and very few public protests. While some Panthers did run for public office, they distrusted the political process. They saw themselves firmly as a working-class organization, dedicated to taking over the means of production and ending the exploitation of their people. Although the COINTELPRO program with the FBI disrupted much of their progress and assassinated their leaders, the legacy of the Black Panthers is still seen in urban Black communities across the country.

Hy Thurman spoke about his work in Chicago, which he explains further in his book, *Revolutionary Hillbilly*. Most of the people involved in the original Young Patriots were from Appalachia, where, he writes, "the US government had neglected sharing wealth and resources with people who were only recognized as resources to be exploited by the coal and textile industry, military recruitment, and a forgotten people by politicians." Hy had himself moved to Chicago from Appalachia at seventeen. As he and the Young Patriots began organizing, he says, they "would explain how these conditions in Chicago and nationally kept poor Southern whites in poverty by being denied proper health care, job training, and employment assistance."

When Black Panther leader Fred Hampton was shot by the FBI in Chicago in 1969, it was the beginning of the end for the Rainbow Coalition. By 1975, the organizers of the Young Patriots were scattered, mostly through gentrification of their communities. Many of them struggled to find work or make their way in a world increasingly hostile to their message. The meeting in Seattle that day in 2018 felt like a time capsule from the past, where leaders could share what they learned decades ago and inspire us to continue the work.

We still needed housing. We still faced police violence. We still faced gentrification. We had fewer job opportunities. We had plenty of drugs but increased incarceration and prison systems. It was time for a new movement of poor people, with poor people themselves taking leadership in that fight.

We met people without judgment, no matter their addiction or criminal history, and we met them with the firm belief that they deserve to be treated with dignity and honor. From their ranks, we recruited volunteers and staff and empowered them to serve their own community and find their own commitment to liberation. We started with a commitment to the basic dignity of every person. As people discovered their own worth and found their own healing, they in turn became leaders in their own right, leading their community toward salvation.

Of the group of young people from Grays Harbor who converged in Seattle that day, several went on to do important organizing work, and some are still doing that work to this day. That day we felt a sense of continuity with movements from the past and across the country, a sense of how our work was connected with a larger struggle.

❧ **28** ❧

WHITE TRASH IN DC

"MY NAME IS Mashyla Buckmaster. I'm twenty-nine years old. I'm a single mother. I was homeless for five years of my life. I'm celebrating two years in recovery. I'm from Grays Harbor County, Washington State."

"We are with Aberdeen. Aberdeen. Aberdeen!" people chanted as Mashyla introduced herself. She was standing in front of thousands of people on the lawn in front of the Capitol in Washington, DC.

"I live in a tiny town where it's easier to get loaded than it is to find food or shelter," Mashyla told the crowd. "The town is so small it only has one stoplight, so it's small, but the people seem so far away from each other. The 'better off' act like all my friends are better off dead. They act like the church I work at, where we love everyone no matter what, is a disgrace to the human race. Because we feed the homeless and addicted, they look at us like scum."

Here we were, fifty years after the Rev. Dr. Martin Luther King, Jr., had announced, just months before his death, the original Poor People's Campaign. People from all over the country were here now launching a new movement of the poor: present, marching, speaking, chanting. Mashyla was speaking at the event, alongside leaders of the Apache Nation, organizers from North Carolina's Fight for $15, mothers with their children exposed to lead in Flint, mothers who had lost their children due to lack of health care, union and labor organizers. Black and brown and white organizers, with one voice, were crying for justice for poor people.

At home on livestream, we were watching the event in DC that signaling the inception of the Poor People's Campaign: A National Call for a Moral Revival, as thousands of people listened. "We're strong," Mashyla was saying. "We've already walked through hell. So they can bring it on."

"Aberdeen. Aberdeen. Aberdeen!" people chanted again.

I had met Mashyla years before, when she came to our community center in Westport. Shyla was quiet and rarely spoke, preferring to hide on the couch in the corner and catch some sleep. Eventually, she came in pregnant. We talked about what she planned to do next, long pauses stretching out our conversation as she shyly weighed her options.

Within just a few months, she had found a couch to sleep on and had quit drugs. She was one of the first and only people I have seen successfully get off drugs entirely on their own while still being homeless. Shyla went back and forth between friends' couches and the women's shelter until her baby was born, so tiny, so perfect. She named her Ella. That same year, we hired Shyla as our first apprentice.

As an organization, Chaplains on the Harbor had joined the Poor People's Campaign early in its formation. We were in the process of working to identify and educate leaders from our community. Mashyla threw herself into organizing with a passion. She developed relationships with the planning teams of the campaign and with the cochairs, and she led our organization into deeper connection with poor communities around the country.

Shyla also developed a sharp political analysis, linking what was happening in our own community with what was happening elsewhere. She saw uncompromising support of Black and brown people's struggle as an integral part of the role of poor white people in organizing. She actively engaged her own community in promoting the Poor People's Campaign and solidarity across race in a struggle to end poverty. Time and again, she overcame her own natural reserve to speak publicly, in venues across the country.

A few months later, we were part of an event in Seattle that brought out the Rev. Dr. Liz Theoharis and Bishop William Barber II, the cochairs of the Poor People's Campaign. Shyla spoke there as well, having worked with Aaron on her speech. She brought forward for the audience the metaphor from the Young Patriots: "When they took out their white trash, they forgot to burn it."

Aaron and Shyla's work to build relationships with the larger campaign served us well. In addition to gathering large groups of poor people from all over the country in the nation's capital to publicize their needs and demands, the contemporary Poor People's Campaign sends delegations to individual communities to build relationships all around the country. This effort to listen to poor people and leaders around the country is powerful, particularly at a time when poor communities often feel so alone and isolated.

In May 2018, several black SUVs rolled into Aberdeen, followed by a train of people from around the region. It was the early days of the Poor People's Campaign, and Bishop William Barber had come to visit the River. For anyone who has met him, Barber is a force, seen by many as someone who has taken the torch from the Rev. Dr. Martin Luther King, Jr. in demanding an end to King's three evils: poverty, racism, and militarism (and the additional threats of ecological devastation and our distorted moral narrative). Barber was touring poor communities across the country, and our connection to the Poor People's Campaign had brought him here, to an encampment on the edge of the world.

A few people were prepared to give a tour of conditions there, while many more warily watched from afar.

"Are there any Black people here?" Barber asked. His question took the predominantly white and Native encampment by surprise. No, we told him, at that time there were not.

Barber nodded. "So poverty in Grays Harbor is almost as large as the poverty in Mississippi," he opined. "It's by design the way this stuff has been racialized."

He stopped and talked to each person, each group. Several people came forward to shake his hand.

We made our way slowly down the River, on the dusty road before it was gated by the city, with the encampment on one side and the railroad tracks on the other. Bishop Barber stood for a long moment, gazing out over the tracks and the people clustered in tents and shacks.

We made it to the end, where a memorial cross to a young Native man was covered in flowers and small gifts, surrounded by a little white fence. "This is a memorial for my younger brother who died this winter," Leon said. "He had a heart attack or stroke due to freaking pneumonia that could not get to the doctor on time."

"Every time we sent him up there," Leon noted, referring to the community hospital, "they sent him back down here. Told him, 'Oh, you'll get better.'"

Bishop Barber stood by the cross a long while, silent. He turned to Leon and pressed his bishop's cross into his hand. "Take this," he told Leon. "I will always remember you." Leon, who always avoided the spotlight and disliked talking to strangers, thanked him, his eyes filled with tears. One of many veterans living at the River, he explained to Bishop Barber how hard it had been to come back from war with no job to be found.

Many people on the street are veterans. In my time as a chaplain, I listened as many people shared their war stories with me—harrowing stories of moral injury, survivor's guilt, and being left without resources. Men who killed children, Indigenous people haunted by being sent to fire on other Indigenous people, and many others who gave their best years to a country that did not have their backs when they returned. Haunted by the trauma of war, many veterans of US military actions and wars—from Vietnam to Colombia, from Iraq to Afghanistan—found themselves on the street and without jobs when their country no longer needed their bodies.

"We were in charge of million-dollar machinery, guns, everything," Leon said that day. "But we can't flip a burger, wash a car, get a job now."

For the first time, many of the poor white and poor Native people camped along the river began to wonder if maybe they were not entirely alone. Bishop Barber's visit shifted something. A Black pastor and activist and national leader in the movement to end poverty—someone who had the ear of politicians and presidents and celebrities—had opened up for them the possibility that, collectively, we might be able to change our material conditions.

The work must be done collectively: this is one of the hallmarks of any move for social and economic change. This is even more pressing in our culture of individualism, our culture that isolates each of us to our individual struggle apart from the whole. Fragmentation is fundamental to capitalism, making every struggle personal, every mistake your own, every financial crisis a personal failure, every sorrow a personal grief.

Our social mess is partly a product of isolation. Our liberation will only be in collective struggle. The economic system that hoards everything for the few and leaves the rest of us to die alone can only be challenged by mass movement building. Leon had a bishop's cross that testifies to this truth.

THE HALLS OF CONGRESS

WE BEGAN THE farm project by leasing three acres that had land on which we could grow vegetables. The goal was to start selling vegetables in a community-supported agriculture (CSA) program, supplying subscribers with weekly vegetables each week for the growing season. It was a low-overhead enterprise to start—even though it required a great deal of skilled work, as we quickly found out—and it allowed us to hire additional apprentices and build out a jobs program. We leased property from a local farmer and rented a shed and greenhouse, to see if we could actually get anything to grow.

The leased land was a half dozen miles up a river valley, near a bend in the river, with a view of the Olympic Mountains, if it was clear and sunny. It is rarely clear and sunny in the spring in Grays Harbor, so most of the time, a light mist hung over the fields of peas or barley that surrounded the three acres we leased. A light rain often fell. All you could see were the towering trees in the hills above the property, and all you could hear was the river, in all its glory, running past.

The first farm team, complete with rubber boots and rain jackets, consisted of one farm manager and four young men and women who were either just getting out of jail or off drugs. Not everyone stayed, and not everyone succeeded. But together, we learned how to start and run a small business, grow food from different soils, and develop leaders accountable for their own healing and recovery.

That summer, one of the apprentices, Chris, was asked to be part of a team speaking with a congressional forum in Washington, DC, organized by the Poor People's Campaign. The afternoon that he was to testify before the congressional committee, the farm team gathered in the shed on the property. Hannah, the farm manager, set up her laptop and livestreamed the Poor People's Campaign's meeting with lawmakers. Convened by Representative Elijah Cummings and Senator Elizabeth Warren, who were joined by a handful of lawmakers, the congressional hearing had invited the Poor People's Campaign to assemble a group of testifiers from poor communities around the country.

Pamela Rush, from Lowndes County, Alabama, spoke about living in a mobile home with raw sewage in her yard due to the sanitation issues in her county. Kenia Alcocer spoke about the struggle of being undocumented. Pamela, who had become a leading activist for environmental justice, would die of Covid just two years later, before her terrible struggle for basic sanitation could be remedied.

Then Chris spoke about his journey, as a small-town kid from Westport who joined the Air Force. Prescribed opiates when he was diagnosed with pancreatitis, he became dependent on them, and his addiction eventually spiraled out of control when he got out of the military.

Watching Chris speak to senators and representatives, I remembered when I first met him. That first winter in Westport, during our one-hundred-day experiment in sheltering people in a church, a friend had brought him in for breakfast. The first thing I noticed was his extensive tattoo sleeves. They were not the typical hand-done tattoos I see so often on the street, but well-designed, slightly mesmerizing geometrical patterns, forming sleeves on both arms.

One of many veterans living on the streets in the United States, he was nodding out a bit over his cereal bowl, but he responded politely when I introduced myself. "I like the mat," he told me, pointing to our now-famous floor mat in front of the church door: "Come Back with a Warrant."

Chris would become a regular that winter and the next, until he landed in jail, where I visited him regularly. His quest for knowledge was insatiable, and we spent hours talking about books and theories of addiction. He received diversion, which allowed him to go to drug treatment instead of to prison, and when he got out, I invited him to visit the farm. His knowledge of mechanics and ability to construct irrigation systems made him quickly invaluable to the farm team, and he was hired.

Now, at the Capitol, he was speaking about his experience. Chris referenced the fact that money was available in the state of Washington to address the crises of homelessness and addiction. "I can only begin to imagine the lives that might have been saved or could be saved if this money were used for things that it is already authorized to be used for," he told the members of Congress. "An inpatient treatment facility, a community center, affordable housing and rental assistance, to name a few."

Chris's leadership abilities were on clear display that afternoon, as he spoke about his own experiences of homelessness and addiction and then used that story to advocate for his community. Tears came to my eyes as I watched him bring together so much of his own pain and the pain of his community into a proposal for change.

🐦 🐦 🐦

Poor people must lead any efforts to end poverty in this country. Far beyond all the rhetoric to which we are all exposed in the media, poor communities do truly have a clear view of the problem. They are the experts on their own struggles, and they often understand—earlier and more clearly than anyone else—what can and should be done. This does not mean that there is not a dire need for education in poor communities on the root causes of their struggle. But their knowledge is not theoretical. It is born of long and painful lived experience. They do not need an academic panel on police reform to know that police violence is real and deadly. They do not need statistics to prove their children are hungry or their communities do not have enough.

Poor communities across race have been surviving the ravages of the greed of the wealthy for a very long time. While formerly economically stable households in the United States now face rising poverty, poor people have survived many generations despite the odds. There is a wisdom born of long struggle that runs deeper than any of the shallow narratives that abound on the internet and TV.

Our involvement in the Poor People's Campaign was allowing us to connect developing leaders in our community with leaders around the country. Young white people from our area were connecting with leaders of color from places like Lowndes County and Flint and Detroit and Washington, DC, and North Carolina. These connections both broke our isolation and exposed our young leaders to communities across race struggling with the same issues. It exposed our group to the wisdom born of long struggle in Black and brown communities, wisdom to which poor white communities often have little access.

It also gave us some access to the halls of power. The senators and representatives who attended that hearing in 2018 were sympathetic. Many of them would make a bid for the presidency in 2020. Their intentions were good, and the need for congressional action on issues around poverty are intensely needed.

Based on these conversations, in the halls of Congress and on the streets, the Poor People's Campaign has developed a list of demands—a moral agenda to bring to politicians and demand concrete change. These demands are an amalgam of the work of thousands of progressive organizations and grassroots organizers, compiled from meeting with poor communities around the country and asking them what issues they faced. In some ways, these demands echo many of the demands of workers in the 1930s, when the New Deal mitigated some aspects of US capitalism and offered workers some protections. They also echo many of the demands of the civil rights movement.

This broad-based movement building is critical. The way the racial divide has functioned in the United States has worked to prevent poor people from uniting across issues. For a long time, organizers in the United States have been relegated to their own silo issues, each nonprofit fighting for funding and lobbying for their particular issues. The Poor People's Campaign unites a broad base of movements across the country, honors the analysis they have built, and brings them together on to the national stage.

Ending this system that is killing us all means demanding that our elected leaders enact policy change to address widespread poverty and neglect. These policy changes in and of themselves will not end poverty. But they are a concrete start to allow people to organize for their own material interests. Sometimes small wins are needed toward a larger goal, to mobilize a large-scale movement for change and build relationships across communities to fight together.

Chris would continue his leadership, both in Chaplains on the Harbor and in the political arena. The Washington State Legislature, after the fiasco of Covid responses in so many rural areas, passed legislation requiring county boards of health to expand. Up until that point, the three elected county commissioners in Grays Harbor also formed the board of health. Generally, people elected to these positions had no expertise in matters of public health. The commissioners were forced to bring in four new members to the board of health, including a doctor, a tribal representative, and two people impacted by the local health systems. Chris was selected to sit on that board, where he was able to bring his vast knowledge of addiction and treatment to the table of local politics.

Leaders know how to lodge the experiences of their own lives within the larger narrative of a people and then tell those stories for the sake of justice. That's exactly what Chris has done. Watching the congressional hearing that afternoon from a little shed on the opposite coast, the team listened as Chris finished his remarks. He had brought some of the issues we faced as a community to national attention and to a national stage. He was studying and learning about the root causes of our poverty and suffering and formulating demands to bring to the halls of power.

⚜ 30 ⚜

TRESPASS FIRST DEGREE

PRIVATE PROPERTY, AS we have seen, forms the ultimate cornerstone of American law. It is sacrosanct. No one is allowed to question if the land itself, or any nonhuman life form on it, belongs to private individuals. While many other countries, born of years of organizing, have added land reform principles to their constitutions, the United States has resisted any effort to do so. Land remains the main body of contention in the United States—land on which poor people struggle to survive and over which the market seeks to maintain absolute power through private property rights.

The contention over land was best illustrated in Grays Harbor by the fight for the River. It was a place to which poor people had been driven in their last effort to survive, a place of lawlessness and desperation, a place of contention between private property owners and people who had literally no land on which to legally stand.

In 2018, the city of Aberdeen purchased the land on which the River camps sat. One day that summer I was walking past the iron gate the city erected at the entrance to the camp when I was stopped by a police officer. "You need to get permission to be down here," the officer told me, not unkindly, leaning out of his vehicle.

I had been walking along the path along the River, checking in with people from tent to tent. And I was aware that I could be arrested for it. The officer who stopped me kept driving, certainly not interested in enforcing anything.

Once the city bought the property, they made some very unusual moves, even for a West Coast city trying to get rid of homeless camps. The mayor announced that everyone had to get written permission to enter the property. The eighty or so people who had stayed in the encampment after the purchase had been given temporary permission to live there until the city figured out what to do with them. Miffed by advocates, including me, who insisted that they find a place for people to go before they evicted them, they chose which social workers, advocates, or organizations they would allow to enter.

I filed for a permit to enter the property. It stated that I was a pastor to many people staying there and that I needed to be able to check in with people and sometimes pick them up for appointments. The city rejected my request, stating that I did not provide specific times when I would be there.

I continued to visit people anyway. I would park my truck near the gate and walk the mile up and down the site to check in with people on foot. It was during this time that someone needed medical care badly enough that his tent mates bundled him into a wheelbarrow and pushed it a half mile to my truck so I could get him to the hospital, since there was no way to drive closer.

A Seattle lawyer called me and suggested that a lawsuit could be brought on constitutional grounds of freedom of religion and freedom of movement. He warned that with continued visits, I was running the risk of arrest and a trespass change. I ignored the warning, knowing that people needed to know that I stood with them, even now.

A few people did get trespassing charges for walking into the encampment without permission. I once ducked behind a trash bin when the police came down. But I suspect they were tired of the issue at this point and definitely didn't want the bad press of arresting a pastor. And when the one officer did stop me, he was sympathetic.

I was not the only one facing issues visiting people. April Obi, who had family members in the camp and visited often, refused to apply for a permit. She insisted she had a right to see her family, and she had a right to engage in Native ceremonies with them. Constitutional rights. These mean very little if you are among the poorest people in our country.

In a place like Aberdeen, if you have the wrong name, you can be stopped and questioned and your name run for warrants. Police can stop you and go through your belongings without your permission. Police can ask for your name, and you have to give it.

If you go to jail for something, the first thing you do is sign away your rights to a speedy trial, because your court-appointed attorney tells you to. And up to 98 percent of all criminal cases in this country never go to trial.

After so many years of ignoring constitutional rights, Aberdeen thought they could tell me who I, as a pastor, could and could not visit. That turned out poorly for them, however. By that time I had enough visibility and publicity to attract an attorney who would take them to court. I filed a civil lawsuit in US district court, along with April Obi, against the Aberdeen mayor and the city itself. Regional media jumped on the story of a pastor and mayor facing off over small-town homelessness.

The reality, of course, was far more complicated.

↓ ↑ ↓

The mayor was nearly a decade my junior. Having become mayor at only twenty-four, he was struggling to push progressive policies in a good old boys' town. In another reality, we might have been friends. We were both small-town millennials who got an education and came back to our hometown. Both of us were eager to foster change and a better life for the people we loved.

An engineer by trade and prone to long but logical arguments, the mayor had declared the city's intention to close the river to camping for good while promising a different place for people to go. Homelessness had become by far the most contentious issue in the city. Community watch groups who advocated running homeless people out of town faced off with the town's drug-addicted, poor, and homeless citizens and their supporters.

The young mayor, caught in the middle, became more and more frustrated. But he went too far when he barred case managers and support people, including family members, from visiting without a city-issued permit. Our lawsuit invoked the constitutional right to freedom of religion, arguing that people had the right to be visited by their pastor, and the constitutional right to freedom of movement, arguing that people had the right to have people visit them, like any other citizen of Aberdeen had. I sat in the courtroom that December with the two other plaintiffs, and the conservative federal district court judge issued a stay on the city's permit system.

After weeks of negotiation, we settled out of court. The city paid $18,000 in damages, with $12,000 going to me and the other plaintiffs being awarded $3,000 each. While rumors flew over how I was getting wealthy off homeless advocacy, I signed the check over to Chaplains on the Harbor to help fund our expanding work.

For the first time in a long time, poor people in Aberdeen had had their day in court. Even if there was a limited basis to fight for people's rights to exist, there were some openings. And there would be more to come.

⬥ ⮝ ⬥

One of the most important legal cases for the West Coast has been *Martin v. Boise*. The decision, handed down by the Ninth Circuit Court of Appeals, ruled that cities in their jurisdiction cannot criminalize unhoused people for sleeping on public property or outdoors unless there is adequate shelter open to them. If there is not adequate housing available for those who are unhoused, criminalizing them for where they sleep makes that punishment is cruel and unusual. This wide-reaching ruling made it possible for homeless people and their advocates to bring cities up and down the coast to court: for evicting homeless encampments or for issuing criminal citations for sleeping outside without adequate shelter available.

We are relegated to small fights in the United States, over whether ticketing someone sleeping in a tent is cruel and usual punishment or whether banning a pastor from visiting people at an encampment is a violation of freedom of religion. This is because we do not have economic rights enshrined in our constitution or our laws. We cannot sue because people do not have homes, since they do not have a right to a home. So we have to wait until conditions get so bad that they can be ruled "cruel and unusual punishment."

After the first lawsuit, the city continued its plan to remove everyone from the property. They were right to assert that it was a dangerous place. Not long before, a woman had crossed the train tracks next to the camps at night and a moving train had severed both her legs. Conditions were indeed dangerous and unsanitary. But people had been driven here as housing became harder and harder to obtain. The city was also ramping up efforts to keep people out of the downtown, with ordinances like one that banned people from sitting or sleeping on the sidewalk during daytime hours.

Even though the mayor had been quoted as saying "if the city doesn't have somewhere for them to go, I have no interest in forcing them off," there were no solid plans developing for a place for people to go. In early April, the Aberdeen City Council drew up an ordinance that would prohibit public access to the River site, still with no plan for moving people to any other location. On April 24, a second lawsuit was filed in US district court. I was a plaintiff on this suit as well, as was April Obi. But the most important names on the suit were the ten people (eight initially, with two later added) who were residents at the River. This time, the lawsuit was a "prayer for relief," asking for an injunction against the city's plan to clear all residents from their camps with no place to go.

We issued a call to clergy in the region to meet us at the courtroom in Tacoma, and Native leaders asked for drummers to gather as well. Two women named on the lawsuit and residents at the camp were there: Misty, who I met with the baseball bat so many years before, and Shawna, who faced off at her camp with the owner's effort to bulldoze her shack. Those of us from Aberdeen arrived in a few carloads. As we gathered on the steps of the Tacoma courthouse, dozens of supporters showed up too. It was a beautiful day, in front of the brick courthouse, its atrium glittering with stained glass and huge chandeliers.

In our ragtag group, people shoved their hands in their pockets as they noticed the security guards and metal detectors, making sure they had left pocketknives behind and making sure they had ID.

We were joined by many people: A fierce Seattle advocate for disability rights who passed out handmade gifts and goodie bags to their friends in Aberdeen camps. Dozens of priests, in their Episcopal collars. Ed, the oldest priest in the diocese, was there, grasping my hand in his own. A group of Native drummers gathered at the doors to sing. The clergy surrounded our group and prayed over us.

We packed the courtroom, trailing down the halls after going through metal detectors. April, Misty, Shawna, and I sat next to the lawyers in front.

The judge opened the court saying that he was uneasy about restricting the city's right to act—in this case, to remove people from their camps and bulldoze the area. He made it clear he was not happy to see the case in his courtroom and that he didn't believe the judiciary branch should decide cases like this.

In the hour that unfolded, as attorneys on both sides battled, those of us in front struggled to remain composed, tensely waiting for the judge's decision. And slowly, we watched with relief and amazement as the tide began to turn. It became clear the city did not have a clear plan for where the nearly hundred residents of the camp should go. And it became clear that the judge was losing patience as he snapped at the city's legal team, "You guys have to give me something!"

While the city maintained that the plaintiffs simply wanted to continue camping at the River, which was unsafe, our attorneys argued that we were simply demanding a reasonable place for them to go. We were not asserting that the River was safe, nor were we demanding that people continue to camp there, in that location, in particular. We were merely searching for a reasonable solution, a place—any place—people might be able to go.

In the end, the judge issued a stay, insisting that both sides negotiate and find a place for people to go. The camp would remain on the River until then.

As the late afternoon sun shone into the little courtroom, we breathed a sigh of relief. There was a stay of execution. We gathered in a big circle in the courthouse atrium, under the gaudy chandelier shining its broken light on the floor, held hands, and gave thanks.

There would be other court dates, other struggles to come. We would find out both the advantages and the limitations of court battles for human rights and dignity. But for the first time in a long time, poor people stood up in Aberdeen and said that they would not take it anymore. They were heard.

We started talking with homeless rights advocates around the country and their legal teams. We talked with people who were re-forming the National Union of the Homeless, an organization that had formed in the 1980s and 1990s and that had taken over foreclosed HUD housing for homeless people. We were moving more deeply into a new phase of our work. We were making common cause with others facing the same issues, even as the numbers of homeless people were exploding across the country.

〔 **31** 〕

#RIVERGANG4LIFE

ON A WARM July day in 2019, the fight between the city and the River ended. While the case itself would not be fully resolved in court until November, the city opened a mitigation site in July. As the final agreement would read, the city will provide "space in the Temporary Alternative Shelter Location (the tent camp behind city hall) for all unsheltered plaintiffs, including those currently sheltered there, until March 15, 2020, so long as they abide by the rules of the camp." The city had also agreed to pay damages for property lost by the final sweep: $2,000 for each of the ten plaintiffs who lost property. It was not the win people without homes needed most in Aberdeen, but it was a small win. There was at least somewhere for people to go.

So on that day in July, big equipment started rolling in to the River. People still camping there called me as soon as they showed up. "Bulldozers are here. You should be here."

The sun was hot early, as police officers started arriving. The police chief, who was keen to keep the sweep as low key as possible, had gathered officers he knew were good at de-escalation and conflict management. They went from shack to shack, marking the dwellings that were vacant for immediate demolition. Some people were planning to go to the mitigation site, and others were going to find other places to camp.

One young man came storming up to me. "They bulldozed my camp. I was still there! They said they were only bulldozing the ones people were not staying in." I walked to the middle of the camp, where his shack lay in pieces, all its contents strewn in a heap.

"I'm gonna protest," he said. Later, when I walked back through from the other side of the camp, I saw the broken pieces of his place arranged on the ground and spelling out the words "RIVER LIFE." Spray-painted next to it were the words "River Gang Will Never Die! #RG4L."

⚑ ⚐ ⚑

The week before, as the eviction had became more and more imminent, we had invited Episcopal priests from the region to join us in solidarity and prayer.

Surrounded by bulldozers, as people stacked up whatever they could carry or had relatives move them out by car or truck, a group of half a dozen priests showed up to pray. Collared, in suits and khakis, they were clearly not used to working in surroundings like this.

We had gathered up the three crosses erected in memory of the dead: for Shawn, for Daniel, and, most recently, for Wendy. Shawn's cross, which had been there for years, towered in the center of the camp. Daniel and Wendy's crosses were smaller, close together. All of them were full of notes and gifts people had left over the months and years. Several family members and close friends of the dead gathered with the clergy group. A smartly dressed priest from Seattle led the group in prayer, acknowledging the loss of loved ones and naming their value and dignity in the eyes of God.

Someone had loaded up the crosses into my truck to be brought to the church we used in Westport, where they could be mounted on the wall. I was glad that had already been done, because now, the day of the eviction, the bulldozers were here and there wouldn't have been much time.

I went to check on several women whose mental health was such that they had no idea what was happening. One woman came out of a little pallet shack, and my heart sank. Two very high-needs women had set up camp right where police were planning to bulldoze that morning. The other was sleeping on a couch sitting in the middle of dirt. The first woman came up to me, gesticulating wildly. "They can't do this! I have legal rights here, and I have this under control. All these guys work for me."

"Honey," I said gently. "They are going to bulldoze this today. They won't let you stay."

I gave them some time to think things over and went to talk with Michael, whose camp was in its fourth or fifth iteration. "Will you go to the city encampment?"

"Hell, no. I won't live like that," he told me. "I'll figure something out." His eyes looked bleak.

As the day wore on, I returned to the women's spot. This time, there were two bulldozers on either side of them, and an officer was trying to convince them to leave.

An advocate called the local crisis team for an evaluation—hoping, I think, that they could get referred to a mental health facility. But neither of them met qualifications to be detained or referred to a bed. Eventually, the first woman wandered off and disappeared.

The second woman meticulously packed a dozen bags or so, and Bonnie, always calm in crisis, loaded them in a vehicle to take her and her belongings to the mitigation site. When the woman got out of the car at the new site and began going through her things, she started yelling.

"You didn't bring all my bags. I am going to sue you! I am going to sue you for stealing my shit. How dare you? You are gonna be sorry."

Bonnie just nodded kindly and left.

We were grateful that the city, for the first time in recent history, was investing in some transition site for those who were unhoused. But the new tent city was rough. It was gated, both to hide people from view and for their own privacy, with 24-7 security that did provide some semblance of safety to vulnerable people. Rules became difficult, however, especially as the months inched toward winter. The city purchased insulated tents it believed to be sufficient, but people ran the danger of frostbite and were forbidden from using any heat source. Many were kicked out for using propane or candles, a serious fire risk that would indeed set part of the camp on fire a few years later. But there were no alternative heat options given either. The woman Bonnie helped move into the camp was kicked out that winter. She spent the rest of the year living in portable bathrooms around the city, to the frustration of anyone who actually wanted to use them.

At a city council meeting, when advocates brought forward these concerns, one woman on council remarked, "We just don't want people to get too comfortable."

When people were driven off, they were driven to land that they had no claim or stake to, places where they were constantly asked to move or criminally cited for doing so. Even in the city-sanctioned tent encampment, they were afforded little autonomy. There was very little risk of "getting too comfortable."

Still, around the town to this day, you will see the spray-painted messages: #RG4L.

🕊 🕊 🕊

It was about land. It has always been about land. Homelessness is just one manifestation of landlessness, which is also another way of saying people need space and resources.

For all of the danger in it—for all of the infections that people got in unsanitary conditions, all of the drugs that were used, all the violence that happened because there was often little protection—the River was a place where people demanded and held on to a place to be. They carved out a piece of land that could be their refuge, and they made that refuge available for others who needed to join them.

It was a place where people built their shacks and staked their flags. Many flags flew there: the American flag, sometimes upside down, the flag of the Quinault Indian Nation, because so many of their number lived there, and, on occasion, a "Don't Tread on Me" flag. They cooked food there, fished there, sometimes grew gardens there. They made their own heat, stacked their own firewood, arranged their own homes, and survived on whatever ingenuity and talent they could use.

The River was now gone. The eight-acre stretch of river was gated and flattened, and people were warned that they would be criminally charged with trespassing if they tried to come back.

It sits there still, an abandoned piece of riverfront. Once a mill site, once a homeless camp, the land is now abandoned, deserted, as the tide ebbs and flows on the Chehalis.

⟨ 32 ⟩

THE UPRISING MEETS ABERDEEN

"GET OUT OF this town! We don't want you here! Get the fuck out of here!!"

The man had an AR-19 with a bayonet, clearly assembled at home, and a military vest with a III% patch on it. At least a dozen armed men and women were following him. A videotape also noted an open container of alcohol in his pocket, which explained his breath as he swore and spit in my face.

I was, of course, *from* here, standing on a street I had walked as a child. It was the spring of 2020. As deaths mounted in the worst worldwide pandemic in a century, the United States was swept into uprising after the police murder of George Floyd in Minneapolis. Police departments across the country made statements condemning the officers responsible for George Floyd's death, every major city in the country saw nightly protests in the streets, and residents of small rural towns turned out for the first time en masse.

All across the country, people were restless from quarantine, frustrated with politicians' inability to meet the needs of the American people, and enraged by Floyd's murder and other incidents of police brutality. Breonna Taylor, a Black woman in Louisville, Kentucky, was shot in her own home in a botched raid not even supposed to target anyone in her house.

Slowly, an alt-right backlash emerged as well. Small towns across the nation began seeing shared Facebook posts warning that "antifa" was coming to their town next to burn it to the ground. As Seattle and Portland saw rising protests, their downtown core already boarded up due to Covid restrictions, property destruction became a main fear. Right-wing organizers stoked the fear of small-town business owners and citizens, warning that protesters would be coming to their town to destroy it next. Alt-right militias up and down the West Coast, already angry at the economic cost of Covid shutdowns, grabbed their guns to prepare for war.

After staff discussion at Chaplains on the Harbor, we decided to stage a protest of our own in downtown Aberdeen, in support of Black Lives Matter and to call attention to people who had died at the hands of police in Grays Harbor.

We were a core group of maybe twenty people—mostly women, many still homeless—who met at our feeding program location and then walked to the main road running into Aberdeen, a popular site for protests and events. Melissa, who wrote an op-ed in the *Daily World*, and Mimi, now out of prison, joined us.

In retrospect, we should have been more careful, noting the strong social media backlash forming against our announcement of the protest. But we had become accustomed to random threats on social media, and I miscalculated just how ready for violence some people were. As we began our march, the park itself was filling with a counterprotest. We decided we would stay on our own side of the street and not approach the full park or the counterprotest itself. In our last protest, we had hired security, even though we had not needed it. This time we were alone.

White and Indigenous and Black women marched together, carrying homemade signs that said "Black Lives Matter" and "Rednecks against Police Violence." Other signs listed the names of George Floyd and Breonna Taylor. They also listed the names of Patrick West and Kristopher Fitzpatrick, along with others who had died in local police-related incidents.

As we came down the street, we saw just how large the counterprotest had become. At least one hundred people were waving flags and holding signs in support of the local police departments. Most were staying on the sidewalk. We stopped short, still on a side street, not yet at the main street where we intended to set up across the street.

I hesitated. Members of our group looked at each other as we assessed what to do.

That moment lasted too long. Before we knew what was happening, a dozen or so people, angry and openly armed, were rushing toward us. As they approached us from a block away, they spread out and separated us, shouting in our faces, using every slur they could—

"tweakers,"* "n*****s," "c***s"—while screaming "all lives matter!" I heard one man yell, "I will put this gun to your head and pull the trigger!"

Every single fiber of my being wanted to retaliate in kind. Our small group was scrappy, most with long experience living on the street. But I knew if I lost my cool, everyone around me would too.

While our group never responded with violence, neither could most among us maintain their calm. They were too used to street culture, where slurs and threats are always matched tit for tat. The two groups' interactions devolved into a screaming match, until I was finally able to disengage our group and move us through the back streets of town.

I stayed completely calm on the outside, de-escalating argument after argument after argument until I could get people regrouped and across the street, walking away. I realized too late how important the preparation phase for a protest is, why many groups spend weeks practicing getting screamed at before holding an actual protest.

Police arrived and, at first, stood by. We finally regrouped and began walking to city hall, armed and angry men following us every step of the way.

Currently homeless women held Black Lives Matter signs in front of armed men. Once we were at city hall, police finally separated the counter-protesters, ensuring they stayed across the street, although the open displays of guns and threats went unchecked as the men continued yelling and revving their truck engines, flying large American flags.

I walked with Grace, a Black woman, as she was being followed by armed white men in tactical gear. She stopped and faced them, and she proceeded to argue reasonably, under great pressure. One of the men finally yelled, "I don't really give a fuck about people!"

She fixed her gaze on him and paused for a moment. Then she said evenly, "Well, now do you see your problem?"

$$\text{🪶 🪶 🪶}$$

Even with all the ruckus, people in our group managed to share stories of police violence. I shared what I have witnessed. Family members of Patrick

---

*The term "tweaker" is a slur directed specifically toward a person under the influence of methamphetamine, or any illegal drug more broadly. It is a frequent slur used in Grays Harbor.

West were there, and even during yells from the other side—that he had had it coming, that he had deserved to die—they stayed calm. An old car circled the block over and over, its driver and passengers likely afraid to get out, honking loudly and flying the Mexican flag.

We lit candles for all the names we had brought and many more that people spoke. Then we did what we could to get everyone safely out of the square.

I have received plenty of harassment in the course of my ministry, but this was the first time I had guns in my face. A little internet research revealed that local guys from around the county had met at the park after a local agitator, who frequently has opposed our work, posted that antifa was coming to town.

The videos on Facebook shook the town. Pictures from the event—armed and angry men screaming in the faces of people in our group, which was composed of mostly women and queer folks carrying a few signs—made it clear that the war for America's soul had made its way to the most remote spots. People were suddenly afraid of each other, and rumors flew. People who had ignored our advocacy in prior years suddenly took notice and publicly called out the perpetrators. Some who had attended the protest were stalked and followed to their homes.

Facebook groups in support of Black Lives Matter formed, and several other smaller demonstrations were carefully planned and carried out. Organizers held those subsequent protests in school zones where guns could not be openly carried, a move that made eminently good sense after the display we had encountered. For a moment, many people recognized that vigilante violence, clearly still alive and well in Aberdeen, needed to be confronted. The Aberdeen City Council issued a statement against racism, perhaps for the first time in their history, and included a note discouraging the brandishing of weapons during protests. It was a weak response, but the fact that they felt compelled to do so was surprising in a town with a long history of turning a blind eye to vigilante violence.

As an organizer, I wrestled with the reality that holding a protest like that in downtown Aberdeen could have gotten someone injured or even killed.

At the same time, I felt less and less comfortable being out in public in Grays Harbor. This was my home, but I had very nearly been killed by fellow citizens, and even worse, so had people who followed me into what felt like a war. My wife had come flying into town when the videos first started getting posted, sure I was dead.

Our day on the streets of Aberdeen revealed the oldest strategies of the American empire, ones first practiced by Aberdeen's timber barons: get poor people to back the perceived interests of the business community and form a vigilante army against other poor people demanding a better life. It revealed that the oldest strategies of violence are not, in fact, merely efforts of the past. They are current and effective strategies to repress poor people struggling for life.

It has become common since the summer of 2020 and especially after Janunary 6, 2021, for journalists to wonder if we are heading into a "second American civil war." But the reality is this: we have been in constant civil war since the first treaty was broken by the first settlers, since the first slave patrols hunted Black people, since the first Indigenous villages were torched, since the first vagrancy laws were enforced.

Our day on the streets of Aberdeen also showed something else. It showed just how much the systems that control our lives fear a ragtag little group of people experiencing racism, homelessness, and police violence. In the end, systems upheld by such violence are fragile. Locally, people who avoided politics were suddenly making statements to support Black Lives Matter. People who had been afraid to speak up started to talk about their own oppression and to stand with their homeless neighbors. For so many years—basically ever since the labor wars of nearly a century earlier—working-class people in Grays Harbor had largely put their heads down and tried not to make a fuss. But the mood was shifting, with more and more people becoming restless and considering how best to organize.

⟪ **33** ⟫

ORGANIZING THE FUTURE

THE FOREST WAS quiet, except for the call of a raven high in a hemlock snag. Years ago I heard a cougar mewling near this spot, but there was no sign today of the giant cats of the coastal rainforests. As a child, I'd seen a black bear here once too, back when the owners, or poachers, still had cruel steel traps set to catch them, posing an equal hazard to children's feet. Wrens were bobbing in and out of the underbrush, with their many songs, as the raven continued to call.

It was cloudy, with a light drizzle, here in the region with the most days of rain in the world. The creek that once provided my childhood swimming hole, blocked up by culverts, was now running free, ready for the first time in probably a century for salmon to return. In a lawsuit won by the Quinault Indian Nation, the state of Washington has until 2030 to replace 90 percent of its culverts, changing them out for systems that allow for fish to travel upstream, in an effort to restore salmon to the rivers and creeks that once provided their main habitat. The giant cedar trees there were getting old; they had watched me grow most of my life, and I had spent hours under them. They whispered in the wind like old friends.

I sat under the largest tree, easily over a hundred years old, and wondered what the tree had witnessed. I wondered what knowledge it carried if only we stopped long enough to listen. I imagined the world of this rainforest, part of a forest that once stretched continuously from the place of my birth in central California to Alaska, providing bounty for whole civilizations.

My best friends as a child were the plant and trees and creatures of this forest. I knew how to track them, I knew their names, and I knew some of what they could be used for. In the spring and summer, this forest was full of salal berries, salmonberries, huckleberries, thimbleberries, and elder berries. I would forage here every year, waiting for the sharp smell of the skunk cabbage in early spring and the bountiful huckleberry harvest in late summer.

Later, as I learned more from Native people of the region, I learned some-thing of the history of this place. The destruction of so much bounty, as big equipment cleared forests that had been tended for thousands of years since the last ice age. I knew that the trees remembered.

Poverty and violence stalk our lives in Grays Harbor, but we are also a place of towering, regrowing forests, plentiful rivers, and the wild Pacific coast, with all its bounty and power. During the summer of 2020, commu-nity members in Grays Harbor increased their engagement with both local issues like homelessness and with larger qustions of justice. Mutual aid groups formed and re-formed, people began openly criticizing the status quo, Indig-enous students staged protests, and new nonprofits gave a growing number of young people in recovery opportunities to both serve their community and reflect on the bigger picture. While the larger business community con-tinued in their harsh persecution of people on the street, individual small businesses turned to help: donating supplies, doing mutual aid, providing meeting places, inviting homeless young people into internships, speaking out for the most vulnerable in the community. A few pastors continued to support whatever programs they could, including ours, and spoke out in their congregations for the rights of Grays Harbor's poorest. I felt change in the air.

For the first time, it felt like the number of people who wanted change exceeded the number of people spewing hate on social media.

Capitalism creates trash. It calls all the mess created on the land after clear-cuts and oil spills and chemical spills "waste." Trash. What system takes all the beauty and power of the world and nature and turns it into trash?

Then it packages everything you need to survive in *more* waste and then calls it trash. Mountains of it. Oceans full of it. Poor communities choked with it. Homeless camps drowning in it.

And then there are the people who are called trash. My people. Our labor, the only thing we have to sell, is not needed, as easier and easier tech-nologies take the place of labor. As machines do more, as even poorer people in the Global South are exploited, more and more trash people are living in cast-off zones. It is time to end a system that sees humans and the earth itself as trash.

Movements to end our oppression have been in the works all over the world. At this moment, communities all over the world are imagining a better world and are implementing it—the Zapatistas in Chiapas, the landless workers movements in Brazil, the Shackdwellers Movement in South Africa, the recent Indigenous triumph in Bolivia, and the ongoing struggles of Indigenous people throughout the world for access to land and resources.

Capitalism might call us trash, but we are actually part of a global working class: the majority of the world's population that has been forced to sell our labor and cut off from our natural relationship with the land. We are the many.

Throughout our history, there have been opportunities to rise up together, across race and across the borders that divide us, and sometimes we have. W. E. B. Du Bois argues that the Civil War and its aftermath was one such opportunity. Then, the white worker and the Black worker, who was enslaved and whose body was owned as real estate until emancipation, could have joined forces. Instead, Irish organizations refused to march with Black workers and the labor movement remained segregated. Reconstruction, the period after the Civil War, became a battle between Northern oligarchs who relied on machines and hired labor and Southern oligarchs who relied on land and slavery. Du Bois writes, "It was not until after the period which this book treats that white labor in the South began to realize that they had lost a great opportunity, that when they united to disfranchise the Black laborer, they had cut the voting power of the laboring class in two."

We do not have to lose another opportunity. Even though we are taught to fight each other across race, even though we are sent to fight wars against other working-class people around the globe, we can find a different path.

As I walked the land, seeking answers, I began to realize that my people's search for home and belonging was futile without acknowledging the sovereignty of the land's rightful stewards. Without addressing the devastation of racialized settler capitalism, which gobbled up land and bodies together for profit. Without going back to the beginning, to the land, and recognizing the interdependence of all life. Capitalism was destroying land and people with equal abandon, baiting poor white people like me with the promise of a home we could never find under a system designed for profit.

It has taken me a long time to learn how to frame my experience as a poor white person from the rural United States, where I was both so connected to the land on which I was raised and also more and more aware that it was stolen land. Poor white people in the United States are desperate to belong somewhere, to have a home somewhere. We also have expected to take, and believed we were entitled to, the home of the Indigenous people of this continent. We have staked out homesteads—even if most of them have been abandoned for the next person or for corporate takeover, all across this country—as places to raise our families and live in a way that was our own. We have felt connected to the land itself, we have dreamed of living off the land, and we have staged multiple "back to the land" movements. However, we never did so as guests on Indigenous land; we did so as settlers, funded by the US government, and we did so as white people claiming the Doctrine of Discovery as our basis for settlement. At best we were "tourists" on the land, as Indigenous scholar Vine Deloria writes—"detached from real relationship with the land." At worst, we were agents of genocide.

White writer Wendell Berry is best known for his stories about coming home to rural America. Like Jayber Crow in Wendell Berry's fictional work of the same name, I had decided I was called to share in the fate of the place in which I was raised. As much as I respect Wendell Berry, and as much as he acknowledges the ecological and agricultural devastation of the modern rural setting, he rarely seems to see or acknowledge the human crisis or the Indigenous people who still live here. The home I came back to was not to the fellowship of Wendell Berry's dreams or his depiction of a nearly classless society. What I came home to was the wreckage and legacy of colonialism and capitalism. I came home to the results of generations of genocide of Indigenous people, extraction from the land, and exploitation of workers.

In an Indigenous worldview, the land is not owned, not by anyone. Once upon a time European peasants would have believed this too. But that belief was lost long, long ago and no longer haunts our memory. To Indigenous people, the land, as Robin Wall Kimmerer says so beautifully, "belonged to itself; it was a gift, not a commodity, so it could never be bought or sold." The land, and other-than-human relatives, are meant to be lived with in relationship. Only capitalism has turned the land into a commodity. As our rivers are drying up, as our climate warms, as our ecosystems fall apart, as species die, and as the end of life as we know it seems imminent, might it not be time to return to a land unbought and unsold, back to a relationship between human and nonhuman life?

And what does all this mean for my people, the poor white people who were once displaced from their own lands and have been taught that this land should be theirs by right? Certainly, white people are taught to see movements for Indigenous sovereignty as a threat. But how well have the last few centuries really gone for us? Indigenous people lived on this land for millennia, from time before memory, and it has only taken five hundred years for greed and plunder to bring the land, with its human and more-than-human inhabitants, to the edge of extinction. Even the promise of a "secure life in a land of plenty" that Will Campbell talks about has not been a reality for poor white people, still fighting every day to survive.

Would it be possible to give up our claim on stolen land in exchange for a culture of reciprocity and generosity? Indigenous sovereignty would be in poor white communities' best interest. Land acquisition and theft in the United States, while in theory meant to benefit white people, tend to only benefit a few incredibly wealthy people in the owning class. Poor white communities find themselves in postindustrial economies, where all that is left to us are polluted water, homeless camps, and little access to decent jobs, decent housing, decent food, education, or hope. There is no blueprint for this, but for so long, we have been hampered by our inability to imagine something outside the confines of the system of which we are a part.

As I walked the woods of my childhood, I was beginning to see that healing can only come from a radical break with an extractive system designed to benefit the few at the expense of the many. It can only come from both recognizing that we can build alliances across the globe with other working-class and poor people, building leaders in our communities who understand the root causes of our poverty and can teach others. It can only come from building alliances across race in the United States, in movements like the Poor People's Campaign, as we meet each other, see each other's pain, and demand our right to survive and thrive. And finally, it can only come from acknowledging, at last, the Indigenous stewards of this land, and the agency of the land itself.

WHEN WE BOUGHT THE FARM

IT WAS IN the middle of the pandemic. We gathered outside, all masked and standing apart, with the local Episcopal bishop and a local pagan priestess. In two different traditions, they prayed over the land.

We were standing just outside the greenhouse that Chris had designed and built, ready for next year's starts. In front of us stretched twenty-two acres of pasture land that was once a part of an old dairy. Here along the Chehalis River, several miles east of Aberdeen, three acres had been converted into a vegetable patch. The struggle with weeds was evident, and an old battered tractor was parked alongside the house we used for office space.

The year after the River was bulldozed, our supportive employment project moved into a permanent farm location. The Episcopal Diocese of Olympia, our sponsoring diocese, bought a permanent piece of property for the farm project. I looked around our circle. There were three farmers that season, and two more would come on in the following year. Learning to farm was slow, difficult work, but it brought a connection to the land and an opportunity for people, often after long stints on the street or having been incarcerated, to get their hands in the dirt.

James was one of the first apprentices on Harbor Roots Farm, which we started as a supportive employment project. He had spent most of the five previous years on the streets, couch surfing in flop houses or camping by the river. He had also spent most of those five years drunk and angry at the world.

I met him first handing out sandwiches under the bridge, and he became a regular at all our programs, talking the ear off anyone who would listen. Under all his words ran deep currents of pain and alienation. At two, James had held his dead baby sister, who had drowned in the bathtub. By age five, he had run away from home. At age nineteen, having been raised by a foster family who then adopted him, he ended up on the streets.

Today James is raising two sons. He and his wife had won their CPS case and had regained custody after a long two-year court battle. He has come such an astonishingly long way from the angry young man I met under the bridge. His children are being raised with all the love he and his wife can give them. He is determined they will lead a very different life than he had, determined to care for them in ways he was never cared for. He has continued to grow as a leader since that day he met with Black Panther and Young Patriot leaders and elders.

The farm was only a first small step on a path toward healing. It was not the large change we need. The land was still private property, owned by a church. The Indigenous people of the region still did not have access to steward the land of their ancestors, and hundreds of people were still homeless in the county. But a group of young people from the streets of Grays Harbor, white and Native, were building a small farm project on a piece of land that was once part of a larger dairy farm. In doing so, they were investing in their healing, their future, and their leadership in a movement to end poverty.

Two years later, we got a small grant to start replanting native food-producing trees and shrubs on part of the property. Just a few hundred years before, the rich land along the river would have been a great forest of red alder and western red cedar and spruce. Under that canopy grew all sorts of food: salmonberries and elder, blackberries and thimbleberries, Bog Labrador and hazelnut. When settlers cut the forests, they converted the land along the rivers into dairy farms, planting grass on the floodplains and often diverting tributaries.

We bought buckets of bare root native plants: berries and wild ginger, alder and cedar and hazelnut. I did not always get to put my hands in the dirt, because I was so busy with other things, but I was determined to be part of planting these.

David and Jon and I plotted where they would all go, using up little corners, making the most of the shade cover of the only half dozen trees left on the property by the former owners for the plants that needed a shade cover. We planted a thicket of huckleberries, my favorite.

To me, this region tastes like the mellow tang of salmonberries in the early summer, and the sharp tartness of red huckleberries—although the blue huckleberries are amazing too. All this abundance of food, which capitalism does not value, once formed a large part of the diet of Indigenous people in this region from time immemorial.

One day, muddy and rainy, we planted the blackcap raspberries. From the time I farmed as a child, I have always insisted on gardening without gloves. I love the feel of the soil, the smell of it. I can tell what will grow in it by its smell, and the sharp tang of this soil seemed to bode well for the berries. It was, after all, the soil that belonged to the plant. We were replacing imported varieties of shrubs and plants with plants the soil still remembered.

In between covering the bare roots of the two-year-old raspberry plants, David looked up at me. "Remember that first year in the shelter?" he asked. I nodded. I had first met David there. He spent most of his time camping out in the woods, where he loved to forage, but he would always come in for food and supplies.

"I could never have imagined, back then, that I would be here now, planting raspberries with you," he said. I felt tears in my eyes. I could never have imagined it either, but here we were. This project had been partly David's idea. When he went to treatment, he was supported by his tribe to go to Northwest Indian Treatment Center. There, his love for the land of his ancestors was nurtured further, as he learned about plant-based medicine and Native healing. He brought that passion to his work on this piece of land, where he coaxed plants to life with a tenderness that few ever bring to this kind of work.

We were beginning to discover that healing must include our other-than-human relatives. So many lifeways and so many ecosystems have been disrupted in the race for the bottom line. When we sank our hands into the soil, we learned from the trees and the shrubs that belonged to that place. We watched the ducks and geese overwinter on the lake that formed in the field every winter, and watched for the trumpeter swans that made their brief visit in the late fall. Eagles hunted and little cedars grew. And we learned from the land.

Supportive employment and a little farm project do not do much to end larger systems of greed and oppression. But it did give a space to grow and nurture leaders who could take the fight to the next steps. It did give a space to learn from the land itself, a space to heal from the hurt inflicted on us by systems of abuse and oppression. And a place to connect with our other-than-human relatives and learn from them.

Perhaps what I learned most clearly, as I planted blackcap raspberries in the mud, was that no resistance is perfect. It is always partial and always flawed. But every move that has helped people survive, every effort to educate poor people and organize them in solidarity with each other: these were chinks in a system bent on our oppression.

EPILOGUE

I SAT IN the quiet of the newly remodeled farmhouse, still smelling of new floors and paint. My little desk looked out over the tulip tree flowering in the yard. Beyond that, twenty-two acres of farmland rolled out, the spring grass catching the glint of the morning sun.

My cross sat on the desk, with the dreamcatcher someone in prison had made for me. I had the ashes of two people I had buried sitting in little necklaces at the foot of the little cross. A stack of jail letters sat on the desk, awaiting my response.

Soon the farm team would start tilling the rich bottomland soil to start their fifth season of farming, their first on land that was our own. I heard the calls of finches and the trill of a pair of thrushes.

I had an email correspondence going with three consultants who were helping us purchase the land, separately incorporate, and come up with a solid business plan. We were starting a worker-run co-op with our team of leaders, designed to create leaders from young people coming out of homelessness and incarceration. Bonnie had been decorating the place, sewing curtains and putting together bedrooms that would house guests and visitors to our work.

There was still deep suffering to attend to, still much work to be done, still many battles to fight. But that morning, the day was beautiful and the sun glinted on the picture of Zach and dozens of others we had lost, waiting to be hung near my desk.

I felt my life coming full circle. Nearly thirty years earlier, I had pulled a little red wagon full of vegetables around my urban neighborhood. Today, I looked over a small farm, worked by the people thrown away by our social systems, who had found the power in themselves to heal and to bring healing to their community.

🕊 🐦 🕊

But those little moments of peace never last long. There is always a new crisis in the abandoned zones of empire. The pandemic had shuttered many social services. The city had closed down their sanctioned tent city, scattering people yet again, pushing them back under bridges and closer to the banks of the River. We witnessed a record number of overdose deaths. Funding became more precarious, as the emergency money of the early years of Covid dried up, placing a great deal of strain on all of us.

One day, as I planned yet another funeral service, my own long experience of poverty and loss, and then of caregiving in poverty and loss, caught up with me. As I prepared the details of the funeral, I began hearing the words I had put together for the service echo strangely, over and over and over again in my head.

> *In the darkness and warmth of the earth, we lay you down.*
> *Into the sadness and smiles of our memories, we lay you down.*
> *Into the cycle of living and dying, we lay you down.*
> *Into a place with the ancestors who watch over us, we lay you*
> *down.*

In those words, my mind bent and warped. I felt an overwhelming wave of despair, planning this funeral for a young man I had known and loved, murdered by an intentionally set fire in the abandoned house he was sleeping in. I could not remember how many funerals I had planned. And my own personal trauma, kept at bay for so many decades, suddenly pulled me under.

For nearly six months, I lost the ability to function. I could not read or write, could not balance a balance sheet, could not have a functional conversation. More than once, I wanted to lay down too, forever. The fallout from that time saw my withdrawal from chaplaincy and ministry altogether. Like so many caregivers in the middle of catastrophic conditions—rising poverty, a global pandemic, and economic collapse—I found my own untended needs had caught up with me. I am only now coming to terms with the weight, not just of what I witnessed as a chaplain, but what I myself experienced as a poor white person on the edge of empire. The weight of being seen as trash for so long, and for so many generations.

When the immediate crisis had passed, I had time to think. I moved, leaving the place I've considered home for most of my life, knowing that the memories of long ago were too painful to live near anymore. Knowing that it was time to tend to myself like I had told so many others to do. Knowing I had to feel safer in my choice of community and could not do that where I was.

These changes gave me space to ask the bigger questions, to process my years of frantic work. I had the time wonder: What is our responsibility now, in this historic moment? What have I learned from this decade of witness, and what is a path forward? This book is the beginning of an answer. I have written it with the awareness that it is only the beginning of a much longer struggle and a much longer time of healing.

⬎ 𓅿 ⬏

In the last five hundred years, poor white people have found many ways to resist the owning class, but they have only rarely done so in any concerted way. What makes me believe that we can now? What makes me believe it is possible that we will recognize our history, that we will recognize our place in the global working class, or that we will acknowledge Indigenous sovereignty? To be sure, this country is full of voices telling poor white people to do the opposite. To continue to be the foot soldiers of the American empire, to continue to enforce the will of the bosses and the state.

In my ten years of ministry in Grays Harbor County, I realized that poor white people are becoming more and more desperate. For young people, particularly, the promises of the American empire of land and jobs to poor whites is a distant dream. The promise of free land and good jobs is dead. As we struggle to make ends meet, as we live either precariously close to homelessness or in tents on riverbanks, we are longing for a way out. We are tired of being treated like trash.

We must dare to dream of a better future and an end to this five-hundred-year experiment in death and destruction. For most of us, this dream is so far out of reach we cannot even imagine a world without private property, without the rule of capital and the almighty dollar, without corporate ownership of land and institutions, without the punishment of prisons.

There are plenty of voices, in the media and in the halls of power, telling poor white people to continue to hold on to the promises of white supremacy. Those same voices also shame us for our poverty and our failure to maintain a decent life. To confront this narrative of white supremacy, we have to say that we are worthy. We have been told we are trash for so long that we believe it.

We have to find strength in the stories and resistance and faith of our ancestors. We have to rediscover our oldest stories, our deepest strength.

We have to reject white supremacy, the claim that our whiteness is superior to other races, while embracing the heritage that is truly ours, the heritage that is our finest moments. We need to lean into the heritage of workers working side by side across race, the heritage of John Brown, a poor white man who fought side by side with enslaved Black people. We have to learn our own history—not the history we are taught of European empires, but our history of dispossession of the lands we once belonged to and our search for home ever since.

We must learn to live as guests in the land to which many of us fled as refugees many years ago. We have to acknowledge that Indigenous people existed on this land for many thousands of years and hold the wisdom to restore the land and its people. There will be no healing possible for us without accepting Indigenous leadership on this stolen continent. In the end, that might be our only hope. The colonial dream was clearly never meant for us, and we have wandered long enough.

We have to face the heritage of our own misdeeds: when we blighted the lives of Indigenous people, when we helped burn villages and destroy land and people, when we patrolled the lives of Black people, when we stood at the lynching tree. We must stop taking orders from empire and turn and join together with other suffering people.

And to do so, we have to lay aside the shame. The shame of our suffering. The shame of our failing a system that was designed to kill us. We must learn that we were never meant to survive.

And yet some of us have. We have survived when we were left to starve; survived when drugs poured into our communities, taking our best and our brightest; survived when our culture turned on its children, blighting our lives; survived when our loved ones fell in wars we never decided on or had any stake in; survived even amid the mockery of politicians and figureheads; survived starvation and disease, even today, on the streets of US cities and towns.

We have survived. We have survived because we are the result of the love of thousands. We have loved each other the best we could, in the grime and dirt and fear of the streets and jails and prisons and slums of this country.

We can rise, but only if we rise together, across race, with all those who live on this stolen land with us. We can rise, but only if we draw on the strength and courage of our true ancestors and our deepest truths. We can rise, but only if we see ourselves as part of a global working class, whose power is greater than that of a few greedy men. We can rise, but only if we acknowledge the legitimacy of the Indigenous people who were and are the original stewards of this land.

We are not trash, like we have been told. The systems that kill us are trash.

We are not trash, and we can rise up against our own oppression and that of our Black, brown, and Indigenous siblings.

We can rise.

ACKNOWLEDGMENTS

SO MANY PEOPLE helped make this book possible.

A profound thank you to Valerie Weaver-Zercher, my editor at Broadleaf, for all the endless hours of feedback, encouragement, and conversation. Thank you for listening when I was frustrated and for pushing me to find the right words. Writing my first book would never have been remotely possible without you.

Thank you to all my professors, but especially thank you to my seminary professors from Episcopal Divinity School: Dr. Kwok Pui-lan, the Rev. Dr. Christopher Duraisingh, the Rev. Dr. Joan Martin, the Rev. Dr. Patrick Cheng, Dr. Julie Lytle, and Dr. Frederica Harris Thomsett, Dr. Angela Bauer-Levesque, among so many others. Thank you to my teachers in chaplaincy: the Rev. Cristina Rathbone, the Rev. Mary Eaton, the Rev. Dr. Elizabeth Mae Magill, and the soon to be Rev. Kae Eaton. To all of the people who have shaped my thinking in the Poor People's Campaign: you are too many to mention. But I want to extend special thanks to the Rev. Dr. Savina Martin, Dara Kell, Idalin Bobe, Clinton Wright, the Rev. Erica Williams, John Wessel-McCoy, Nijmie Dzurinko, Kevin Kang, Dr. Adam Barnes, Kristin Colangelo, and scholar for our times: Willie Baptist.

Thank you to Borja Gutiérrez, Anu Yadav, Carolyn Baker, Tracy Clayton, Reg Richburg, Dara Kell, Jean Ramos, and Ruby Sales for reading my manuscript and giving me feedback, and to Aaron Scott for encouraging me to write it in the first place and reading multiple drafts. Thank you to Shailly Gupta Barnes, Dr. Colleen Wessel-McCoy, and Dr. Tom Womeldorff, for your technical assistance and advice. I also want to thank you, Tom, for teaching my first course in economics in college: what I learned left a profound impression on me. Your feedback was amazing; all mistakes are solely my own. Thank you to the Rev. Dr. Liz Theoharis for your encouragement to write this book and your support through the process, and most of all for your incredible leadership in the Poor People's Campaign.

Most importantly, thank you to each person who touched my life, each person who gave me permission to tell their stories, each person who taught me the lessons included in this book. A special thanks to the family members and friends of people who died who are remembered in this book. Thank you to the folks of Grays Harbor's streets and jails and back alleys. This book, in some ways, is my gift to a community I can no longer serve. I hope that I have told people's stories as truthfully as they would want them told.

I want to specifically thank those who truly took the time to teach me about life on the streets, about hope, about survival, who have continued to be friends through years of hard work together: Pixie, JoyceAnn, Ang, Ava, Michelle, Shirley, Melissa, Brian, Mimi, Misty, Blaine, Randy, Christina, John, Larry, Shawna, Charles, Michael, Matt, and so many more.

I want to thank the staff at Chaplains on the Harbor, past and present, who allowed me to lead them, stood by and supported me when I fell on my face (pretty often, if I recall), and made our mission possible: Chris, James, Mashyla, Jon, David, Angela, Janet, Tracy, Skye, Donnie, Levi, and many others. More than anyone, I want to thank Bonnie for her personal support, for her incredible pastoral presence and care to me and to Grays Harbor, and to always cheering us on and holding down the fort. Bonnie's husband, Jim, was one of my best friends, and he did most of the behind-the-scenes work at Chaplains on the Harbor, doing the bookkeeping for the organization as it grew. His story does not show up in these pages, but none of it would have been possible without him. His loss leaves a great hole in my heart.

And Aaron: We were partners in ministry from the first, through successes and mistakes, through wins and losses. Thank you for your vision, your commitment to the bigger work, and for putting up with me. Thank you for bringing your analysis and love to this work and for your continued work for justice.

Most of all, thank you to my partner, Emily, whose faith in me and love for me has been my light in darkness. Thank you, Emily, for all you contributed to this book in conversations about what it means to be a "broke-ass white person," for your humor and encouragement, for your feedback, and most of all for supporting me through the final stages of this project. This would never have been possible without you.

A final thanks to the baristas at Rhythm's Coffee and Barnes and Noble Café for your kindness and for filling me with enough caffeine to finish this book.

NOTES

Introduction

1 *"searching but never finding a secure life in a land of plenty":* Will Campbell, "Elvis Presley as Redneck," First Elvis Presley Symposium, University of Mississippi, August 7, 1995, http://www.canopicpublishing .com/juke/contents2/willcampbell.htm (accessed March 25, 2013).

2 *"freedom to flounder, to drift, to wander westward in a frustrating search of what had been promised but never delivered":* Campbell, "Elvis Presley as Redneck."

2 *roughly 20 percent of the US population:* Shailly Gupta Barnes, Lindsay Koshgarian, and Ashik Siddique, eds., *Poor People's Moral Budget: Everybody Has the Right to Live,* (Institute for Policy Studies, Kairos Center, and Repairers of the Breach, 2019), https://www .poorpeoplescampaign.org/wp-content/uploads/2019/12/PPC -Moral-Budget-2019-report-FULL-FINAL-July.pdf, 49. There are several different ways to determine poverty levels. The federal poverty level has been widely deemed an inaccurate measure of real poverty, since it fails to account for inflation and serious increases in the cost of living over the past fifty years. The Census Bureau developed Supplementary Poverty Measure (SPM), and those are the numbers used by this report.

4 *poor white people, who he calls the "white worker," have few revolutionary leaders:* W. E. B. Du Bois, *Black Reconstruction in America* (New York: The Free Press, 1998), 17. Du Bois stated, "But the poor whites and their leaders could not for a moment contemplate a fight of united white and black labor against the exploiters. Indeed, the natural leaders of the poor whites, the small farmer, the merchant, the professional man, the white mechanic and slave overseer, were bound to the planters" (27); and also, "This meant that the mass of ignorant poor white labor had practically no intelligent leadership" (349).

5 *Why are 33 percent of white people poor, and why are 43.5 percent of Americans poor:* Gupta Barnes, et al., *Moral Budget.*

5 *Some 140 million people in this country . . . are poor and low income:* Gupta Barnes, et al., *Moral Budget,* 49.

7　***who challenged the white theological community when she said:***
Ruby Sales, interviewed by Krista Tippett, *On Being*, "Where Does It
Hurt?", September 15, 2016, https://onbeing.org/programs/ruby-sales
-where-does-it-hurt/.

1. Canaries in a Coal Mine

15　***concludes that this is a vast undercount:*** National Law Center on
Homelessness and Poverty, *Housing Not Handcuffs: Ending the Criminal-
ization of Homelessness in US Cities*, 2019, https://homelesslaw.org/wp
-content/uploads/2019/12/HOUSING-NOT-HANDCUFFS-2019
-FINAL.pdf, 28.

15　***This report revealed:*** This information is not public in its full form. My
source is email correspondence with Cassie Lentz, Housing Resource
Coordinator, Grays Harbor Public Health, on April 13, 2018. Part of
the data (but only by county, not by city) is available in online housing coalition records from April 2018, https://static1.squarespace.com
/static/53ee83dee4b027cf34f1b520/t/5daf716d46ed800117c33eed
/1571778930438/10.22.19+Slides.pdf. The full source is from ESA
EMAPS Report #4397 using the ACES Data Warehouse, running a
report for "Cash, Food, and Medical Clients Reported as Homeless in
the Grays Harbor Area, By Zip Code, December 2017," produced on
February 8, 2018.

18　***number of sentenced inmates in US state and federal prison
of all races has grown exponentially:*** Saurav Sarkan and Shailly
Gupta Barnes, eds, *The Souls of Poor Folk: Auditing America 50 Years
after the Poor People's Campaign Challenged Racism, Poverty, Mili-
tarism/ the War Economy, and our National Morality* (Institute for
Policy Studies and Kairos Center, April 2018), 35, https://www
.poorpeoplescampaign.org/wp-content/uploads/2018/04/PPC
-Audit-Full-410835a.pdf.

19　***wildly increasing overdose rates:*** Brian Mann, "Street Fentanyl Surges in
Western US, Leading to Thousands of Deaths," National Public Radio,
November 17, 2020, https://www.npr.org/2020/11/17/934154859/street
-fentanyl-surges-in-western-u-s-leading-to-thousands-of-deaths.

2. Poor White Trash

24　***she died of hypothermia and abuse:*** Kathryn Joyce, "Hana's Story:
The Tragic Death of an Ethiopian Adoptee and How It Could Happen

Again," *Slate*, November 9, 2013, http://www.slate.com/articles/double
_x/doublex/2013/11/hana_williams_the_tragic_death_of_an_ethiopian
_adoptee_and_how_it_could.html.

24 *most of us lived on what scholars call "common land":* Roxanne
Dunbar-Ortiz, *An Indigenous Peoples' History of the United States*, (Boston: Beacon Press, 2014), 34.

25 *"from time immemorial":* Karl Marx, *Capital Volume I*, (London: Penguin Books, 1990), 891.

26 *It was not just land that could be waste:* Nancy Isenberg, *White Trash: The 400 year Untold History of Class in America*, (New York: Penguin Books, 2016), 20.

26 *In the Scottish Highlands, the Duchess of Sutherland decided to clear her lands of fifteen thousand people to make way for sheep farms:* Marx, *Capital Volume I*, 891–92.

27 **An Gorta Mór** *opened up Ireland's land for plunder:* Marx, *Capital Volume I*. Marx writes: "Therefore her [Ireland's] depopulation must go still further, in order that she may fulfil her true destiny, to be an English sheepwalk and cattle pasture," 869.

27 *These displaced people:* Dunbar-Ortiz, *An Indigenous Peoples' History*, 35.

27 *"To many minds, the migrant poor represented the United States' re-creation of Britain's most disposed and impoverished class: vagrants":* Isenberg, *White Trash*, 105. Isenberg writes, "Land was the principal source of wealth, and remained the true measure of liberty and civic worth. Hereditary titles may have gradually disappeared, but large land grants and land titles remained central to the American system of privilege."

27 *Yet Jefferson dreamed of such a republic while sitting as a Southern aristocrat and enslaver:* Lina Mann, "The Enslaved Household of President Thomas Jefferson," White House Historical Association, https://www.whitehousehistory.org/slavery-in-the-thomas-jefferson
-white-house#:~:text=Despite%20working%20tirelessly%20to%20
establish,most%20of%20any%20U.S.%20president.

27 *Isenberg writes, "Land was the principal source of wealth . . .":* Isenberg, *White Trash*, 63.

3. The Family Curse

31 *the "Quiverfull" movement:* This name comes from Psalm 127:4–5: "Like arrows in the hand of a warrior, so are children born in one's

youth. Blessed is the man whose quiver is full of them." It is a reference both to the movement's refusal to use birth control and its stated goal of raising enough children to "take over America."

33   ***Psychotherapist Resmaa Menakem writes:*** Resmaa Menakem, *My Grandmother's Hands: Racialized Trauma and the Pathways to Mending our Hearts and Bodies* (Las Vegas: Central Recovery Press, 2017), 62.

34   ***Doug Wilson of Moscow:*** Southern Poverty Law Center, "Doug Wilson's Religious Empire Expanding in the Northwest," https:// www.splcenter.org/fighting-hate/intelligence-report/2004/doug -wilson%E2%80%99s-religious-empire-expanding-northwest.

4. Naming My Story

35   ***She was telling the story of her childhood rape:*** Maya Angelou, *I Know Why a Caged Bird Sings*, (New York: Ballantine Books, 1997), 87.

38   ***it would make me worthy of death:*** James Perron, "The Man Who Wants to Kill the Gays," Aug 12, 2018, https://medium.com/the-radical -center/the-man-who-wants-to-kill-gays-397d4acfa30e.

5. Class War in Graduate School

40   ***the last acceptable slur in polite company:*** Campbell, "Elvis Presley as Redneck."

"It is an ugly word," Cambell wrote, "an invective used to defame a proud and tragic people—the poor, white, rural, working class of the South. . . . But hearing the equally offensive insult, redneck, draws not a flinch in most circles. Only a chuckle."

40   ***In 2018, NPR ran an article:*** Leah Donnella, "Why is it Still Ok to Trash Poor White People," NPR, Code Switch, August 1, 2018, https://www.npr.org/sections/codeswitch/2018/08/01/605084163 /why-its-still-ok-to-trash-poor-white-people.

44   ***"your legs are your passport, valid forever":*** Eduardo Galeano, interviewed by Juan Gonzalez and Amy Goodman, Democracy Now, May 19, 2006, https://www.democracynow.org/2006/5/19/voices_of _time_legendary_uruguayan_writer.

45   ***American corporate interests have written the future for most countries south of the US-Mexico border:*** For more information, see Eduardo Galeano, *Open Veins of Latin America*, trans. C. Belfrage (New York: Monthly Review Press, 1996).

6. The Beginning

51 *had reduced the Indigenous population by up to 92 percent:* Charles Wilkinson, *The People are Dancing Again: The History of the Siletz Tribe of Western Oregon*, (Seattle: University of Washington Press, 2010), 57.

51 *sold 900,000 acres of land in 1900 to Weyerhaeuser:* Joni Sensel, *Traditions Through the Trees: Weyerhaeuser's First 100 Years* (Seattle: Documentary Book Publishers, 1999), 16.

51 *the most dangerous job in the United States:* ISHN, "Top 25 Most Dangerous Jobs in the United States," November 20, 2020, https://www.ishn.com/articles/112748-top-25-most-dangerous-jobs-in-the-united-states. Per a 2018 study, logging is still ranked as the most dangerous job in the country: you are thirty-three times more likely to die logging than in any other industry.

51 *White people did not recognize Indigenous agriculture:* Andrew Curry, "Pacific Northwest Forest Gardens were Deliberately Planted," *Science*, April 22, 2021, https://www.science.org/content/article/pacific-northwest-s-forest-gardens-were-deliberately-planted-Indigenous-people.

52 *the tribe has bought back up to 40 percent of that land:* Olympic Peninsula Intertribal Cultural Advisory Committee, *Native Peoples of the Olympic Peninsula: Who We Are*, Norman: University of Oklahoma Press, 2015.

53 *At one time, the Northwest coast was a region where, in the words of Roxanne Dunbar Ortiz:* Dunbar-Ortiz, *An Indigenous Peoples' History*, 25.

54 *"One by one the canoes were welcomed ashore by Quinault Nation leaders . . .":* Fred Shortman, "Paddle to Quinault," *The Chehalis Tribe*, https://www.chehalistribe.org/tribal-journeys/paddle-to-quinault/.

54 *Indigenous people on Turtle Island depended on a culture of reciprocity:* Robin Wall Kimmerer, *Braiding Sweetgrass: Indigenous Wisdom, Scientific Knowledge, and the Teaching of Plants* (Minneapolis: Milkweed Editions, 2013).

55 *Grays Harbor County declined to prosecute it as such, handing down a charge of manslaughter:* Cary Rosenbaum, "Quinault Member Jimmy Smith-Kramer Killed in Alleged Racially-Charged Confrontation," *Indian Country Today*, May 28, 2018, updated Sept 13 2018, https://indiancountrytoday.com/archive/quinault-member-jimmy-smith-kramer-killed-alleged-racially-charged-confrontation-2; KXRO News, "Guilty Pleas in Donkey Creek Death of Jimmy Smith

Kramer," May 1, 2018, https://www.kxro.com/walker-pleads-guilty-for-death-of-jimmy-smith-kramer/.

7. The River

63 ***effort to deregulate the economy and roll back social service programs at federal and state levels:*** There is extensive documentation and many studies on the steady rollback of social services and housing in the United States. Some resources for further reading include:

Western Regional Advocacy Project, "Without Housing: Decades of Federal Housing Cutbacks, Massive Homelessness, and Policy Failures," 2007 https://wraphome.org//wp-content/uploads/2008/09/WRAPWithoutHousingfederalcutbacks2007report.pdf.   WRAP also has continuing research, especially from the west coast, that is valuable.

Matthew Desmond, *Evicted: Poverty and Profit in the American City* (New York: Crown, 2017).

Nell Berstein, *Burning Down the House: The End of Juvenile Prison* (New York: The New Press, 2016).

63 **the Poor People's Campaign concluded:** Gupta Barnes, et al., *Moral Budget.*

8. "The American Dream" and Its Signs

68 ***Nearly 40 percent of the land area in Grays Harbor is owned by five or six timber companies:*** Grays Harbor County GIS Department, "Major Timberland Ownership," https://cms5.revize.com/revize/graysharborcounty/GIS/Maps/Major_Timberland_Ownership.pdf.

9. Baptism on the Edge of Loss

73 ***one in fifteen kids have been accepted to a CPS referral:*** Grays Harbor Public Health and Human Service, "Community Health Improvement Plan: Creating a Healthier Grays Harbor," April 26, 2016, slide 15. https://static1.squarespace.com/static/53ee83dee4b027cf34f1b520/t/573b9b5d04426254ad906d56/1463524205004/GreaterGH_4.26.2016.pdf, accessed through healthygh.org.

75 ***The abuse that children endured in these schools is extensively documented:*** In Canada, the Canadian state held a Truth and Reconciliation Commission, in response to the largest class-action lawsuit in

Canadian history (https://www.rcaanc-cirnac.gc.ca/eng/1450124405592
/1529106060525#chp2). The commission documented extensive first-
person testimony and collected extensive documentation of residential
schools. These reports are housed at the National Centre for Truth and
Reconciliation and available online at https://nctr.ca.

75 ***Secretary of Interior Deb Haaland initiated the first report of Indian
boarding schools:*** US Department of the Interior, "Federal Indian Boarding School Initiative," https://www.doi.gov/priorities/strengthening
-indian-country/federal-indian-boarding-school-initiative. The first
volume of this report was released in May 2022, saying: "This report
shows for the first time that between 1819 and 1969, the United States
operated or supported 408 boarding schools across 37 states (or then-
territories), including 21 schools in Alaska and 7 schools in Hawaii.
This report identifies each of those schools by name and location, some
of which operated across multiple sites. This report confirms that the
United States directly targeted American Indian, Alaska Native, and
Native Hawaiian children in the pursuit of a policy of cultural assimilation that coincided with Indian territorial dispossession. It identifies the Federal Indian boarding schools that were used as a means for
these ends, along with at least 53 burial sites for children across this
system- with more site discoveries and data expected as we continue
our research." Federal Indian Boarding School Initiative Investigative
Report: May 2022, available online at https://www.bia.gov/sites/default
/files/dup/inline-files/bsi_investigative_report_may_2022_508.pdf.

75 ***the ways that "child-bearing was a profitable occupation" for
enslavers:*** Du Bois, *Black Reconstruction*, 44.

75 ***one in ten Black children removed from their parents:*** Janel Ross, "One
in Ten Black Children in America are Seperated from Their Parents By
the Child-Welfare System: A New Book Argues this is No Accident,"
Time Magazine, April 20, 2022, https://time.com/6168354/child-welfare
-system-dorothy-roberts/. This is an article on the new book by Dorothy
Roberts, *Torn Apart: How the Child Welfare System Destroys Black Families
and How Abolition Can Build a Safer World* (Basic Books, 2022).

10. Childhood Nightmares

77 ***when the laws changed:*** Melissa Santos, "It's an Issue of Liberty: WA
will stop jailing kids who run away or skip school," *Crosscut*, May 9,
2019, https://crosscut.com/2019/05/its-issue-liberty-wa-will-stop-jailing
-kids-who-run-away-or-skip-school.

77 ***incarcerated only 180:*** Seattle Times Editorial Board, "State Needs to Divert Resources for Jailing Homeless Youth to Prevention," *Seattle Times*, Dec 19, 2015, https://www.seattletimes.com/opinion /editorials/state-needs-to-divert-resources-for-jailing-homeless-youths -to-prevention/

77 ***We live in a country:*** Sarah Mehta, "There is only one country that hasn't ratified the convention on children's rights: US," November 20, 2015, *ACLU*, https://www.aclu.org/news/human-rights/theres-only-one -country-hasnt-ratified-convention-childrens.

79 ***MD spent a total of about seventy-five days locked in a room or in a padded cell with little human interaction:*** ACLU, "Grays Harbor County Policy Putting Kids in Solitary Confinement Unconstitutional," March 15, 2016, https://www.aclu-wa.org/news/grays-harbor -county-policy-putting-kids-solitary-confinement-unconstitutional -asserts-teens.

80 ***He told the newspapers, in his defense of widespread youth incarceration:*** Melissa Santos, "Washington No.1 for jailing noncriminal kids, spurred by law named for Tacoma runaway," *News Tribune*, January 31, 2016, www.thenewstribune.com/news/politics-government /article27129946.html.

11. The Theatrics of Terror

84 ***Policing in the United States exists as "theatrics of terror":*** Mark Lewis Taylor, *The Executed God: The Way of the Cross in Lockdown America* (Fortress Press, 2015), 57–58.

85 ***the largest sweep in the Northwest in a decade:*** Erik Lacitis, "$1 Million Razor and Barbed Wire Fence Proposed for the Jungle," *Seattle Times*, Feb 25, 2016, https://www.seattletimes.com/seattle-news/politics /1-million-razor-and-barbed-wire-fence-proposed-for-the-jungle/.

85 ***"We cause no harm to that area but just want to sleep or rest, yet some of you people just can't let us be":*** Melissa Hill, "A Homeless View," *Daily World* (Aberdeen, WA) July 29, 2020, https://www .thedailyworld.com/letters/letter-to-the-editor-a-homeless-view.

12. On the Run

88 ***His body was found days later:*** KBKW, "Missing Hoquiam Man Identified as Brooke Sandbeck," September 26, 2016, https://kbkw .com/missing-hoquiam-man-identified-as-brooke-sandbeck/.

88 *the rates are much higher for young Black men:* Gwen Aviles, "Police killings are the sixth leading cause of death among young men, study shows," *NBC News*, August 13, 2019. https://www.nbcnews.com /news/nbcblk/police-killings-are-sixth-leading-cause-death-among -young-men-n1041526.

88 *The People's Policy Project did a study:* Justin Feldman, "Police Killings in the US: Inequalities by Race/Ethnicity and Socioeconomic Position," People's Policy Project, https://www.peoplespolicyproject .org/wp-content/uploads/2020/06/PoliceKillings.pdf.

89 *group most likely to be killed by police are Native Americans:* Mike Males, "Who are Police Killing," Center on Juvenile and Criminal Justice, August 26, 2014, http://www.cjcj.org/news/8113.

90 *Kevin's picture appeared in the newspaper that day:* Louis Krauss, "Police Arrest and Use Taser on Alleged Safeway Shoplifter," *Daily World*, October 28, 2018, https://www.thedailyworld.com/news/police -arrest-and-use-taser-on-alleged-safeway-shoplifter.

90 *correlation between the early formation of slave patrols . . . and the formation of municipal police forces:* NAAPC, "The Origins of Modern Day Policing," https://naacp.org/find-resources/history-explained /origins-modern-day-policing. This book does not have the space to trace this history in detail, but poor whites historically had the role of policing Black people who were enslaved and kept the system of slavery intact and stable. Du Bois points out, "In the South, on the other hand, the great planters formed proportionately quite as small a class but they had singularly enough at their command some five million poor whites; that is, there were actually more white people to police the slaves than there were slaves . . . The result was that the system was held stable and intact by the poor white." (Du Bois, *Black Reconstruction*, 12).

91 *The coroner ruled her cause of death as natural:* Dan Hammock, "Coroner: Hoquiam woman died of 'sudden unexpected death due to excited delirium' after struggle with police," *Daily World*, February 8, 2017, https://www.thedailyworld.com/news/coroner-hoquiam-woman-died-of -sudden-unexpected-death-due-to-excited-delirium-after-struggle-with -police/.

92 *The family came forward later with a civil lawsuit:* Mike Carter, "3 WA Cities will pay $3 million to settle lawsuit after man is killed in a SWAT-like assault," *Seattle Times*, February 2, 2022, https://www .seattletimes.com/seattle-news/law-justice/grays-harbor-area-police

-agencies-pay-3-million-to-settle-lawsuit-by-family-of-man-killed
-during-swat-like-assault/.

92 *it does not appear that he has a weapon:* Drew Mikkelsen, "Family
of Man Killed by Aberdeen Police Wants Answers," King5.com, September 11, 2019, https://www.king5.com/article/news/local/family-of
-man-killed-by-aberdeen-police-wants-answers/281-b5c35b12-8fd3
-4488-af01-40528a0630e5.

13. The Value of Punishment

93 *the highest county [incarceration] rate in the state:* Prison Policy Initiative, "New Data Reveals Where People in Washington Prisons Come
From," August 3, 2022, https://www.prisonpolicy.org/blog/2022/08/03
/waorigin/.

93 *Nearby reservations, such as the Squaxin Island Reservation, experience staggering incarceration rates:* Emily Widra and Colin Cole,
"Where People in Prison Come From: The Geography of Mass Incarceration in Washington State," August 2022, Prison Policy Initiative,
https://www.prisonpolicy.org/origin/wa/2020/report.html.

95 *Corporate labor is often farmed out to state prisons:* Michael Berens
and Mike Baker, "Broken Prison Labor Program fails to keep promises, costs millions," December 13, 2014, *Seattle Times*, https://projects
.seattletimes.com/2014/prison-labor/1/.

95 *Prisoners in Washington State, however, make between 65 cents and
$2.70 an hour:* Drew Mikkelsen "Legislator fighting to increase work-
ing inmate's wages," December 16, 2022, *King 5 News*, https://www.king5
.com/article/news/local/pay-inmates-minimum-wage-prison-jobs
/281-3c42badf-52ba-41af-93f5-e20d790c47ae#:~:text=Current%20
pay%20for%20prisoners%20ranges%20from%2065%20cents%
20to%20%242.70%20an%20hour.&text=OLYMPIA%2C%20
Wash.,for%20work%20done%20behind%20bars.

96 *for the poorest economic group, 43 percent of white men and 47 percent
of Black men had been to jail:* Nathanial Lewis, "Mass Incarceration:
New Jim Crow, Class War, or Both?", January 2018, People's Policy Project, https://www.peoplespolicyproject.org/wp-content/uploads/2018/01
/MassIncarcerationPaper.pdf.

96 *Black men are five times more likely than white men to be in prison:*
Nathanial Lewis, "Locking Up the Lower Classes," January 2018, *Jaco-
bin*, https://jacobin.com/2018/01/mass-incarceration-race-class-peoples
-policy-project.

14. Death on the River

101 **Gustavo Gutierrez says that poverty is defined as "early and unjust death":** John Dear, "Gustavo Gutierrez and the preferential option for the poor," *National Catholic Reporter*, November 8, 2011, https://www .ncronline.org/blogs/road-peace/gustavo-gutierrez-and-preferential -option-poor.

101 **In his groundbreaking book, A Theology of Liberation, Gutierrez expounds further:** Gustavo Gutierrez, *A Theology of Liberation: History, Politics, and Salvation* 15th anniv. ed. (Maryknoll: Orbis Books, 1988), xxi.

105 **As Salvadoran liberation theologian Jon Sobrino says:** Jon Sobrino, *No Salvation Outside the Poor: Prophetic-Utopian Essays* (Maryknoll: Orbis Books, 2008), 30.

15. Shaker Funeral

108 **"Native Americans are the original sustainable society,":** Coast Works Alliance, "Coast Works Builds Sustainable Connections," April 17, 2017, https://www.wacoastworks.org/2017/04/coast-works-builds-sustainable -connections/.

109 **it is a unique and beautiful syncretization of Christian and Native traditions:** Squaxin Island Tribe, "Indian Shaker Church," https:// squaxinisland.org/indian-shaker-church/.

109 **jailed for practicing their belief in Jesus through the Indian Shaker Church:** Squaxin Island Tribe, "Indian Shaker Church."

110 **Indian Country's needs—particularly in the areas of health and infrastructure—have been neglected:** Written testimony of President Fawn Sharp, National Congress of American Indians to US House Committee on Oversight and Reform From Recession to Recovery: Examining the Impact of the American Rescue Plan's State and Local Fiscal Recovery Funds, March 1, 2022, https://docs.house.gov/meetings /GO/GO00/20220301/114462/HHRG-117-GO00-Wstate-SharpF -20220301.pdf.

17. Kneeling in Chains

119 **In 2016, EMS services had administered naloxone:** Wilma Weber and Kristina Alnajjar, "Grays Harbor County Public Health and Social Services Department," "Opiate Needs Assessment and Response Plan," February 2018, 10–11, https://static1.squarespace.com/static/53ee83dee

4b027cf34f1b520/t/5a99e51dc830255b24067ebb/1520035105024/Op
ioid+Needs+Assessment+and+Response+Plan.pdf.

119 *"The opposite of addiction isn't sobriety. It's connection":* Johann
Hari, *Chasing the Scream: The First and Last Days of the War on Drugs*
(New York:Bloomsbury, 2015), 293.

18. Seeking Redemption

121 *The Grays Harbor electorate swung red in 2016 for the first time
in ninety years:* Claire Galofaro, "Trump Won Places Drowning in
Despair. Can He Save Them?" *Associated Press*, August 18, 2017, https://
apnews.com/article/north-america-aberdeen-ap-top-news-us-news-wa
-state-wire-21cc9528cabd4578996c3f118d8d656f.

125 *a study showed that 64 percent of unhoused people in Los Angeles County have lived there for more than ten years:* Inyoung Kang,
"Where Does California's Homeless Population Come From?," *New
York Times*, November 6, 2019, https://www.nytimes,com/2019/11
/06/us/homeless-population.html.

19. A Rainbow Coalition

129 *Hy Thurman, a cofounder of the Young Patriots, recalls:* Hy Thurman, *Revolutionary Hillbilly: Notes from the Struggle on the Edge of the
Rainbow* (Berkeley, CA: Regent Press, 2020), 141.

130 *surrounded the police car and demanded Bobby's release:* Amy
Sonnie and James Tracy, *Hillbilly Nationalists, Urban Race Rebels, and
Black Power - Updated and Revised: Interracial Solidarity in 1960s–70s
New Left Organizing* (New York: Melville House, 2011), 76–77.

130 *"Back then, there were Minutemen militias who weren't too happy
about whites and Blacks in a rural area cooperating with one
another":* Sonnie and Tracy, *Hillbilly Nationalists, Urban Race Rebels,
and Black Power*, 93.

130 *Armsbury would end up spending ten years in prison:* Sonnie and
Tracy, *Hillbilly Nationalists, Urban Race Rebels, and Black Power*,
94.

130 *"We are the living reminder that when they threw out their white
trash, they didn't burn it":* Sonnie and Tracy, *Hillbilly Nationalists,
Urban Race Rebels, and Black Power*, center pictures.

131 *"The Rainbow Coalition was their worst nightmare":* Sonnie and
Tracy, *Hillbilly Nationalists, Urban Race Rebels, and Black Power*, 84.

20. A Poor People's Campaign, Then and Now

133 *The fact is that Capitalism was built on the exploitation and suffering of black slaves and continues to thrive on the exploitation of the poor:* Martin Luther King, Jr, "The Three Evils of Society," delivered at the National Conference on New Politics, August 31, 1967, transcribed online at https://www.nwesd.org/ed-talks/equity/the-three-evils-of-society-address-martin-luther-king-jr/.

133 *King had been assassinated just the month before the first march:* Kairos Center, "The Poor People's Campaign: A National Call for a Moral Revival," https://kairoscenter.org/ppc/.

133 *Abernathy explained that the intention of the Poor People's Campaign:* Kairos Center, "Building a Poor People's Campaign for Today," https://kairoscenter.org/poor-peoples-campaign-concept-paper/.

134 *the march allowed them to also protest for Native rights:* National Park Service, "Native Americans in the Poor People's Campaign," https://www.nps.gov/articles/000/native-activism-poor-peoples-campaign.htm.

21. Facing Off with Vigilantes

137 *The town was desperately poor:* Data pulled from MissionInsite, a database open to churches, on 6/16/2015, prepared for the Episcopal Diocese of Olympia on zip code 98595. MissionInsite uses US Census Data.

137 *Westport was still one of the top five commercial landings on the West Coast:* Fisherman's News, "West Coast Fishing by the Numbers," May 1, 2018, www.fishermansnews.com/story/2018/05/01/features/west-coast-fishing-by-the-numbers/532.html, accessed June 10, 2018.

140 *gathered a mob to drive out the remaining Chinese families who had refused to leave:* "What is suprising about the expulsion of Aberdeen's Chinese residents is the degree to which the historical record of it is filled not with white workers who resented competition with Chinese labor, but with Aberdeen's merchant elite." From Aaron Goings, Brian Barnes, and Roger Snider, *The Red Coast: Radicalism and Anti-Radicalism in Southwest Washington*, (Corvalis: Oregon State University Press, 2019), 25.

140 *None were ever convicted:* Goings, et al., *The Red Coast*, 29–32.

140 *The business community responded not only with police but with a variety of strikebreaking efforts:* Goings, et al., *The Red Coast*, 63.

140 *a hired gun shot and killed striking worker William McKay:* Goings, et al., *The Red Coast*, 111.

23. Raising the Flag

153 *These are the Fourteen Words:* These words are written by David Eden Lane, inspired by Hitler.

153 *openly propagate theories of "white genocide":* Southern Poverty Law Center, "Asatru Folk Assembly," https://www.splcenter.org/fighting -hate/extremist-files/group/asatru-folk-assembly. Asatru Folk Assembly, "Statement of Ethics," https://www.runestone.org/statement-of-ethics/.

154 *Most practitioners:* Andie Sophia Fontaine, "Pagan Chief Says Racists Co-Opt Elements of Ásatrú," *The Reykjavik Grapevine*, August 28, 2014. "Hilmar Örn Hilmarsson, the head chieftain of the Ásatrú Society, spoke candidly with Vísir about white supremacist groups who evoke elements of Ásatrú . . . 'There are groups to the right of Hitler who in some cases use Ásatrú as a pretext,' he said. 'We do not want our name used to give these beliefs any kind of credence.'"

155 *Brown had made this vow at a funeral for an abolitionist:* Aaron Scott, "Sermon: 13th Sunday After Pentecost," Aug 22, 2015, https:// aaronheartsjesus.wordpress.com/2015/08/22/sermon-thirteenth -sunday-after-pentecost/.

155 *"conspiring with Negroes to produce insurrection":* Fergus M. Bordewich, "John Brown's Day of Reckoning: The abolitionist's bloody raid on a federal arsenal at Harpers Ferry 150 years ago set the stage for the Civil War," October 2009, *Smithsonian Magazine*, https:// www.smithsonianmag.com/history/john-browns-day-of-reckoning -139165084.

155 *Aaron Scott preached these words in a Seattle church:* Scott, "Sermon."

156 *"Whenever black people have entered into a mutual relation with white people,* James Cone, *God of the Oppressed* (Maryknoll: Orbis Books, 1997), 220.

24. Healing Is Revolutionary

159 *Sandra wrote an article about her experience:* Quinault Indian Nation, *Nugguam* (Taholah, WA), August 2018 newsletter.

160 *"Blessed are the meek":* Matthew 5:5.

25. Mustard Seed Movement

163 *"What I hope for is an awakening of awareness of the need to care for the homeless in ways that are just and loving":* Scott D.

Johnson, "Bishop Curry Speaks at Aberdeen Affordable Housing Rally," *The Daily World*, June 18, 2018, https://www.thedailyworld .com/news/bishop-curry-speaks-at-aberdeen-affordable-housing-rally.

26. An Ode to Joy

167 ***20 percent of young people in juvenile justice systems:*** Daiana Griffith, "LGBTQ youth are at greater risk of homelessness and incarceration," Prison Policy Initiative, January 22, 2019, https://www.prisonpolicy.org /blog/2019/01/22/lgbtq_youth/.

27. Anniversary of the Black Panthers

173 ***the US government had neglected sharing wealth and resources with people who were only recognized as resources to be exploited:*** Thurman, *Revolutionary Hillbilly*, 121.

173 ***would explain how these conditions in Chicago and nationally kept poor Southern whites in poverty:*** Thurman, *Revolutionary Hillbilly*, 175.

28. White Trash in DC

178 ***We were in charge of million-dollar machinery:*** Most of this dialogue and story is told through a video recorded by Bishop Barber's team on May 1, 2018. Repairers of the Breach, "Homeless Vet: "Walk a Mile in Their Shoes"| Grays Harbor Homeless Encampment Visit," https://www.youtube.com/watch?v=pwsQQ-pdwLM.

29. The Halls of Congress

180 ***the congressional hearing had invited the Poor People's Campaign to assemble a group of testifiers:*** Sarah Ruiz-Grossman, "Sens. Warren, Sanders Hear Directly From America's Poor At US Capitol," *Huffington Post*, June 12, 2018, https://www.huffpost.com/entry/warren-sanders -cummings-poor-peoples-campaign_n_5b2048ece4b09d7a3d782673.

180 ***Chris referenced the fact that money was available:*** Louis Krauss, "Formerly Homeless Man from Grays Harbor Speaks at Congressional Forum," *Daily World*, June 29, 2018, https://www.thedailyworld .com/news/formerly-homeless-man-from-grays-harbor-speaks-at -congressional-forum/.

183 ***Chris was selected to sit on that board:*** Dan Hammock, "Four
Selected for Expanded County Board of Health," Grays Harbor Public Health, June 23, 2022, https://www.healthygh.org/in-the-news-1
/2022/6/23/four-selected-for-expanded-county-board-of-health.

30. Trespass First Degree

186 ***up to 98 percent of all criminal cases in this country never go to***
trial: John Gramlich, "Only 2% of Federal Criminal Defendants Go to
Trial," Pew Research Center, June 11, 2019, https://www.pewresearch
.org/fact-tank/2019/06/11/only-2-of-federal-criminal-defendants-go
-to-trial-and-most-who-do-are-found-guilty/. The study documents
further: "Statistics about trial rates in state courts are harder to come
by because each state runs its own court system and no standardized
record-keeping system covers all states. But trial rates in criminal cases
tend to be very low in the states for which data is available. . . . In
2017—the year with the most recent data—jury trials accounted for
fewer than 3% of criminal dispositions in 22 jurisdictions with available data."

188 ***made it possible for homeless people and their advocates to bring***
cities up and down the coast to court: City of Boise, "Settlement
Reached in Groundbreaking Martin v. Boise Case," https://www
.cityofboise.org/news/mayor/2021/february/settlement-reached-in
-groundbreaking-martin-v-boise-case.

188 Scott Greenstone, "At Aberdeen's 'Hobo Beach,' a Priest and a Mayor
Battle over Homelessness," *Seattle Times*, December 28, 2018, https://
www.seattletimes.com/seattle-news/homeless/at-aberdeens-hobo
-beach-a-priest-and-a-mayor-battle-over-homelessness/.

188 ***"if the city doesn't have somewhere for them to go, I have no interest***
in forcing them off": Louis Krauss, "Aberdeen Finalizing Purchase of
Riverfront Homeless Camp Land," *The Daily World*, July 14, 2018,
https://www.thedailyworld.com/news/aberdeen-finalizing-purchase
-of-riverfront-homeless-camp-land/.

189 ***This time, the lawsuit was a "prayer for relief":*** Louis Krauss, "Another
Federal Lawsuit Filed Against Aberdeen to Stop Homeless Evictions,"
Daily World, April 24, 2019, https://www.thedailyworld.com/news
/another-federal-lawsuit-filed-against-aberdeen-to-stop-homeless
-evictions/.

31. #RiverGang4Life

191 ***While the case itself would not be fully resolved in court until November, the city opened a mitigation site in July:*** Dan Hammock, "Settlement Reached in Second Aberdeen Homeless Lawsuit," *Daily World*, Novemeber 5, 2019, https://www.thedailyworld.com/news /settlement-reached-in-second-aberdeen-homeless-lawsuit/.

33. Organizing the Future

203 ***Irish organizations refused to march with Black workers:*** Du Bois, *Black Reconstruction*, 10 and 367.

203 ***Reconstruction . . . became a battle:*** Du Bois, *Black Reconstruction*, 349.

203 ***It was not until after the period:*** Du Bois, *Black Reconstruction*, 353.

204 ***At best we were "tourists" on the land:*** Vine Deloria, Jr., *For This Land: Writings on Religion in America* (New York: Routledge, 1999), 257.

204 ***Like Jayber Crow in Wendell Berry's fictional work of the same name***: Wendell Berry, *Jayber Crow: A Novel* (Berkeley, CA: Counterpoint, 2001), 143.

204 ***the land . . . "belonged to itself; it was a gift, not a commodity, so it could never be bought or sold":*** Wall Kimmerer, *Braiding Sweetgrass*, 17.

Epilogue

212 ***In the darkness and warmth of the earth, we lay you down:*** Adapted from a rite of passage from *Celtic Daily Prayer: Book Two*, copyrighted by The Northumbria Community Trust, published by William Collins, 2015.